S0-BTC-876

Traditional Egyptian Christianity

✠ ──────── ✠ ──────── ✠

A History of the Coptic Orthodox Church

Theodore Hall Partrick

✠

Fisher Park Press

BX
133.2
.P37
1996

Front photo: Altar piece at St. Macarius' Monastery, Wadi Natrun, Egypt.
Back photo: Author with Brother Jeremias, guestmaster, St. Macarius' Monastery.

Fisher Park Press
P.O. Box 14561
Greensboro, NC 27415

Suggested cataloging data:

Partrick, Theodore Hall
     Traditional Egyptian Christianity : a history of the Coptic Orthodox Church.
     Includes bibliographical references and index.
     ISBN: 0-9652396-0-8 (alk. paper)
     1. Coptic Church—History.
     2. Egypt—Church history.

     Call numbers:
          LC   BX 133.2   .P37 1996
          Dewey   281.7
Library of Congress Catalog Card Number 96-84373

Copyright © 1996 Theodore Hall Partrick

All rights reserved.

Printed in the United States of America by Versa Press, Inc., East Peoria, Illinois. Pre-press preparation by North Star Press of St. Cloud, Inc., St. Cloud, Minnesota.

Preface

✠ ——————————————————————————————————— ✠

    This book began with a master's thesis on Origen of Alexandria, learning the Coptic language, and a graduate seminar on Athanasius of Alexandria. Teaching early church history for twenty years helped me develop a good grasp of the evolution of Egyptian Christianity in its first four centuries.

    The greatest impetus, however, came during a three-week trip to the Eastern Mediterranean in 1974 where I encountered several Coptic laymen and clergy in Cairo, Luxor, and Jerusalem who received me with unusual cordiality. As a result, I made the decision to research the historical development of the Coptic Church to bring my knowledge of it up to the present.

    Initial efforts included the purchase of books and subscriptions for study and making frequent visits to the libraries of Duke University and the Universities of North Carolina in Greensboro and in Chapel Hill. During the decade beginning in 1982, I spent every spare moment in this project, beginning with a solid fourteen weeks in the British Library, the Bibliothèque Nationale, and the Hebrew University library and St. Anne's library in Jerusalem.

    In 1984 and in 1989 I was able to spend a month each back in Egypt, where I visited the St. Macarius and Muharraq monasteries and used their libraries and the libraries of the Société d'Archéologie Copte, the Coptic Institute at the Patriarchate, and the Jesuit, Dominican, and Franciscan institutes in Cairo. I also visited a number of urban and rural Coptic churches and institutions and interviewed a variety of Coptic Christians.

    I herewith express my gratitude to the librarians for the unfailing help I was given in each of the libraries mentioned above—to which I should add the libraries at the Harvard Divinity School, at the Virginia Theological Seminary in Alexandria, at the University of Kentucky and at the Catholic University of America. The bibliography shows how much has been made available to me.

Sincere thanks are due the Coptic Christians at the Patriachate, at the monasteries that gave me hospitality, at Beni Suef and Suhag, at St. Mary's Coptic Church in Raleigh, North Carolina (where I worship when I can), and the Copts in Los Angeles who have greatly helped in getting this book into print, above all, Mr. Hany Takla, president of the St. Shenouda the Archimandrite Coptic Society.

I owe special thanks to my sister and her husband, Louise and Francis Newton. She tutored and read Arabic with me, and they offered me a generous subvention to help publish this book.

I am especially grateful to Fr. Maurice Martin, S.J., of Cairo and professors Birger Pearson of Santa Barbara and Orval Wintermute of Duke who read my manuscript, encouraged me to publish, and suggested a number of helpful improvements.

No one has helped me more than my son, Ted Partrick, who has shared hours of his time and much of his computer expertise in preparing what you are about to read. Alice Rice saved me many errors and inelegancies in style.

My gratitude to all those mentioned above, however, can only approximate what I owe my wife, Charlotte, who always encouraged me, read every word I wrote, and never once mentioned the time and money I was investing in the search and the writing of this book. Those who know her will not be surprised.

Table of Contents

✠ ———————————————————————————— ✠

Introduction

✠ ———————————————————————————— ✠

EGYPTIAN CHRISTIANITY IS AS OLD as Christianity itself and has survived intact from the first century. The Egyptian Church is a case study for anyone curious about how a religious community could survive for fifteen centuries in the face of discrimination and hardships of all kinds, including active persecution.

There is a sense of mystery about Egyptian Christianity, partly because it is so little known. Even the Coptic[1] language of its worship is mysterious. The written form looks like Greek but has no relation to it. And who read it other than a little band of scholars of early Christian literature?

The Egyptian Church is so little known mainly because it was cut off from the Eastern Orthodox Churches and all Western Christians after 451. It has been only in recent years that Coptic Churches have begun to appear in a few Western Countries like Britain and France, but above all the United States, Canada, and Australia where there are concentrations of immigrant Copts.

Indeed, simply being Egyptian makes Egyptian Christianity interesting. Foreigners have had a fascination with Egypt at least since the Greek historian Herodotus visited there in the fifth century before Christ and was astonished by the antiquity of the great monuments of Egyptian culture.

The Nile River itself is legendary. The pyramids of Gizeh are still counted among history's great architectural and engineering feats. So are temples like those of Karnak and Abu Simbel, and the paintings and bas reliefs on the tomb walls of Upper Egypt amaze us with their still brilliant colors and artistic excellence. Pyramids, temples, and tombs were already ancient when Herodotus first saw Egypt. In the ancient world it was always assumed that Egypt's civilization was the oldest because such a high level of civilization was achieved there so very early in human history.

There are some interesting paradoxes in Coptic Christianity. For example, it is strongly traditionalist; some might say quite tradition-bound. Indeed, one can experience directly much of the tone and flavor of primitive Christianity by observing Coptic Church life. And yet in the 1990s, the Coptic Church is a lively movement by most standards. Young Coptic adults are thronging into the churches, in some places almost overwhelming their own organizations. In many of the churches, Coptic children crowd every meeting area for church school classes after the regular school day on Sundays. Monasteries are attracting more vocations than they have for centuries, and today's monks and nuns are often found to be university graduates and professionals.

Sunday worship in Coptic Churches is still quite long by Western standards and the standing can be quite tiring. But the high level of congregational participation, the singing and the cymbals, the incense and the movement make the Sunday Eucharist an exciting experience for anyone making any effort to enter into what is going on.

These factors which make the study of Egyptian Christianity interesting also make it important, particularly for those already interested in Egypt or in Christianity. The former will want to understand the place of Christianity in Egyptian history. Those interested in Christianity will want to expand their knowledge of what forms Christianity can take, and how a Christian tradition can survive and even thrive in an often unfriendly environment.

Also important was the Egyptian Church's role in the origin of the Christian monastic movement. From the beginnings of Christian monasticism, Egypt was a center both of the hermit type associated with the name of Anthony of the Desert and the community type, which Pachomius is usually thought of as organizing in Upper Egypt for the first time in history. It is hard to overestimate the importance of monasticism in church history—even in secular Western history—and we cannot know it well without some knowledge of its origins in historic Egyptian Christianity.

Then there is Alexandria, the capital of Egypt throughout the early centuries of Christianity. The theologians of Alexandria's Christian "school" took the lead in developing between 200 and 450 A.D. enough consensus on key Christian doctrines that it is still possible for Christians of widely varying traditions to communicate reasonably well with one another on essential questions of Christian teaching. It is important that this theology, so crucial in the development of Christianity, be seen in the context of the evolution of Egyptian Christianity.

Before sketching out our plan for the chapters to follow, let us review briefly some of the background to Egyptian Christianity. In style of government the ancient pharaohs originally set the standards for centuries to come. Pharaohs were divine kings, ruling absolutely whenever they could and claiming title to all the incredibly fertile valley of the Nile.

Subsequent rulers tried to do the same, first the Assyrians, then the Persians, then Alexander the Great of Macedon. They incorporated Egypt in their vast empires and exploited Egypt's extraordinary productivity. On the death of Alexander in 323 B.C., General Ptolemy gained control of Egypt. His dynasty held it for almost three centuries. Ptolemaic rule was by foreigners (Macedonians and Greeks), but at least they were foreigners living in Egypt.

Upon the defeat and death of the last (and most famous) Cleopatra in 30 B.C., Egypt was taken over and made an imperial colony by Rome which proceeded to ship much of Egypt's production to Italy. It looked as if Egyptians would be forever governed by foreigners, with the fruits of their labors largely confiscated, and often sent abroad.

For Egypt was a source of great wealth. The Nile deposited each year rich new topsoil along its banks and supplied the fields with water for irrigation, so Egypt was unusually productive in agriculture. Also, trade was prosperous because Egypt's strategic location made her a market for goods from South Asia and the Eastern Mediterranean. Finally, Egyptian craftsmen manufactured valuable products like papyrus and jewelry. Who would not covet Egypt's riches?.

As to social background, at the base of the ancient Egyptian social and economic pyramid were the artisans and the large class of agricultural workers. Between them and an upper class of priests, scribes, and administrators was a great gap, although under strong rulers everyone was a servant.

When the Ptolemies took over, they created a privileged class of Greeks and Macedonians, who could be joined by those Egyptians or Jews who by wealth and education fit in well with them. This gave the Ptolemaic rulers a powerful class who would support them. The Romans continued this practice, except that they excluded all Egyptians and Jews from the privileged class.

Turning to the cultural background, we find that writing was always a highly prized skill in Egypt. (The figure of the scribe was a popular pose for statues of Egyptian nobility.) The first Egyptian script was the artistic but linguistically awkward hieroglyphics. It was followed by the simpler hieratic and then the still simpler demotic script. The truly alphabetic Coptic script developed under the rule of the Ptolemies.

Ancient Egyptian painting and sculpture and architecture achieved a high esthetic level very early, but their style soon became fixed, with little if any variation. The literature had characteristics surprisingly similar to

Israel's, especially to the Psalms and other Wisdom literature. Egyptian narratives were good short stories.

Ancient Egypt was famous for its religion. One pharaoh, Akhenaton, even insisted on monotheism, although it is hard to relate his beliefs to Jewish or Christian monotheism. Ancient Egyptian religion was better known for its many animal gods, although in fact the principal divinities were sun gods like Ra and Amon and river gods like Isis and Osiris. Egypt's daily sunshine and the regularity of the rise of the Nile helped give Egyptian religion a characteristically optimistic outlook. At the same time, the agricultural cycle and the rise and fall of the Nile flood went well with an emphasis on death-and-rebirth in religion.

The social and political power of priestly hierarchies, and the dominance of temples and tombs (including pyramids, of course) among the permanent buildings in ancient Egypt clearly illustrate the important place both of religious ceremonial and also of life after death in classic Egyptian religion.

Egyptians were notoriously religious. The Macedonians and the Romans, like Egypt's earlier conquerors, made no particular effort to reform her traditional religions, except to identify some Egyptian deities with their own, and to favor the Serapis cult in Alexandria as a symbol of Greco-Egyptian syncretism.

A determinative element in the background to Egyptian Christianity was Egypt's most important religious minority, which became important in Egypt a few centuries before Christianity, the Jews.[2] A Jewish historian in the first century A.D., Josephus, tells us that Alexander the Great himself brought in Jews to help settle his new capital, Alexandria, but it was more likely Ptolemy I who initiated this migration, largely under compulsion.[3]

There were Jews in other population centers of Egypt. Another first-century Jewish writer, this time an Alexandrian named Philo, stated that there were a million Jews in Egypt. There certainly were quite a few, but probably not that many.[4] We have seen that under the Ptolemies some Jews qualified for Greco-Macedonian status. Jews also had municipal and religious self-government, they had the right to live according to their ancestral customs, and they were allowed to send the temple-tax to Jerusalem.

Jews served in the military in Egypt, owned land, practiced crafts, were agricultural workers, engaged in trade, and even served in government.[5] Economic activities did not significantly distinguish Jews from others in Egypt.

But in culture, Jews were less likely to assimilate. A strong sense of community, linked inevitably to the synagogue, made real assimilation rare, even though the Jews in Egypt did not take long to forget their traditional Hebrew language. Their traditional Hebrew scriptures were soon translated into Greek so they could understand them. This translation was called the "Septuagint" because of the tradition of there being seventy translators. (The reliability of the translation was promoted by the tradition that all seventy came up individually with identical translations.) The Torah of Moses remained the definitive body of law on which the Jewish community was based, even if there was a certain tendency among Jews to turn sometimes to Hellenistic law, especially in commercial matters.

Judaism in Alexandria, and in other cities in Egypt, was certainly Jewish but also predominantly Hellenistic. The reason for this is simply that Alexandria was the most important center of Hellenistic Civilization. Hellenistic Civilization had emerged in the Eastern Mediterranean as a result of Alexander's conquests in the fourth century before Christ. His plan seems to have been to spread Greek Civilization South and East, and his major strategy to achieve this plan was to establish cities like Alexandria in Egypt and Antioch in Syria which would be centers from which Hellenism would radiate.

Greek language, arts, philosophy, and education were the dominant influences in Hellenistic Civilization, but by no means was Hellenistic Civilization simply Greek. It incorporated many elements of the arts and sciences of the older Eastern Mediterranean civilizations. But Hellenistic Civilization was perhaps the world's first ecumenical culture, and as such it became invaluable to Christianity's aspirations to be a universal religion.

The history of Egyptian Christianity can be divided into eleven segments. We begin with the first Christians in Egypt, down to about 175 A.D. It is interesting and important to lay that initial foundation, but extremely difficult, as we have surprisingly little direct knowledge of the church in Egypt in that period. We shall see that this ignorance may be due to the "heretical" character of early Egyptian Christianity but more likely to its Jewish character, which allowed it to be hidden in the mass of Egyptian Judaism.

Then we turn in chapter 2 to the exciting period which roughly corresponds to the third century. The Christian school of Alexandria places Christianity for the first time at the highest intellectual and spiritual levels of the Hellenistic world. Meanwhile the bishops of Alexandria are creating a strong hierarchical government for the church in Egypt. What is more, Christian monasticism is having in Egypt its earliest beginnings. Egyptian Christianity is clearly poised to lead the Christian movement.

In chapter 3 the achievements recorded in the preceding chapter put Alexandria in the position to lead the ecumenical Christian Church in her efforts to resolve the crises that arose after the Emperor Constantine adopted Christianity. In words and deeds Bishop Athanasius of Alexandria leads the long effort to unite the universal church behind the Nicene Creed and the doctrine of the Trinity. In the next (fifth) century Bishop Cyril of

Alexandria leads what came the closest to being a truly successful effort to formulate a universally accepted doctrine of Christ. Meanwhile, Egyptian monks are developing for the Christian world both a dramatic new way of life and a positive theology of spiritual life and growth.

In chapter 4 we find that the ecumenical impact of Alexandria and Egypt virtually ends in 451 after Bishop Dioscorus of Alexandria overreaches himself in trying to dominate the church leadership in both capitals of the Empire, Constantinople and Rome. We shall see how isolation from these two great centers helps make Egyptian Christianity into a national church which will turn more and more to the native Coptic language and culture.

Chapter 5 begins with the Arab conquest of Egypt, made easier by Persians, but mainly by the Christian Byzantine Empire centered in Constantinople. We will see how in the three centuries from 640 to about 970 the Copts find ways to survive and make themselves needed. But they also begin to lose their place in their own country.

In the next three chapters, which bring us down to Napoleon's invasion in 1798, we will see how the Arab conquest has more drastic effects in Egypt than any earlier conquest of Egypt. Even Hellenistic Civilization did not have as much cultural impact on Egypt as the Arabs and Islamic Civilization were to have. Only Egypt's conversion to Christianity had a comparable influence in redirecting Egypt's history and culture. In 1800 many must have wondered if Egyptian Christianity would ever again be anything more than an historical relic.

In chapter 9 we begin to encounter the forces that make Coptic Christianity a lively twentieth-century religious movement, a striking balance to its strong traditionalism. Napoleon's 1798 invasion is short-lived, but it brings along a host of eager French investigators and innovators who initiate Western influences on Egypt. Then, the Albanian adventurer, Muhammad Ali gains control of Egypt and makes a massive effort to wrestle it into position as a "modern" economy and society. Simultaneously, Western missionaries in Egypt arrive to find it easier to evangelize Copts than Muslims and introduce elements into Egyptian church life that eventually become important forces in the Coptic Church itself. We also see the great reforming Patriarch, Cyril IV, laboring for seven years to push his views and programs for the Coptic Church, and how these new directions, which make the Coptic Church what it is today, survive powerful efforts to stall or even reverse reforms.

In chapter 10 we shall see how the late nineteenth century brings British occupation and rule, with paradoxical results for Egypt, for the Copts, and for the Copts' relationship to Egypt. We find that many of the developments in Egypt and the Coptic Church from 1882 to 1952 have mixed results for the church's future, which had looked so bright at the beginning of the twentieth century. The first half of the twentieth century sees massive struggles and outbursts of ideas and organizations which make the period interesting as well as important. Personalities begin to emerge who still in the 1990s incarnate the true greatness of Coptic Christianity.

Our final chapter focuses on the "Renaissance" in the Coptic Church since 1959. Since this is what originally motivated the writing of this book, our temptation is to depict the present as the long-awaited golden age of the Copts, now emerging after fifteen hundred years of vicissitudes. Unfortunately, despite their religious renaissance, which is quite real, the Copts are scarcely better off politically, economically, and socially in Egypt today than they were in the nineteenth century. We shall see why, and end the history proper with a consideration of the place of the Coptic Church in Egypt in the late twentieth century. In a brief Conclusion, the question of continuity in traditional Egyptian Christianity is addressed.

[1]Essentially the word Coptic simply means Egyptian. But it also refers to the last stage of written Egyptian; Coptic uses the Greek alphabet plus seven letters from Demotic (the next-to-last stage of written Egyptian). In speaking of church or Christianity, we normally substitute the adjective "Coptic" for "Egyptian" for the time since Coptic replaced Greek as the dominant language of Egyptian Christianity or for the time since the Egyptian Church became separated from most Eastern and all Western churches. All members of Egyptian Christian families are called "Copts," unless they convert to Islam, so it has become a quasi-ethnic term.

[2]For the place of Jews in Alexandria and Egypt, I am largely dependent on V. Tcherikover, *Hellenistic Civilization and the Jews*, trans. S. Applebaum (New York: Atheneum, 1970), especially Part II.

[3]Tcherikover, e.g., pp. 58, 272, 321.

[4]Tcherikover, p. 286.

[5]Tcherikover, p. 281.

Chapter One

The First Christians in Egypt

✠ ———————————————————————————————— ✠

to about 175 A.D.

W E SHOULD KNOW MORE ABOUT the beginnings of Christianity in Alexandria and Egypt than anywhere else outside of Jerusalem. The Christian Church in Egypt would seem to have been destined to lead Christianity from its earliest days through its triumph in the Roman world.

A. F. Shore, considering the role in world history of early Christianity in Egypt, tells us: "On the early development of the Christian Church Egypt exercised an important, and, at times, a decisive influence; at no other period of its history is the legacy of Egypt to the modern world so direct and so demonstrable."[1]

Nature herself was able to preserve for us ample evidence of a strong and influential Christian community in Egypt from the church's earliest days. Egypt's dry climate and soil are such that documents of all kinds, some of them simply thrown away or used for wrapping or packing, survive for centuries, just waiting for us to dig them up and decipher.

Also, communication between Judah and Egypt was short and direct— so short that the First Gospel has Joseph take Mary and the infant Jesus from Bethlehem to Egypt until Herod's death. In a number of Egypt's towns they would have found Jewish communities, some of them large and important. There was a lot of back-and-forth of Jews between Egypt and the Holy Land. And Jesus and all his early followers were Jews.

Indeed, Christianity began among Jews, and Jews had been in Egypt for centuries. Central to Jewish self-understanding was their long stay in Egypt before the Exodus. In the great exile of Jews in the sixth century B.C., a Jewish community was formed in Egypt that did not disappear. From the fourth century B.C., Alexandria had a large and influential minority of Jews. As they progressively forgot their traditional Hebrew language, they developed a Greek-speaking Judaism and a Greek translation of the Hebrew scriptures, the Septuagint, which was to be the first Bible of spreading Christianity.

In fact, the entire New Testament was written in Greek, the language of the spread of Christianity, and Alexandria was the principal center of the Greek-speaking culture we call Hellenism. Hellenistic culture was to provide the primitive Church not only with its language but also with a whole way of thinking that made Christianity comprehensible to the world of the Roman Empire and its near neighbors.

Finally, we would expect early Egyptian Christianity to be well known to us because by the early third century Alexandria was the intellectual and theological capital of the universal Christian movement, as evidenced by the writings of Clement and Origen. Simultaneously, Bishop Demetrius of Alexandria was developing a pattern of leadership and government of the church in Egypt that was to make the Alexandrian patriarchs the most powerful church authorities anywhere, except perhaps for Rome. There must have been a lot of history behind such achievements in theology and church organization which did so much to influence the evolution of Christianity. According to the expert opinion of J. M. Creed, "no city has affected the development of the Christian religion more profoundly than has Alexandria."[2]

We should know more about the first century and a half of Christianity in Egypt than almost anywhere else, yet we know very little about it. The New Testament, which contains all or almost all the oldest Christian writings that have come down to us, is of almost no help in seeing how the Christian Church got started in Egypt. The Book of Acts gives a lot of information about Christian beginnings in the great city of Antioch in Syria, and about Paul's churches in Asia Minor, and Macedonia, and Greece. And the New Testament epistles attributed to Paul give us important insights into primitive Christianity in many of the cities where he and his co-workers were active. Other epistles and the Book of Revelation mention various cities with Christian congregations. But none is in Egypt.

If Paul's missions had taken him to Egypt, we would know a great deal about Christian beginnings there. As it is, only one Egyptian is identified as a Christian in the New Testament—Apollos, a Jew born in Alexandria and learned in the Scriptures—but we are not told that he became a Christian in Egypt (except in one family of manuscripts of the Book of Acts). The only New Testament writing often associated with Egypt is the Epistle to the Hebrews, largely because it handles sacred scripture very much like the influential first-century Jewish writer, Philo of Alexandria. Martin Luther guessed that Apollos wrote the Epistle to the Hebrews.

It is striking that we read more in the New Testament about Christians from neighboring Cyrene than from Alexandria. Simon of Cyrene carried Jesus' cross, and Acts 11:20 and 13:1 suggest that missionaries and prophets from Cyrene were prominent in establishing and leading the Christian movement in Antioch. In Acts 2:20 and 6:9, Egypt is mentioned but is paired with the Cyrene area. Cyrene had a large and important Jewish population until the Jewish rebellion there in 115 A.D. It is not surprising that an important Christian group emerged there, but Cyrene was a city culturally and economically subordinate to Alexandria, so Cyrene should have gotten its Christianity from Alexandria and Egypt. However, there is no evidence that it did.

Why do we know so little of the early Christianity of Egypt? Walter Bauer[3] developed a brilliant explanation for our ignorance of early Egyptian Christianity: "orthodox" Christianity was brought to Egypt from Rome rather late and then covered up earlier evidences of Christianity because they would show that the earlier Christianity in Egypt was "heretical" Gnosticism. The theory is helped by the fact that the best known names of the Christians of the first half of the second century in Egypt were Gnostics like Basilides, Valentinus, and Carpocrates. Bauer also suggested that Mark was proposed by the orthodox as the apostolic founder of Alexandria for the simple reason that he was thought of as the disciple and interpreter of the Apostle Peter in Rome. Bauer's theory quickly drew attention, and opposition. The theory's greatest weakness was lack of concrete evidence in its favor.

Recently, Bauer's thesis has been rather effectively discredited by Colin H. Roberts,[4] who has argued that the earliest Christianity in Egypt was brought from Jerusalem to Alexandria, was Jewish rather than Pauline, and left few traces because Christians were not distinguished from Jews until the Jewish troubles of 117 A.D. growing out of the Jewish rebellion under Emperor Trajan. Upon reviewing the evidence, Birger A. Pearson[5] came to essentially the same conclusions, making them even more convincing.

For its first three centuries, Christianity was not recognized in Egypt (or elsewhere) by the Romans as a legal religion. Among other things, this meant that congregations had no protection and could not own property. Christianity's not being legal encouraged Egyptian Christians to try to be included within the Jewish community's "ethnic rights," at least until 117 A.D. This helps explain how Christians could have been virtually hidden among the large Jewish population.

What, then, do we know about the earliest Christianity in Egypt? Let us begin with direct evidence from archeological discoveries of literary fragments. We find that by the early second century the canonical Gospels of

Matthew and John are circulating in Upper Egypt, along with writings like the *Shepherd of Hermas* and *Gospel of Thomas*. And the important second century anti-Gnostic work by Bishop Irenaeus of Lyon in faraway Gaul was known in Egypt only a few years after he wrote it. In the words of Henry Chadwick[6]: "Papyrus fragments show that in the second century the [Christian] mission had moved far up the Nile valley." There is direct evidence of an early Christianity in Egypt.

Indirect literary evidence of early Egyptian Christianity is found in a number of writings thought to have originated in Egypt. We have already mentioned the canonical Epistle to the Hebrews. There was also a *Gospel of the Hebrews*, angled towards Jewish Christian concerns, which was known to writers in the third and fourth centuries, although we now have only fragments of it. We have even fewer fragments of the *Gospel of the Egyptians*, which opposed marriage for Christians. There is every reason to believe that these two Jewish-Christian writings were Egyptian. But they do not tell us much about the early church in Egypt except for its Jewish connection and tendency toward self-denial.

The *Epistle of Barnabas*, the *Preaching of Peter*, and even the *Book of James* were probably Egyptian writings also. Clement and Origen believed that the *Epistle of Barnabas* was written by that well-known leader from the Book of Acts and that it was authoritative. It contains a very Jewish description of the "two ways" between which we must choose. But it is mainly concerned to show that the Jewish Bible can only be correctly understood by Christians and really belongs to them—in this way sounding rather like the Epistle to the Hebrews. The first *Pseudo-Clementine Homilies*, probably written later and in Syria, links Barnabas to Alexandria when it claims that Clement of Rome was taught Christianity by Barnabas in Alexandria.

The *Preaching of Peter* may go back as early as the first century and was quoted by Clement of Alexandria as authentic teaching from the apostle. The few fragments we have (mostly in Clement's writings) emphasize the oneness of God and criticize idols, both of which emphases sound Jewish. But readers are also warned not to imitate those Jews who worship angels and archangels, the months and the moon. Israelites are said to need to repent and believe in Jesus, and their prophets need to be interpreted as speaking of Jesus Christ if they are to be properly understood.

The second century *Book of James* purports to be the story of Jesus' mother Mary, written by Joseph's son James. It begins with her marvelous conception and continues up through the birth of Jesus—with a subordinate interest in the origins of John the Baptist. The writing is Jewish in tone and attempts to fill in some of the gaps in the earlier Gospels about the backgrounds of Mary and her husband Joseph, and the parents of John—all devout Jews, of course.

The *Second Epistle of Clement* and the *Epistle of the Apostles* are believed by some to be Egyptian. *Second Clement* quotes the *Gospel of the Egyptians* and shows similarities with Alexandrian theology. This does not prove that it was written in Alexandria, though it is quite possible that it was. It is a sermon which insists on Jesus' divinity and on the reality of his flesh, on our being the children of the Church, which is Christ's body, and on repentance and the need for good works.

The *Epistle of the Apostles*, which may well have been composed in Asia Minor, circulated in Upper Egypt in a Coptic version and was known in Ethiopia. It is presented as the words of the resurrected Christ giving further instructions to his Apostles. As in *Second Clement* there is a focus on the divinity and the flesh of Christ and on the need to obey Jesus' commandments. We see that all these writings have some distinctly Jewish characteristics.

In fact, all the literature we associate with early Egyptian Christianity fits well with the ideas that it was, indeed, Jewish Christianity and that the Christians were part of the Jewish community until the terrible reaction against the Jews after the Jewish rebellions of the early second century. The depicting of Jesus as revealer and as the Wisdom and Word of God but also truly in-the-flesh, along with the insistence on Jesus as the key to understanding the Jewish scriptures, all fit well with the Jewishness and the Christianity of the earliest Christians in Egypt.

When we say that Jewish Christians were part of the Jewish community in Alexandria, this does not mean that there was not a majority of Jews who rejected the Christian message. Indeed, refuting the claims of the non-Christian Jewish majority seems to be a common thread in the writings we associate with the Alexandrian Christians of that period, e.g., the Epistle to the Hebrews and the *Epistle of Barnabas*. That Jewish Christians were part of the Jewish community does mean that Jewish Christians of Egypt and their Jewish disputants shared a common Bible, the Septuagint. The dispute was about what the Jewish Law means, not whether the Jewish Law is authoritative.

Jews had flourished in Alexandria from the time they had been welcomed and cultivated by the early Ptolemies who ruled Egypt two or three centuries before Christ. The Ptolemies recognized Jews as an essentially self-governing community, and this helped maintain in-group loyalty in the Jewish community. Individual Jews, however, could also qualify through their education and wealth for the privileged citizenship granted Macedonians and Greeks. Jews also flourished under Roman rule in the first century. The Palestinian rulers of the Jews, Antipater and his son, Herod the Great, had backed Julius Caesar and Octavian who won the struggles for leadership of Rome in the first century B.C. So we are not surprised that the

Romans quickly recognized the Jews in Alexandria as a community with religious rights.

Then, a crucial change emerged for Jews in Egypt after 5 A.D. A new Roman poll-tax on everyone in Egypt not classified a Greek or Roman disqualified many Jews and resulted in their "social and psychic dislocation." Thus, "this disenfranchised Jewish minority group would have been extremely receptive" to Christian missionaries, especially after 70 A.D., when in Egypt the emperors confiscated land previously granted to private owners, and in the Holy Land Jerusalem was captured and its temple destroyed. It is not too surprising that the new and promising Christian movement within Judaism would attract many Jews.[7]

The early Egyptian Christians owed a great deal to Philo, a contemporary of Jesus and the Apostles, and perhaps the most influential Jew in Alexandria in his day. In addition to his work as an advocate for the Jewish community, in his writings he traced out a way of interpreting the Jewish Law and a way to use the language and culture of Hellenism to explain the faith and practice of the Jewish people. Philo had the same basic motive as the translators of the Septuagint: to make Judaism comprehensible and convincing to Jews whose language and culture were no longer Hebrew, Aramaic, or Palestinian. Egyptian Christians were to take full advantage of the methodology of Philo, as well as the Greek Old Testament, to build up a comprehensive understanding of God and God's relation to the world and its history, which was destined to capture the imagination of the heirs of Egypt's intellectual and spiritual traditions.

The works of Philo were a model for the Christian writers of Alexandria, even if they did not slavishly copy him in detail, for their readers were even more Hellenized than Philo's. In his *Church History* the fourth century Bishop Eusebius of Caesarea in Palestine assumed that the Egyptian Jews called "Therapeutae," whom Philo described, were Christian converts of Mark.[8] For Eusebius, the ascetical way of life described seemed more characteristic of Christians than Jews. Then Eusebius went on to report[9] rather extensively on various other writings of Philo, illustrating the dependence of Christian theology on this leader of Alexandrian Judaism.

The "Jewish" Christians of Alexandria would have included not only ethnic or observant Jews who accepted the Christian Gospel; they would also have included Christian converts who had been "godfearers," that is, Gentiles who worshipped in the synagogue and admired Jewish faith and worship and morals but did not want to be circumcised or take on the dietary laws or become ethnic Jews.

The variety of the first Christians in Alexandria would mirror the diversity among Jews there, economic and social, and also religious. All the Christians would have insisted that Jesus was the Messiah and would have accepted the authority of his teachings, but otherwise they could be conservative or liberal, traditionalist or modernist, broad or narrow in their acceptance of what was sacred literature, enthusiastic about Hellenism and philosophy or hostile to both.

As we shall be seeing in the evolution of Christianity in Egypt, not all Egyptian Christians favored the spiritual interpretation of Scripture popular with Philo and Christian theologians, not all accepted or rejected the Book of Revelation, not all believed that God is pure spirit and has no body, not all preferred the Greek language to Coptic, and not all the Alexandrian clergy backed their patriarchs in the great Trinitarian controversy against their fellow priest, Arius.

This diversity among Christians in some cases perpetuated differences going back to Alexandrian Judaism and in other cases is reminiscent of its variety. For example, as one scholar has observed, "one can plausibly trace. . . a first-century religious Platonism represented on the Jewish side by Philo and on the Christian side by Apollos. . .[but]. . .less sophisticated varieties of Christianity [e.g., that found in the *Epistle of Barnabas*] existed in first-century Alexandria."[10]

For most of the early period we are considering in this chapter, Christians, as a part of the Jewish community, reflected the diversity within that community. Early Egyptian Christianity has been called "a movement more than. . .a church" and a "movement [which] took shape in a number of esoteric groups. . . .[with] their roots in Jewish wisdom-schools."[11] There is no early contemporary evidence to suggest that there were any official Christian leaders who might have tried to standardize Christian teaching in Alexandria.

Among the variety of Christian groups, we know of Christian "gnostics" who viewed themselves as by nature spiritually superior to average Christians as well as to non-Christians. Alexandria seems to have produced the most famous teachers of Christian Gnosticism in the first half of the second century, Basilides and Valentinus. Both focused on the sharp distinction between the inferior creator and law-giving God of the Old Testament and the hitherto unknown and unknowable superior God, with whom the "gnostic" elite had a natural affinity.

Christian Gnostics thought of Jesus as a revealer of such knowledge, by which Gnostics were "redeemed" from the low and the false self-image which had previously handicapped them. This knowledge was available only to those to whom it was handed down in a secret and private tradition; it was not something even philosophers could figure out for themselves. Christian Gnostic teachers claimed to have direct links with apostolic tradition.

Basilides, like other Gnostics, was concerned with the problems of evil and of suffering. He was the "first Christian theologian to interpret the New

7

Testament allegorically" and wanted to downplay its connection with the Old. In this matter he may have been "echoing the extreme anti-Jewish feeling of Alexandria of the time."[12]

Of the Gnostic teachers perhaps the most influential was Valentinus, who may well have been Egyptian and educated in Alexandria,[13] although he spent most of his mature years in Rome,[14] where he may have hoped to become bishop.[15] The greatest "hammers of heretics" at the end of the second and beginning of the third century—Bishop Irenaeus of Lyon and Hippolytus, learned presbyter and anti-pope in Rome, and Tertullian, a brilliant Christian writer of Carthage—exposed and refuted Valentinus and his followers. He not only had adherents but also disciples who were perpetuating and expanding on his teachings.

Gnostic and other expressions of Egyptian Christianity seem to have had much in common: preaching "individual salvation with an emphasis on gnosis and askesis [discipline]," stressing "a spiritual and heavenly rather than a corporeal and earthly citizenship," and combining "the language of contemporary religious philosophy and its Platonic concepts with traditions based on Jewish Scriptures."[16] Thus we are not surprised that a Gnostic library should be discovered at Nag Hammadi in Upper Egypt in the vicinity of an ancient Christian monastery—and with bindings manufactured by the monks.[17] Whether these writings had ever formed part of the monastery library is still debated.[18] It is notable that "none of these texts are polemics against either Gnosticism or Manichaeism,"[19] and it is not hard to see that Nag Hammadi works like *The Gospel of Truth, On the Origin of the World, The Gospel of Thomas,* and *The Teachings of Sylvanus* would have been valued by Coptic-speaking monks and other Christians who aspired to a more mystical and mysterious presentation of spirituality than they might discover in the translations they had of books of the Bible—or hear from the pulpits of their churches.

Irenaeus' attack on Gnosticism, already circulating in Upper Egypt before the end of the second century, shows that church authorities were hoping from an early date to discredit the movement, but it is likely that Gnosticism was driven underground only with the fourth-century focus of church authority in Egypt on the dangers of heresy. The great Alexandrian theologians of the third century quoted Gnostics like Theodotus and Heracleon (who may have been the first to write a commentary on a Gospel and may have influenced Origen[20]), and they shared some spiritual ideas with Gnostics. But we shall see in the next chapter that it was they, Clement and Origen, rather than the Gnostics who pointed the way to mature Alexandrian theology. The Gnostics failed the crucial test of taking seriously the humanity of Jesus;[21] and their tendency to deny human free will and to reserve real salvation to a few elect natures was inconsistent with the basic theology of Clement and Origen and the Alexandrian theologians who inherited the tradition they created.

All Christian groups in Alexandria found it easy to conceive of Jesus as the embodiment of the divine Wisdom or Word ("logos"), who could bridge the gap between the human race and the eternal and almighty God who is quite above and beyond everything in our experience. The divine Wisdom is personified both in the canonical Book of Proverbs (e.g., chapter 8) and in the Alexandrian book, *Wisdom,* (especially chapters 7-10) which formed part of the Septuagint. The divine Word is a crucial concept in Philo, and the prologue to the Gospel of John is dominated by the Word—which comes close to being the same as the creative Wisdom of Jewish tradition. Both Word and Wisdom were quite familiar to first-century Alexandrian Jews.

Christians in Alexandria were intensely interested in how Jesus' teachings and achievements should be related to Moses' covenant and laws and to the Jewish scriptures as a whole. For them, the Epistle to the Hebrews, and perhaps the *Epistle of Barnabas* as well, provided useful answers that would be worked out carefully by Clement and Origen in response to Judaizing efforts within the Christian community of their own day. Also, the challenge of non-Christian Judaism remained sufficiently important in Alexandria that the learned Origen prepared himself to defend Christian claims by studying Hebrew and compiling a Hebrew text of the Old Testament with five parallel columns, one for a Hebrew text using Greek letters, one for the Septuagint, and three for other Greek translations, all extremely literal.

For many centuries, Egyptian Christians have considered Saint Mark to be the founder of their church. Clement of Alexandria reported[22] late in the second century that Mark came from Rome to Alexandria after Peter was martyred and produced there a "more spiritual" edition of the Gospel he wrote in Rome, presumably the New Testament Gospel of Mark. Eusebius of Caesarea reported[23] the tradition that the Mark who wrote the Gospel of Mark "was the first who was sent to Egypt. . .and first established churches in Alexandria." In his *Chronicle*[24] Eusebius dates Mark's arrival in the third year of Emperor Claudius (43 A.D.); and in his *Church History*[25] he stated that Mark was succeeded as head of the church in Alexandria in the eighth year of Nero (62 A.D.). A tradition that Mark died a martyr in Alexandria may go back as far as the fourth century.

This Mark who is featured in Christian tradition as the author of a canonical Gospel is well known from the Book of Acts as a companion of Barnabas and Paul. He is also pictured in New Testament epistles attributed to Paul and Peter as a junior co-worker of both. Any church would be proud to claim as her founder one so close to the original church in Jerusalem

(Acts 12:12) and a companion of both Peter, the Apostle to the Jews, and Paul, the Apostle to the Gentiles. Mark was not one of the Twelve, but neither was Paul nor were the anonymous founders of the Church in Antioch (Acts 11:19-21.) A review of evidence of Mark's work in Egypt can show that it is more likely that Mark was in Alexandria than many critical historians have thought.[26] The problem of establishing Mark's foundation of Christianity in Egypt is simply the problem of our startling lack of knowledge of the earliest Christianity there.

Traditional Egyptian emphasis on religious observances and on life after death would strongly influence Egyptians converting to Christianity. Jewish emphasis on synagogue worship and strict moral teachings and a strong sense of community also influenced evolving Egyptian Christianity. Coptic Christianity has always had more specifically Jewish characteristics than almost any other Christian tradition except its daughter church in Ethiopia.

The Septuagint gave the first Egyptian Christians a complete and authoritative Old Testament as the necessary background for their own developing canon of apostolic writings which eventually became the New Testament. Philo the Jew provided Egyptian Christians with a method of reconciling their traditional teachings with a new culture. Thus the early Egyptian Christians confronted their world with great confidence. They had both an authoritative literature and a host of associated writings that showed them God's plan, located them in it, and gave them a detailed way of life appropriate to their present and their future—but with a flexibility which allowed the Christians to transcend language, culture, and ethnicity. In chapter 2 we see it all blossom.

[1]A. F. Shore, "Christian and Coptic Egypt" in *Legacy of Egypt*, ed. J. R. Harris, 2nd ed. (Oxford: Clarendon Press, 1971), p. 390.

[2]J. M. Creed, "Christian and Coptic Egypt," in *Legacy of Egypt*, ed. S.R.K. Glanville, 1st ed. (Oxford: Clarendon Press, 1942), p. 300.

[3]*Orthodoxy and Heresy in Earliest Christianity*, trans. and ed. R. A. Kraft et al. (Philadelphia: Fortress Press, 1977).

[4]Colin H. Roberts, first in "Early Christianity in Egypt: Three Notes," *Journal of Egyptian Archaeology*, 40 (1954), 92-96, then in detail in *Manuscript, Society and Belief in Early Christian Egypt* (Oxford: Oxford Univ. Press, 1979).

[5]Notably Birger A. Pearson in "Earliest Christianity in Egypt," in *The Roots of Egyptian Christianity*, ed. B. A. Pearson and J. E. Goehring (Philadelphia: Fortress Press, 1986), pp. 132-156.

[6]*The Early Church* (Baltimore: Penguin Books, 1967), p. 64.

[7]H. A. Green, "The Socio-Economic Background of Christianity in Egypt," in *The Roots of Egyptian Christianity,* pp. 109-111.

[8]*Church History* II, chap. 17, trans. A.C. McGiffert, in Eusebius: *Church History et alia,* Vol. 1 of *Nicene and Post-Nicene Fathers of the Christian Church,* 2nd ser., ed. H. Wace and P. Schaff (New York: Charles Scribner's Sons, 1925).

[9]*Church History* II, p. 18.

[10]Pearson, p. 149.

[11]A. F. J. Klijn, "Jewish Christianity in Egypt," in *The Roots of Egyptian Christianity,* p. 173.

[12]W. H. C. Frend, "Basilides," *Coptic Encyclopedia,* 1991.

[13]According to Epiphanius, *Panarion* 31,2, 1-3 trans. P. R. Amidon, *The Panarion of St. Epiphanius, Bishop of Salamis: Selected Passages* (New York: Oxford Univ. Press, 1990), p.108.

[14]According to Irenaeus, A *Refutation and Subversion of Knowledge Falsely So Called (or Against Heresies)* III, 4, 3 trans. A. Roberts, W. H. Rambaut et al., in *The Apostolic Fathers - Justin Martyr - Irenaeus,* Vol. 1 of *The Ante-Nicene Fathers,* ed. A. Roberts and J. Donaldson (New York: Charles Scribner's Sons, 1926).

[15]According to Tertullian, *Against the Valentinians* IV, trans. A. Roberts, in *Latin Christianity: Its Founder, Tertullian,* Vol. 3 of *The Ante-Nicene Fathers,* ed. A. Roberts and J. Donaldson (New York: Charles Scribner's Sons, 1926).

[16]Samuel Rubenson, *The Letters of St. Antony: Origenist Theology, Monastic Tradition and the Making of a Saint* (Lund: Lund Univ. Press, 1990), p. 101.

[17]Conveniently presented in *The Nag Hammadi Library in English,* 3rd ed., trans. and intro. by Members of the Coptic Gnostic Library Project of the Institute for Antiquity and Christianity, Claremont, California, J. M. Robinson, gen. ed. (San Francisco: Harper and Row, 1988.)

[18]Rubenson, *The Letters of St. Antony,* pp. 123-124 and the literature cited.

[19]D. W. Johnson, "Coptic Reactions to Gnosticism and Manichaeism," *Le Muséon,* 100 (1987), p. 199.

[20]W. H. C. Frend, "Heracleon," *Coptic Encyclopedia,* 1991.

[21]T. Hall Partrick, "Jesus of Nazareth in Second-Century Gnosticism," Diss. Univ. of Chicago, 1969.

[22]M. Smith, *Clement of Alexandria and a Secret Gospel of Mark* (Cambridge: Harvard Univ. Press, 1973), p. 446.

[23]*Church History* II, p. 16.

[24]In Jerome's reworking of the Chronicle, 7:7 in *Eusebius Werke in Griechische christliche Schriftsteller* 47. See Pearson's note 30 in "Earliest Christianity in Egypt," in *The Roots of Egyptian Christianity,* p. 139.

[25]*Church History* II, p. 24.

[26]This is L. W. Barnard's conclusion in "St. Mark and Alexandria," *Harvard Theological Review,* 57 (1964), pp. 145-150.

Chapter Two

Foundations for Leadership

✠ —————————————————————————————— ✠

from about 175 to 313

THE YOUNG CHRISTIAN MOVEMENT was convinced it had a universal message, the Christian Gospel, which was calling the entire human race into a universal community, the Christian Church. The grandeur of this conviction was rivaled by the universal thrust of Hellenistic Civilization, which assumed that reason was common to all humanity and that Hellenism could educate all races and peoples to use reason to create human unity based on their common humanity.

At first, Christianity and Hellenism seemed to be at war with one another. The Church early adopted the Greek language, but the Hellenistic writers like Celsus, the pagan philosopher, and the Roman historians held Christians up to scorn; and the Roman Empire, which had become the political arm of Hellenism, refused to accept Christianity as legal.

Informed observers must have thought Christianity and Hellenism quite incompatible. At least two Christian writers thought so: the Syrian Tatian and the Carthaginian Tertullian. In one of his famous sayings, Tertullian asked sarcastically whether Athens had anything to do with Jerusalem, implying a strong "no"; and Tatian wrote a long *Discourse to the Greeks* denying that they had made any original positive contribution to humanity. And had not Paul contrasted the wisdom sought by the Greeks with the foolishness of the cross of the Christians (I Corinthians 1:18-25)?

If Christianity was to be able to use Hellenism to universalize its impact, it "needed the services of the more highly developed minds and personalities that were to be found in the cultural environment of Alexandria, capital of the Hellenistic world." Philo had tried to reconcile the Jewish heritage with Hellenism; "thus it was not unprecedented when two centuries

13

later the Hellenic and Christian traditions came face to face with one another at this crossroads of history."[1]

It was first with Clement of Alexandria and then with the greater Origen that "the Christian faith and Greek philosophical tradition became embodied in one and the same individual."[2] With the evolution of Christian Alexandria, neither Christianity nor Hellenism would ever be the same again.

This marriage of Christianity and Hellenism was not the only development in Christian Egypt in the hundred years plus between late in the second century and early in the fourth century. Egyptian Christianity was also making itself a principal contributor to evolving Christianity by developing along two other lines as well. The first was a pattern of leadership worked out through a hierarchy of bishops. The other was a strenuous type of Christianity resulting from the fruitful combination of Saint Anthony's pioneering monastic life with the vast numbers of Egyptians' showing the character of their loyalty to Christ by dying as martyrs. These intellectual, organizational, and heroic efforts of third-century Egyptian Christianity are also interrelated, as we shall see.

"The Christian hope had its roots in Palestine; Christian theology and, above all, Christology have theirs in Alexandria."[3] We begin with the theological achievements of the early third-century Christian "school" of Alexandria. Like the philosophical schools, it was a school in the sense of successive teachers with similar emphases and a substantial body of teachings that did not depend on any individual or external support to guarantee its continuing influence. Still, it was the two writers, Clement and Origen, who constitute almost everything we mean when we talk about the Christian "school of Alexandria."

Let us note three other generalizations about the school: it was Alexandrian and therefore Hellenistic; its relation to the official church leadership seems to have fluctuated rather widely; and third, the school began and ended this crucial period in Egyptian church history in obscurity for us. We know nothing of any writing of Pantaenus, at the beginning, and we have only tiny fragments of the writings of Theognostos and Pierius, at the end. Because of, or in spite of, these factors, the Christian school of Alexandria was to have an incalculable influence on Egyptian Christianity, and on world Christianity.

The first great writer, Clement of Alexandria, c. 150 to c. 215 A.D., was very much influenced by the writings of Philo. Although Clement's interests were primarily philosophical, he was always conscious of the learned traditions of Alexandria's Museum and Library and the role of Alexandrians in literary scholarship in the Greek classics. Of special interest to Clement was explaining and advocating Christianity while avoiding both the excessive simple-mindedness associated with Christian orthodoxy and the false pretensions to knowledge associated with what were coming to be considered the heterodox theories of the Gnostics.

Of Pantaenus, we infer from Clement[4] that he was from Sicily and from Eusebius[5] we learn that he was a Stoic philosopher before he was a Christian and that he traveled to India before he became head of the school. Clement particularly valued Pantaenus' ability to interpret Holy Scripture in accordance with the doctrine of the Christian Apostles.

Clement himself was probably from Athens and, as a convert to Christianity and a philosopher, he had traveled widely to seek out distinguished Christian teachers. After successes elsewhere, he found in the city of Alexandria and the person of Pantaenus exactly what he was looking for; and there in Alexandria Clement initiated a fruitful career as a writer and as head of the "school." We do not know much more about Clement the man except that he was a presbyter, that he left Alexandria about 202, probably because of an outbreak of persecution, and that he died shortly before 215. His influence on Origen, who is supposed to have succeeded him at the "school," is undoubted, although, oddly enough, Origen never mentioned Clement in any of his writings which we still possess.

Clement's career was dedicated to showing thoughtful Christians and potential converts how Christianity can fulfill their highest intellectual, spiritual, and moral aspirations. He rejected fanciful strictures on sex, on wealth, on poetry or philosophy and went on to use his learning and his philosophical skills to expound the emerging Christian "orthodoxy" in a new way designed to be attractive to educated Alexandrians. He had had a good Hellenistic education in poetry and philosophy. He used anthologies of each, as was the custom, but he also knew the major classics themselves.

Instead of attacking Greek philosophy, Clement depicted it as God's gift to the Greeks to compensate them for not enjoying God's revelation to Israel. Thus philosophy cannot contradict the Christian revelation, since they are both from God. Rather, philosophy deepens and enhances our understanding of the faith by increasing our knowledge and our capacity to know and understand. By growing in knowledge Christians fulfill their faith and become authentically Christian "gnostics."

Clement was an optimistic theologian who assumed that Christian growth in knowledge is naturally paralleled by spiritual and moral growth. Creation itself is good, and humanity is by its very nature free to learn and to grow. Throughout history, God leads humanity through a set of learning experiences which move humanity on toward the goal of Creation.

For Clement, the Bible recounts the incomparable history of the people of God and their moral and spiritual journey; moreover, while God established the Bible as the norm for all truth, he also implanted other disciplines in human minds which would provide for growth for the People of God as well as for those still in partial darkness.

Clement did not limit himself to such general speculations. He gave a great deal of practical advice to those who wanted to know what it means to be a sincere and knowledgeable Christian. According to Clement, one does not have to be poor or celibate or ignorant to be a good Christian. Thus Christians need help on how to handle wealth, sex, and knowledge in responsible and positive ways that contribute to spiritual and moral growth.

Clement did not want to ease Christian consciences. In fact, he was rather puritanical, with no patience with luxury or self-indulgence. He preached restraint rather than abstinence. Like the Stoics, he was suspicious of the passions. It is also true that, as a good Platonist, Clement assumed that growth in knowledge and morality moves us progressively away from the worldly and the carnal toward the spiritual and the intellectual.

In sum, for Clement, the whole creation is good and we are to learn much from the various ways it has been understood. But it is in Christ that creation reaches its fulfillment, and we perfect our "education" by following the moral and spiritual path Christ has laid out, using our intellectual abilities to their fullest as we try to understand precisely where to go and how to get there. Thus Clement wed his faith to the humanistic dimension of Hellenism.

If Clement pioneered in embodying in himself Christian faith and Greek philosophical tradition, it was Origen who became the master of explaining Christianity at a level equal in every respect to the highest intellectual achievements of Hellenistic Civilization. The victory of Christianity in the ancient Mediterranean world was in part political, when emperors became Christian and sponsored Christianity. But the victory was also spiritual, intellectual, and literary, and no one did more toward achieving that victory than Origen of Alexandria, 185-253 A.D.

To the task of improving on Clement's beginnings, Origen brought an early start, a brilliant and massive intellect, an enormous appetite for work, and a deep and lifelong religious commitment. It is no wonder that this combination resulted in so many achievements, and Origen was above all an achiever.

We will describe only three of Origen's writings, but we will want to remember that Origen left a mass of literature, mostly on the Bible, greater than the vast majority of readers ever get around to reading in the course of a lifetime. Origen's literary output was greatly helped by a team of stenographers and scribes provided by Ambrosius, a rich Christian Origen had converted away from what he considered a heterodox group.

We mention first Origen's compilation in parallel columns of a Hebrew text of the Old Testament, a Greek transliteration, and four Greek translations—a massive work of scholarship we call the Hexapla, to which we alluded in Chapter One. This required him to know "the textual criticism and exegetic literature developed by the Alexandrian school of philology"[6]— and to learn Hebrew and to invest countless hours of work. Furthermore, Origen "was also a trained teacher of literature in the tradition of the great Alexandrian scholars. He was, in fact, one of the greatest interpreters of the Bible on the literal level in the early church."[7]

Next we mention Origen's book *On First Principles,* a topic Clement wanted to write on but apparently never did. In this bold work, Origen set forth his views on creation, on how humanity got itself into its present situation, on human freedom and God's grace, on our relations with Father, Son, and Holy Spirit, on our future, and on how Holy Scripture can be interpreted so that authoritative answers to such challenging questions can be found. Unfortunately, we have only fragments of the original Greek, for Rufinus' Latin translation is suspected of trying to make Origen's bold speculations more "orthodox."

The third work we single out is Origen's book *Against Celsus.* This was by no means the first Christian effort to answer pagan objections to Christianity, but it is qualitatively superior to all earlier ones. Origen gives a fair exposition of Celsus' most telling criticisms of Christianity, and he answers these objections in detail and with a level of learning and style equal to or superior to Celsus.'[8]

Ironically, despite the grandeur of his achievements, much of Origen's theology seems strange and unconvincing to us, and, over the years, quite heretical to most Eastern Christians. He tells us that human beings and angels and demons all find themselves in the exact state which they deserve after an original falling away from their pristine creation, God being just; but the states we are in now have been so arranged by God in a second creation as to lead us together toward the perfection for which we were first created, God being both gracious and omnipotent.

Origen claims to find these and a multitude of other remarkable ideas in the Bible, by deciphering the allegorical or "spiritual" meanings that are supposed to underlie the stories, poems, prophecies, wise sayings and detailed laws and instructions found in the Scriptures. Origen believed that the same techniques of Bible interpretation are found not only in Philo the Jew but in the writings of Paul and in the Epistle to the Hebrews and in many early Christian writings. For the modern reader, however, most of Origen's spiritual interpretation seems fanciful, even though it is also clear that Origen had an unmatched knowledge of the contents of the Scriptures.

Origen assumed that the Creator willed to bring all rational beings to their natural perfection (even Satan might be saved!), but the Creator also gave them freedom. To the problem of preserving our free will in the face of God's determination to see us brought to perfection, Origen posed the solution of a whole series of existences. In the course of them, we errant creatures would sooner or later choose of our own free will to dedicate ourselves wholly to obedience to God. For this theory, Origen was accused of teaching reincarnation but is credited with laying groundwork for the Western doctrine of purgatory—a doctrine the Coptic Church has denied for centuries.

In common with Clement, Origen perceived the heart of the human enterprise to be spiritual progress. Progress begins with taking the letter of the Bible seriously, sincere efforts to live according to the letter of God's laws, and attachment to "Jesus Christ and him crucified." Without leaving aside those beginnings or any of the intermediate steps, progress climaxes with the ability to discern the Bible's spiritual meaning, the heroic virtues exemplified in the martyr, and a clear understanding of the mysteries of God and all God's creation.

As we have already intimated, while these church writers were laying the foundations of a spirituality and a learned theology, Bishop Demetrius was initiating a hierarchy which would place Egyptian Christianity in the forefront of leadership in the Christian world. Tradition yields contrasting pictures of the man. Eusebius, the first real ecclesiastical historian, was an extravagant admirer of Origen. He shows us a Demetrius so jealous of the brilliant Origen that he drives Origen away from Egypt and gets him condemned by a Roman as well as an Egyptian synod of bishops. The much later, and much less generally reliable (for that period) *History of the Patriarchs of Alexandria* pictures Demetrius as a miraculous personality who was married but was a virgin, was illiterate but became a Bible scholar, and whose ability to perceive that a communicant was a sinner resulted in a sharp drop-off of church members coming forward to receive communion! Origen is depicted as an archheretic, against whom Demetrius protected his flock. This all reflects the Origenist controversies of a later period.

Before Demetrius, it seems that the presbyters governed the church in Alexandria, in which case it would have been Demetrius himself who created the Egyptian episcopate[9] by consecrating three other bishops, to be followed by the consecration of twenty more by his successor, Heraclas.

Although he was ultimately to turn against Origen, it was Demetrius who appointed him head of the catechetical school in Alexandria, thus demonstrating his right of oversight of the school. As both Heraclas and his successor Dionysius were heads of the school before they became bishop of Alexandria, the link between bishop and school is noteworthy.

By 313 there were about seventy-two bishops in Egypt and the adjacent territory of Cyrenaica and Libya and twenty-eight more after 325,[10] but the bishop of Alexandria maintained strict supervision over them all, perhaps because the Empire was so slow in granting municipal status to any of the other cities.[11] This hierarchical structure initiated by Demetrius was a primary factor in making the heads of the church in Alexandria such important leaders in world Christianity, until the 451 explosion which resulted in the separation between Alexandria on the one hand and Rome and Constantinople on the other.

The third element making the third century so important for Egyptian Christianity and its influence was the beginning of monasticism. As to its background, we know of pre-Christian solitaries associated with the Egyptian temples; and Philo wrote about the Therapeutae in Egypt, who had much in common with the future Christian monks. Elements of Christianity from the first easily blended into communities and asceticisms which produced fourth-century monasticism.[12] It has been suggested that the rise of monasticism was influenced by the Jewish-Christians called "Ebionites."[13] Even Saint Anthony of the Desert, often called the first Christian monk, was said by a tradition promoted by Jerome to have been preceded by Saint Paul of Thebes who became a model for Anthony.[14]

But we must begin somewhere, and Anthony,[15] or at least Anthony as Saint Athanasius publicized him in his widely read *Life of Anthony*, is a good place to start. His decision to obey Jesus' injunction to the rich man to sell everything (Mark 10:21), his continuing disillusionment with the level of commitment of most church people, his titanic struggles with demonic powers of the desert, and his willingness to be a spiritual adviser to the aspirants to the life of the Christian hermit made him a complete model to the solitary monk.[16]

Anthony was born about 251 to a family in comfortable circumstances but he does not seem to have been given a Greek education, although Greek education was available in various parts of Egypt and the ignorance or intellectual naiveté of the early monks may have been seriously exaggerated.[17] After the death of Anthony's parents about 270 he provided for his sister, gave away his wealth, studied the advice and example of other ascetics, practiced rigid self-denial, and progressively sought solitude.

Anthony also became in the minds of Christians who encountered him, or his reputation, a healer and an inspired teacher. It does not seem to have occurred to anyone that his search for solitude meant that he was fanatical or that he was selfishly trying to save his own soul in isolation from other Christians. Disciples took up residence in nearby caves to learn from him and to be near him as an example and as a source of practical wisdom. Thus a kind of community would form, but without rule or vows or organization, and a steady stream of visitors came for counsel and inspiration from the holy man.

Anthony and his fellow monastics strove for mortification, to put to death any worldliness within themselves that hindered their spiritual development. Their efforts closely paralleled the literal dying experienced by Christian martyrs. Origen's father was a martyr under Emperor Septimius Severus, and he had the encouragement of the young Origen, who also urged his pupils to be ready and happy to die for their faith and loyalty,[18]and in 236 Origen wrote an influential *Exhortation to Martyrdom* for his friend Ambrosius. Under the persecution of Emperor Decius in 250, Origen was tortured,[19] and there was a host of martyrs in Egypt, as reported by Bishop Dionysius of Alexandria.[20]

Not all Egyptian Christians were willing to suffer for their faith, and even Bishop Dionysius was criticized for fleeing his city.[21] But he joined other bishops in creating guidelines about what was legitimate in avoiding persecution and about how bishops should deal pastorally with Christians who denied their faith to escape the rigors of the confiscation of property, prison, torture, or death. Disputes over the reconciliation of these "lapsed" Christians were a very destructive result of the persecution of the church. Dionysius was able later to show courage and practicality in taking his punishment for being a Christian and bishop.[22]

The ideal of martyrdom remained a strong influence on the Egyptian Church. The persecution which was to become the worst ever was initiated under Emperor Diocletian in 303. It was not long before Egypt supplied the Christian movement with its largest number of martyrs ever.[23] Bishop Peter of Alexandria himself was martyred[24] in 311, one of the last martyrs before Constantine. It says something interesting about Egyptian Christianity that the church of Egypt selected the first year of Diocletian's rule, 284 A.D., as their year 1, i.e., 1 A.M. (for *anno martyrium*.) Ironically, it was under Bishop Peter the Martyr that Bishop Melitius of Lycopolis began a schism by going about ordaining clergy while Bishop Peter was prudently staying in exile. The debate was still over what measures could be properly taken to avoid persecution and how to deal with penitent Christians who gave over in order to avoid torture or death.

If we return to Dionysius, we see that he incorporates within himself some of the more important features of third-century Egyptian Christianity.[25] He was a pupil and then an assistant to Origen in the Christian school of Alexandria. He became head of the school, and then bishop when Heraclas, his predecessor both at the school and as bishop, died. Dionysius himself had to face persecution. He was a prolific writer and wrestled with such crucial questions as how to deal with penitent "lapsed" Christians, Biblical literalism and the authenticity of the Apocalypse of John (he rejected it on the basis of the different literary styles in the Gospel and in the Apocalypse), and the Doctrine of the Trinity. When his namesake from Rome took issue with Dionysius' epistles against Sabellius (who did not recognize any distinctions within the godhead) the Alexandrian explained himself in four books—unfortunately lost, but alluded to in the next century by Athanasius and Basil the Great.

We see that the famous "school" and the bishop's office were related in Bishop Demetrius' asserting his authority over the school and in Heraclas' and Dionysius' going from head of the school to bishop. There was a natural tendency for a bishop to assert the authority of his office and for a theologian to assert the authority of learning. But except in the Origen-Demetrius conflict, Alexandria showed itself able to unite both. It is not surprising, then, that two of the greatest theologians of the fourth and fifth centuries were bishops of Alexandria.

In third-century Egypt, there was a close interweaving of theology, monasticism, and martyrdom. Both Clement and Origen, and also the last two Origenist heads of the "school," Theognostos and Pierius, emphasized spiritual discipline, spiritual growth, and the "education" of the soul in their theologies. This fit well with the heroic asceticism of nascent monasticism. Origen himself was famous for his strenuous life of self-denial as well as for his study and teaching of the Bible. The heroic Christianity Origen advocated in his writings and the leadership of the people these writings influenced the most were to have a determinative impact on all later Christian monasticism.

The interrelation of monasticism and martyrdom is even clearer. Both were attempts to literalize the total demand that Jesus seemed to make upon his followers in the Gospel. It was not until the triumph of Christianity in the Roman world in the fourth and fifth centuries that Eastern monasticism was to have its explosive growth, which was closely related to the virtual disappearance of martyrdom as a possibility for heroic Christians.

One striking result of third- and early fourth-century persecutions was the spread of Christianity in all corners of Egypt. As Christian leaders like Dionysius escaped the cities to avoid persecution they took their message with them.[26] The heroism of confessing Christians in the face of persecution had a strong impact on those who viewed their sufferings.

So far in this chapter we have focused on the remarkable intellectual, spiritual, ascetical, organizational, and literary achievements of third-century Egyptian Christianity. It is equally important for those interested in history to see other characteristics of the Christians of that period.

The other side of martyrs and confessors is the prudence or even cowardice of other Christians. It seems clear that large numbers of the threatened church members hastened to comply with the Empire's orders to sacrifice to the emperor's image.[27] Few people are brave enough to accept confiscation of their possessions, much less face torture or death, as the price of loyalty to their faith. The many defections caused the church much searching of heart about whether and how to bring the lapsed back into the fold. We have seen Dionysius' effort to deal with the problem, and the rise of the Melitian schism.

The increasing worldliness of most Christians during the period we are discussing is evidenced by the reaction shown in the rise and popularity of the monastic movement. Clement's efforts to set forth a simplified life of self-restraint for upper- and middle-class Christians appears to have appealed only to the few.

Origen frequently complained in his sermons about people's inattentiveness (some even went to sleep) and of their reluctance to strive for a mature understanding of their faith. His altercation with Bishop Demetrius also illustrates how jealousy and ambition resulted in Alexandria's banishing the most famous Christian in the world at that time.

Average third-century Egyptian Christians were probably neither very brave, intellectual, alert, studious, nor cooperative. But they had available to them a surprising number of heroic models, an increasingly well-organized church, and a new level of intellectual and spiritual Christian literature—if they could read Greek.

Finally, Christians like Anthony were hearing and reading and writing more and more in their native Egyptian, i.e., Coptic. Portions of the Bible and also other early Christian writings[28] had been translated into Coptic and Anthony was to write his *Letters* in Coptic.[29] There may have been a center in Upper Egypt for translating Greek writings from Asia with a more literal Bible exegesis than was popular in Alexandria.[30] Thus the Alexandrian emphasis on Greek would sooner or later fade. The monastic movement, although it was just starting, was always largely Coptic-speaking and spreading the use of Coptic.

Although it did not come right away, the future of Egyptian Christianity was to lie with Coptic. In the meanwhile, however, we shall be seeing in Chapter Three that Alexandria's world leadership in church affairs until 451 was still dependent on the universal language of Hellenistic Greek.

---

[1]Werner Jaeger, *Early Christianity and Greek Paideia* (Cambridge: Harvard Univ. Press, 1961), p. 37. The first 75 pages of this book have greatly influenced the opening section of our Chapter Two.

[2]Jaeger, p. 38.

[3]A. D. Nock, quoted in *Coptic Egypt* (New York: Brooklyn Museum, 1944), p. 28.

[4]Stromata I, 11, trans. Wilson, in *Fathers of the Second Century*, Vol. 2 of *The Ante-Nicene Fathers*, ed. A. Roberts and J. Donaldson (New York: Charles Scribner's Sons, 1926).

[5]*Church History* V, 10, trans. A. C. McGiffert, in *Eusebius: Church History* et alia Vol. 1 of *Nicene and Post-Nicene Fathers of the Christian Church*, 2nd ser., ed. H. Wace and P. Schaff (New York: Charles Scribner's Sons, 1925).

[6]Jaeger, p. 58.

[7]J. Trigg, *Origen: the Bible and Philosophy in the Third Century Church* (Atlanta: John Knox, 1983), p. 153.

[8]Henry Chadwick has done a masterful translation and commentary on this work, *Origen Contra Celsum* (Cambridge: Cambridge Univ. Press, 1953, 1965).

[9]The consensus is that before Demetrius, the presbyters of Alexandria selected and consecrated one of their number to be bishop. See Jerome, Letter CXLVI, 1, trans. in *Jerome: Illustrious Men et al.*, Vol. 6 of *Nicene and Post-Nicene Fathers of the Christian Church*, 2nd ser., ed. H. Wace and P. Schaff (New York: Charles Scribner's Sons, 1925); W. Telfer, *Journal of Ecclesiastical History*, 3 (1952), 1-13; also the answer of E. W. Kemp in *Journal of Ecclesiastical History*, 6 (1955), 125-142. Annick Martin in "Aux Origines de l'église copte: l'implantation et le développement du Christianisme en Égypte," *Revue des études anciennes*, 83 (1981), 35-56, cites the sixth-century Patriarch Severus of Antioch and Eutychius' *Annales* in support of Jerome.

[10]Annick Martin, pp. 35-56.

[11]H. I. Bell, *Cults and Creeds in Greco-Roman Egypt* (Chicago: Ares, 1945), p, 86.

[12]See, e.g., J. C. O'Neill, "The Origins of Monasticism," in *The Making of Orthodoxy: Essays in Honour of Henry Chadwick*, ed. Rowan Williams (Cambridge: Cambridge Univ. Press, 1989), pp. 270-287.

[13]W. H. C. Frend, "Ebionites," *Coptic Encyclopedia*, 1991.

[14]A. Guillaumont, "Paul of Thebes," *Coptic Encyclopedia*, 1991.

[15]For an important recent and revisionist picture of Anthony, see S. Rubenson, *The Letters of St. Antony: Origenist Theology, Monastic Tradition and the Making of a Saint* (Lund: Lund Univ. Press, 1990).

[16]S. Rubenson argues, e.g., pp. 130-132, that Athanasius' depicting of Anthony aims to show him as a model monk who sides with church authority against heretics and interlopers.

[17]S. Rubenson, pp. 119-121.

[18]Eusebius, *Church History* VI, pp. 2-4.

[19]*Church History* VI, p. 39.

[20]*Church History* VI, pp. 41-42.

[21]*Church History* VI, p. 40.

[22]*Church History* VIII, pp. 7-10, and 13:7.

[23]*Church History* VII, p. 11.

[24]*Church History* VIII, 13:7.

[25]*Church History* VII, pp. 24-26.

[26]*Church History* VII, p. 11.

[27]*Church History* VI, p. 41.

[28]T. Orlandi, "Coptic Literature" in *The Roots of Egyptian Christianity*, ed. B. A. Pearson and J. Goehring (Philadelphia: Fortress Press, 1986), pp. 53-58.

[29]S. Rubenson, *The Letters of St. Antony*, chapter 1 (pp. 15-34).

[30]Orlandi, pp. 58-59.

Chapter Three

Ecumenical Leadership

✠ ——————————————————————————————— ✠

from about 313 to 451

A new era began for the Christian Church throughout the Roman Empire when the Emperors, Constantine in the West and Licinius in the East, agreed in Milan in 313 to grant freedom of worship to Christians and restoration of confiscated church property. In Egypt the advanced theology and the powerful bishops of Alexandria and also the growing monasticism of vernacular Christianity of the countryside were poised to combine to make Egyptian Christianity foremost in the East, and in some ways in the West as well.

For the century and a quarter leading up to 451, Egypt's patriarchs, monks, and theologians were the vanguards and leaders of the Christian movements which were to come together in the official Christianity of the first "ecumenical" councils. It was only at the end of the period under consideration, when Bishop Dioscorus of Alexandria was declared deposed by the Council of Chalcedon in the middle of the fifth century, that the Egyptian Church began to change from being a leader in the Christian world to being a national, Coptic Church. By then, the monks had created a Coptic culture capable of ending Egyptian Christianity's dependence on Hellenistic Civilization.

Because of two slightly related controversies, the Melitian and the Arian, the first third of the fourth century gave few hints of the accelerating importance of the Egyptian Church. First came the Melitian schism referred to in Chapter Two. It had begun as an effort to replace clergy who had left their posts to escape persecution and continued as a rejection of Alexandrian Bishop Peter's schedule of penances for those who "lapsed" during the persecution. Like most schisms, the Melitians continued as a community long after there was any sufficient basis for division.

The "Arian" movement, on the other hand, triggered one of the most bitter and complex controversies in Christian history—even if it was ultimately resolved without permanent divisions, a rare development in church history. The slight link between Arians and Melitians was that Arius began with the Melitians, although it may have been they who first called attention to his "heresy."

Arius' controverted teaching was that the Son of God is a creature and that the Son did not always exist. Arius was the disciple of a famous Bible teacher in Antioch in Syria before he became a prominent presbyter in Alexandria, pastor of a large and prestigious church. He tried in 318 to impose his views on Alexandria, unsuccessfully, and Bishop Alexander brought him to trial. Arius and his teaching were condemned by an Egyptian council.[1]

When Arius found powerful supporters outside Egypt, the case was brought before a great council of mostly Eastern bishops convoked by Constantine, now sole Emperor, at Nicaea in 325. Arius' position was rejected and a creed was drawn up that was to become (with additions to the third clause made at a follow-up council in 381) the Nicene Creed, the closest there is to a truly ecumenical creed, which was to become the basis of the Christian doctrine of the Trinity, one God in three divine "persons."

The council also confirmed the Alexandrian bishop's traditional jurisdiction in Upper Egypt and Libya (beyond the provincial borders) and developed a plan to reconcile the Melitians, which worked only temporarily. Arianism did not find wide popular support in Egypt, but in the rest of the Eastern half of the Empire variants of Arianism strongly contended against Nicene orthodoxy for decades, often with strong support of one emperor or another. Eastern Christians were in turmoil for a long time , and not all who had doubts about Athanasius or the creed of Nicaea could properly be called "Arians."

Origen's teachings underlay several of the debated points. His insistence on a real distinction between the Father and the Son, including the subordination of the Son to the Father (based on texts like Jesus' saying in the Fourth Gospel, "the Father is greater than I"), and the question of the creaturehood of the Spirit may have seemed to back Arius' position. On the other hand, Origen's doctrine of the eternal Sonship of the Second Person of the Trinity would seem to contradict Arius.

Also, Nicaea's *homoousios* (traditionally translated as "consubstantial" or "of one substance", more recently as "one in being") had two objectionable features for most Eastern bishops: it was not a biblical word, and it had materialistic connotations. Also, it did not help Nicaea's supporters that Alexandrian Bishop Dionysius had expressed doubts about the *homoousios* of Son and Father taught the century before by the condemned Bishop Paul of Samosata.

What made the Arian controversy important for Egypt was the unflagging leadership of the Alexandrian Patriarch Athanasius in opposing all efforts to compromise with the Arian point of view or to back away from the creed of Nicaea. Athanasius had been at Nicaea as Bishop Alexander's young archdeacon, and succeeded him as bishop and patriarch three years later, in 328.

Athanasius spent more than a third of his forty-five years as Patriarch in five periods of exile. From the time of his election and consecration, the factions in Alexandria challenged his character and leadership.[2] Emperors felt they could not tolerate his impatient treatment of Melitians, his refusal to lift Arius' excommunication, and his curt rejection of all councils of Eastern bishops which proposed compromises with Arians or Arianism in any of its variants.

Athanasius was much more than a controversialist. His youthful writings, *Against the Pagans* and *The Incarnation of the Word of God*, foreshadowed his formidable gifts as a theologian, Bible interpreter, and spiritual writer, and, late in his career, he appointed the distinguished Origenist biblical scholar, Didymus the Blind, to head the church's school in Alexandria. By widespread visitations in his vast jurisdiction in his first six years as patriarch, Athanasius "had acquired an acquaintance with his Patriarchate such as no other of the ancient Bishops of Alexandria seems to have had."[3]

Athanasius also cultivated the leaders of the growing monastic movements. His *Life of Anthony* was not only an important step in the spread of Christian monasticism in Egypt and the West but also showed Athanasius' solidarity with the movement. Athanasius wanted to ordain Pachomius, the father of organized monastic community life under a common rule. Pachomius avoided the ordination, but soon after his death Athanasius ordained Theodore, then head of the Pachomian communities. When the imperial authorities once again banned Athanasius from Egypt and forced him out of Alexandria in 356, he was able to spend most of the next six years with the monks in Egypt. Despite the imperial threat, he was never betrayed by the Egyptians. This testifies to the intense loyalty they could show their patriarch, even to the extreme of the eventual lynching by the Alexandrians of Bishop George whom the Emperor intruded in 356 as a replacement for Athanasius.

In earlier exiles, Athanasius was in the West, and later in Rome itself, strengthening ties there, mobilizing the powerful support of the Roman pope for his position, and introducing Egyptian monasticism to the West through his *Life of Anthony* and the presence of the monks he brought with him.

27

In the Christian East, Athanasius eventually laid the foundation for theological unity after the turbulence over the Trinitarian issue. He allowed Basil of Ancyra's *homoiousios* (of like essence) as an acceptable interpretation of the troublesome *homoousios* (of the same essence) of Nicaea to express the Son's unity with the Father. In the words of Henry Chadwick, "In the last fifteen years of his life. . . [Athanasius became] the elder statesman whose authority had been vastly enhanced by his record of unbending firmness. . .[and] his answers to questions [from the rising men of the new generation] were esteemed by them as decisive encyclicals."[4]

Athanasius was a determined, unwearying, and perhaps even ruthless combatant for Christian truth as he understood it. He was sustained by the sharp focus in his spirituality on the incarnation of the Word of God—a focus which assumed both the full divinity of the Word and the reality of the humanity of the Word-made-flesh. The incarnation sanctified humanity but in no way diminished the divinity of the Word, who "was made man that we might be made God."[5] This exalted view of human destiny drew Athanasius to Anthony, and we may assume that the spiritual disciplines so admiringly set forth in the *Life of Anthony* represented Athanasius' views as much as Anthony's.

During the long patriarchate of Athanasius there were other momentous developments in the Egyptian Church: in particular the flowering of monasticism, the ordination of leadership for the Christianizing of Ethiopia, and the establishment of a new capital of the Eastern Roman Empire, Constantinople, potentially Alexandria's replacement as the unofficial capital of Eastern Christianity. We will take up each development in order.

In most ways the fourth century was the golden age of Christian monasticism, certainly of Egyptian monasticism. It saw the peak of Anthony's influence, and the careers of Pachomius and Macarius the Great, who led the development of monastic community life. Literature followed: the letters of Anthony, the collection of the still widely read and influential *Sayings of the Fathers* and the writings of pilgrims like Jerome, the great Bible scholar and translator of the Latin Bible, and John Cassian, whose "Collations" have spiritually fed generations of Western monks and nuns— all these spread the spirituality and message of Egyptian monasticism throughout the Christian world.

In Chapter Two, we noted pagan and Jewish foreshadowings of Christian monasticism in Egypt and the crucial influence of Gospel injunctions like Jesus' "go, sell all you have," calling for entire and radical commitment on the part of his followers. Of equal importance were the examples of Jesus or of John the Baptist or Elijah, and Paul's clear preference for celibacy over marriage as a Christian vocation. We also noted the strenuous Christianity set forth in the teachings and example of Origen. It may be, however, that the most important single factor in the spread of monasticism was the ending of the persecutions under which Christians had been able to demonstrate the heroic character of their faith. The unsympathetic but perceptive Arab historian, al-Makrizi, saw that and reported that Anthony was the first to practice this metamorphosis of martyrdom.[6]

Saint Anthony is often counted as the first Christian monk, and his influence is great, as we saw in the preceding chapter. Christians sought out Anthony mainly for instruction in how to be a monk but also for his wisdom and his healing power. The influential *Life of Anthony* by Athanasius was published just one year after Anthony died in 356 at the age of 105.

That book and seven letters attributed to Anthony plus sayings attributed to Anthony in the *Sayings of the Fathers* are our sources for his spirituality.[7] A recent study finds that the letters are the primary source and concludes with the words, "With burning love for his monastic brothers he wrote to them about God's compassion for man, about repentance and demonic assault, but above all about the joy and peace that can be gained by true self-knowledge and by the return to the Creator through the coming of Jesus and the granting of the Spirit of adoption."[8] The letters contain parallels to Origen's basic notions of spiritual growth which show that the writings of the Alexandrian intellectual significantly influenced evolving monastic piety.

Anthony's spirituality was simple and heroic. God's kingdom, with its virtues, is within; so spiritual growth begins with self-knowledge, which brings knowledge of God and contact with the soul's "natural" or original state of innocence. But the human body is "heavy" with many needs, so Anthony's path is "discipline" or the "service of righteousness": battling demons and dying daily through prayer, fasting, sleeping little, reciting the Psalms, virginity, humility, contempt of wealth and fame, charity, and, above all, faith in Christ. This way is heroic, as martyrdom is heroic, and assumes that human life is a dramatic struggle. But since the end is our transformation by God from servanthood to adoption as sons and daughters, the appropriate mood in our approach to life is not fear but joy.

The solitary monks in Anthony's tradition normally depended on others to make some of life's necessities available to them. They earned their own way, however, especially in occupations like weaving, which went well with constant prayer and spiritual collectedness.

Parallel to these hermits were widows and virgins who led sheltered lives dedicated to prayer and works of mercy, under careful supervision of church authorities. Similarly dedicating themselves to evangelism and charity were male "apotactics" (the set apart) who lived together in houses in villages and cities. One city was reported to have 10,000! They were sometimes called "monks," but they could own property.[9]

Pachomius, a former soldier, started as a monk of Anthony's type but soon began to use his talent for organizing communities of monks, and later communities of nuns (he placed his own sister as the head of a community of virgins). The first Pachomian community was founded about 320, in Tabennisi in Upper Egypt, where most of these communities were eventually located.

The Pachomian communities practiced the self-denial and strenuous spiritual exercises of the solitaries, but in community, with specific rules for the community life we know technically as "cenobitism." These communities were also self-sustaining, often functioning like minor industries with close ties to village commerce. The chief purpose of monks and their communities, however, was to practice heroic Christianity, and to provide a rich source of intercession and spiritual power and advice of all kinds to the broader Christian community.

Macarius the Great, c. 300-390, was one of the many other monastic leaders of the fourth century who did much to make Egyptian monasticism the wonder of the Christian world. He went out as a solitary about 330 to Scetis, west of the present Cairo-to-Alexandria toll road. After a visit to the Eastern Desert to learn directly from Anthony, perhaps at Anthony's suggestion, he allowed himself to be ordained priest about 340 so that he and other monks of the neighborhood would not have to walk twenty miles each way for Eucharist.

Macarius attracted disciples, and it was not long before monastic communities developed in Scetis, today called Wadi Natrun. There are still four monasteries there; one is named after Macarius, where he is very much remembered, even after 1600 years. Scetis was the principal source of the *Sayings of the Fathers* (one should add, "and Mothers"), which has long been, in its multiple translations, a second Bible for monastics and others who want to draw on the spirituality of that heritage. The monastic tradition developed at Wadi Natrun combined individualist features of the desert solitaries with some of the community life of the Pachomian monasteries. We shall see that, for some time after the Arab invasion in the seventh century, Saint Macarius' monastery functioned as a second patriarchal seat and produced many of the patriarchs.

Egyptian monasticism began as a purely lay movement and continued to be largely made up of lay persons.[10] We have seen how Pachomius evaded ordination and Macarius only accepted priesthood as a ministry to his many companions. The monks were also mostly Coptic-speaking, from the earliest days of Anthony and Pachomius.

It is striking that this overwhelmingly lay and Coptic movement was the major force in shaping the Christianity of the mass of non-urban Egyptians, that it was a major support of Patriarch Athanasius and his Nicene

Orthodoxy, and that eventually the patriarchs and the other bishops were to be chosen from among the monks so that the hierarchy in later years would be spiritually formed in these communities. Fourth-century visitors to Christian Egypt may well have exaggerated the numbers, but they were everywhere in great numbers.

In the fifth century it was to be another kind of abbot and archimandrite, Shenoute of Atripe, who was to create a more rigid and disciplined and popular tradition of monasticism. Shenoute is remembered for the large number of monks and nuns (4000-5000) he attracted to his White Monastery. The building still there is so large it was long thought to be the whole monastery; but it turned out to be only the chapel! Perhaps the requirements for disciplining this huge number of rugged peasants in the monastic way were responsible for Shenoute's reputation for giving beatings to recalcitrant religious, in one case with fatal results. But he is also remembered as an effective champion of the poor peasants against the rapacious landlords and for making his monastic community a haven for refugees from desert marauders. In the tradition, he is also pictured, like Anthony, as a major support in a doctrinal controversy for his patriarch, Cyril. He also had the distinction of creating the earliest truly Coptic literature through the preserving of many of his sermons and letters in a clear and forceful Sahidic Coptic.

In the early days of the Arian controversy, about 320, two brothers who were Christians from Tyre, Frumentius and Aedesius, were brought as captives to Ethiopia. They rose high in the administration of Ethiopia, and began to make Christian converts, assisted by Christian traders there.[11] Frumentius went to Alexandria and was consecrated bishop by Athanasius, about 340, and thus began the strong and often fruitful relationship of the Egyptian and Ethiopian churches. This relationship continues, although in the 1950s the Ethiopian Church became autonomous.

The creation of Constantinople in 330 as New Rome in the East was to have an even greater impact on Egyptian church history than did the Ethiopian relationship. It was the Eastern branch of the Empire that had most of its people and most of its wealth and productivity, so that it was inevitable that this new capital city in the East would sooner or later challenge Alexandria for dominance in Eastern Christianity.

For a long time, the church in Constantinople suffered from having "heretical" bishops, from conflicts over who was the bishop, and from Alexandrian patriarchs dabbling in the selection or even the deposing of its leadership. Alexandria could usually count on Rome's support. The two worked closely together, for Rome also looked with suspicion on Constantinople as a rival for leadership among the churches. Once Alexandria took on Rome and Constantinople combined, however, the days of Alexandria's leadership in world Christianity were over. But let us not get ahead of our story; the crucial role of the patriarch of Alexandria in church leadership did not by any means end with Athanasius.

The next strong patriarch of Alexandria was Theophilus, often thought of as one of the most unpleasant church leaders in ancient Christianity, who occupied that seat from 385 to 412. He is remembered as the scourge of the monks who admired Origen's ascetical theology, as the nemesis of John Chrysostom, one of the leaders in that golden age of Christian literature in Greek, and as the person responsible for the destruction of the great temple of Serapis in Alexandria.

John Chrysostom had become the patriarch of Constantinople in 398 and thus a natural target for Theophilus when the much admired monks from Egypt, the Origenist "Tall Brothers" sought refuge in Constantinople from Theophilus. Theophilus' visit to the capital was only a partial success but helped start a train of events that brought John down for good. The result was a bitter dispute with Rome, resentment against Theophilus' high-handedness, and the eventual recognition (even in Egypt) of the great contributions of John to the development of Christianity, especially in the East.

The move of the mass of Egyptians from traditional religious loyalties into the churches had been going on since before the end of persecution; as Eusebius had said, "It was clear to the most unobservant that the Egyptians were deserting their hereditary superstition and were greeting every form of death for their duty to Christ."[12] Then, under the Emperor Theodosius in the late fourth century, Christianity became the official religion of the Empire. Pagan rites were proscribed and Christians were not discouraged from taking over the temples, as Egyptian monks had already begun to do. Between the efforts of the enthusiastic bishops in the cities and monks in the countryside Egypt was becoming overwhelmingly Christian.[13] Pagans were still to be found among the aristocrats and the proponents of philosophy, of history, and of classic literature and art. But even when the anti-Christian Julian had earlier tried to restore traditional rites and priesthoods, he could make little impact on the majority in Egypt, or elsewhere. The future lay with the Christians, in all facets of life, and Christian leaders were not always scrupulous about their weapons in the uneven contest with paganism in the waning days of classical civilization. This puts Theophilus' brutality in context.

Pagan resistance certainly did not simply collapse in the fourth century. The municipal pagan aristocracy was tolerated in Alexandria, which, especially because of its university, also remained for long a center of the old learning and philosophy. And officials were reluctant to condemn pagan intellectuals. Pagan power was still shown when Theodosius pardoned all the rioters after a serious disturbance, except those who had actually killed Christians. Also, the biographies of Shenoute and other fifth century Coptic leaders show that pagan resistance was found among peasants and villagers as well as intellectuals and aristocrats.[14] By the middle of the fifth century, however, the pagans were a minority and rapidly losing converts to Christianity, perhaps in part because of the relation of persevering paganism to the century-long scourge of the marauding Blemmyes. From the time of Justinian, paganism was only a relic and no rival to Christianity in Egypt.[15]

Cyril was Patriarch Theophilus' nephew and immediate successor and was, like him, a controversial figure. He stimulated riots against the Jews in Alexandria and he does not escape all blame for the brutal lynching in 415 of the brilliant woman philosopher, Hypatia. But Cyril was also an acute theologian, whose writings laid foundations for much of the subsequent agreement on the Christian doctrine of Christ.

We must turn now to the growing crisis over Christology, the doctrine of the person of Jesus Christ. The course of Egyptian church history cannot be understood apart from this controversy, which was eventually to be the doctrinal basis of the separation between the Coptic Church (and other non-Chalcedonian churches in the East) on the one hand and, on the other, the Catholic Church of the West and the Orthodox Churches of the East which have maintained communion with Constantinople.

The controversy[16] grew out of the Trinitarian position hammered out at the Council of Nicaea in 325 and at the council at Constantinople in 381, and the efforts led by Athanasius in the intervening years. The churches had come to agree that the Son of God was divine in exactly the same sense as God the Father, and that in "essence" they are identical, though in "person" they are distinct.

The question then arose as to how the divine Jesus Christ can also be human as he is pictured in the Gospels and as he is declared to be in the more theological New Testament writings, e.g., the "born of a woman" of Paul's Epistle to the Galatians, the "tempted in every way as we are" of the Epistle to the Hebrews, and "the Word was made flesh" of the Fourth Gospel.

Alexandria had been the leader in theology since the days of Origen and then of Patriarch Athanasius, and the Alexandrian tradition tended to focus sharply on the oneness of Jesus Christ. On the other hand, the tradition of the great patriarchate and school of Antioch in Syria focused on the literal and historical sense of the Bible and on the duality of Jesus Christ, trying in this way not to lose his specific humanity.

The leading bishops quickly rejected the apparent solution of viewing Jesus as a composite being, e.g., Appolinaris' theory that the eternal Word took the place of Jesus' soul. More consequential was the contest between Patriarch Cyril of Alexandria and Nestorius, who had become patriarch of Constantinople in 428. Nestorius was a leader of the Antiochene "school" and held strong opinions, which he vigorously prosecuted. In his effort to preserve the humanity of Jesus, Nestorius insisted that the mother of Jesus should be called "Christotokos" or "Mother of Christ," but not "Theotokos" or "Mother of God," since God had no mother who bore him.

Cyril attacked Nestorius (and in a sense the whole Antiochene school), accusing him of having no real understanding of the unity of Jesus Christ, in which case the essence of Christianity, the Incarnation, would have no real meaning. The Roman Pope, Celestine, backed Cyril and wrote Nestorius demanding a recantation, another case of Rome's support for a patriarch-theologian of Alexandria.

A council was convoked to Ephesus in 431 to try to settle the explosive issue. Nestorius' supporters were late arriving, Nestorius' position was quickly rejected, and Cyril's position accepted as being more in accord with the Council of Nicaea. The unity of humanity and divinity in Jesus Christ was assured. Cyril dominated the council and succeeded in getting Nestorius condemned for heresy, a stunning victory, it seemed.

The Eastern churches, however, found themselves once again in turmoil. Constantinople had had its patriarch condemned, and the many partisans of the Christology of Antioch felt the council had gone much too far— not to mention the fact that Cyril had initiated the council before Patriarch John of Antioch and his sympathizers arrived four days late.

The situation was temporarily prevented from breaking up when Cyril and John were able to come up with a compromise Formula of Reunion in 433. But the contest between Alexandria on the one hand and Constantinople and Antiochene Christology on the other was by no means over. Antiochenes wondered if Jesus' humanity had not been lost or the difference between humanity and divinity obscured. Some Alexandrians were unhappy that Cyril had signed the Formula of Reunion.

Only two years after Cyril died in 444 and was replaced by Dioscorus as patriarch of Alexandria, the new patriarch went on the attack to undermine the 433 compromise. He took up the case of a prominent archimandrite in Constantinople, Eutyches, who was teaching that there were not two "natures" of Jesus Christ "after the union" of the divine and the human that took place in Jesus' conception and birth. Eutyches was condemned by Patriarch Flavian of Constantinople and a synod in that city.

Another council was called to Ephesus in 449. In that same year, Pope Leo I of Rome addressed to Patriarch Flavian a supportive "Tome" that insisted on "two natures" of Jesus Christ "after the union." Leo assumed that his Tome would be read and accepted at the council to settle the dispute. But Dioscorus managed the council so as to get it to ignore the tome of the Roman pope, to remove the patriarchs of Constantinople and Antioch from their positions, and to rehabilitate Eutyches.

Thus the patriarch of Alexandria challenged the other three patriar-chates, Rome and Antioch and Constantinople, combined. This was the boldest bid ever for Alexandrian domination of the universal church. Disaster was virtually inevitable.

The apparent triumph of Dioscorus and Alexandrian Christology at the 449 council at Ephesus lasted little time. After the sudden death of Theodosius in July of 450, imperial officials convoked another, greater council in 451 at Chalcedon which simply reversed that of Ephesus in 449. This time church leaders in Rome and Constantinople were together against Alexandria, as were also the new chief officials of the Empire. The bold Dioscorus was deposed for his conduct, though not his doctrine, and went off to exile on orders of the imperial government and died three years later.

It was by no means clear in 451 that the Council of Chalcedon would occasion a break between Egyptian Christianity and most of the rest of the Christian world that would last up to the present. Nestorius' claim that Chalcedon's formula agreed with his teaching, however, helped convince the Egyptians that the formula of Chalcedon undermined the true unity of Jesus Christ and thus was heresy that must be fought at whatever cost.

The implacable hostility of the majority in Egypt to the doctrine of "two natures *after* the union," coupled with Rome's insistence on it, created a bitter separation between these two hitherto closely allied churches for which no successful compromise could be found. For a while Egyptian Christians were sometimes able to get emperors and patriarchs in Constantinople to make concessions to them, but Roman popes character-istically opposed them, even if the cost was rupture with Constantinople, as we shall see in our next chapter.

Christians in the West, and many in the East, looked upon the Egyptian Church as being Eutychean or Monophysite, since it insisted that Jesus Christ had only one nature after the union—presumably by absorbing the human into the divine. Needless to say, anti-Chalcedonians resented being called "Eutychians" as much as pro-Chalcedonians resented being called "Nestorians." The fact that twentieth-century theologians in the East and Popes of Rome and an Archbishop of Canterbury in the West can now issue joint statements on Christology with Coptic Orthodox leaders is very encouraging to those who believe in church unity. But it does not erase the fact of fifteen centuries of separation, which meant for the Copts a profound isolation from most other Christians.

No later patriarch of Alexandria would be a leader of world Christianity, and no later Alexandrian theologian would have the influence of an Origen or an Athanasius or a Cyril. But the Egyptians' loyalty to the traditional Alexandrian Christology and the strength of the Coptic civiliza-tion created largely in the monasteries and the villages, combined to create a national Egyptian church—what we call the Coptic Church, strong enough to endure harassment from Byzantine rulers for much of two centuries and then from Islamic rulers up until the present time. In our next chapter we will see how the Coptic Church began its long journey to the present in this virtual isolation.

[1]R. C. Gregg and D. E. Groh in their *Early Arianism: A View of Salvation* (Philadelphia: Fortress Press, 1981) argue that Arius' ideas were based on a biblical view of salvation, rather than on philosophical theology.

[2]See the exhaustive summary of ancient and modern arguments about Athanasius' conduct in D. W.-H. Arnold, *The Early Episcopal Career of Athanasius of Alexandria* (Notre Dame, Indiana: Notre Dame Univ. Press, 1991).

[3]E. R. Hardy, *Christian Egypt: Church and People* (New York: Oxford Univ. Press, 1952), p. 56.

[4]in *The Early Church* (Baltimore: Penguin Books, 1967), p. 145.

[5]*Incarnation of the Word*, 54, 3, trans. A. Robertson, in *St. Athanasius: Select Works and Letters*, Vol. 4 of *Nicene and Post-Nicene Fathers of the Christian Church*, 2nd ser., ed. H. Wace and P. Schaff (New York: Charles Scribner's Sons, 1925), p. 65.

[6]found in paragraph 6 of the appendix, "account of the monasteries and churches of the Christians of Egypt," of Abu Salih the Armenian, *The Churches and Monasteries of Egypt*, trans. and ed. B. Evetts and A. J. Butler (Oxford: Clarendon Press, 1895), p. 306.

[7]S. Rubenson has recently published a detailed study of the comparative reliability of these sources for the thought of Anthony, in *The Letters of St. Antony: Origenist Theology, Monastic Tradition and the Making of a Saint* (Lund: Lund Univ. Press, 1990).

[8]Rubenson, p. 191.

[9]See E. A. Judge, "The Earliest Use of Monachos for 'Monk' and the Origins of Monasticism," *Jahrbuch für Antike und Christentum*, 20 (1977), 72-89.

[10]W. H. C. Frend, "The Church of the Roman Empire, 313-600," in *The Layman in Christian History*, ed. S. Neill and H.-R. Weber (London: SCM Press, 1963), pp. 79-80.

[11]cf. Socrates, *Church History* I, 19 and Sozomen, *Church History* II, 24; both of these works are found in English translation in Vol. 2 of *Nicene and Post-Nicene Fathers of the Christian Church*, 2nd ser., ed. H. Wace and P. Schaff (New York: Charles Scribner's Sons, 1925).

[12]See W. H. C. Frend in "The Winning of the Countryside," *Journal of Ecclesiastical History*, 18 (1967), 5; he takes the quote from Eusebius' *Proof of the Gospel* IX, 2, 4.

[13]See, above all, Ewa Wipszycka, "La Christianisation de l'Égypte aux 4ème-6ème Siècles: aspects sociaux et ethniques," *Aegyptus*, 68 (1988), 117-165.

[14]Wipszycka, 126-128, and 157-159.

[15]R. Remondon, "L'Égypte et la suprême résistance au Christianisme (Ve.-VIIe siècles)," *Bulletin de l'Institut Français d'Archéologie Orientale*, 51 (1952), 72-73.

[16]A useful outline of this controversy is found in R. A. Norris, ed., *The Christological Controversy* (Philadelphia: Fortress Press, 1980).

Chapter Four

National and Coptic

✠ ———————————————————————————————— ✠

451 to 641

H OW COULD ANYONE HAVE KNOWN in 451 that the Egyptian church would never be reconciled with Roman popes and only very rarely and briefly with Patriarchs of Constantinople? Alexandrian Patriarch Dioscorus had been deposed by the Council of Chalcedon in 451 and exiled by the East Roman Empire. But this was not necessarily going to mean anything more than the condemnations and exiles of his predecessor in the previous century, the great Athanasius, who died triumphant, with the prestige of the Alexandrian patriarchate greater than ever.

The situation this time was different, however, for Athanasius had been supported by the church in Rome, whereas now it was Rome which was the nemesis of the church in Egypt, that is, the church of the Egyptian majority. At Chalcedon, Rome had humbled both Alexandria and its patriarch who had challenged Rome's leadership.

Rome was adamant on the issue of "two natures after the union" of the human and the divine in Jesus. Pope Leo I wrote it and the Council of Chalcedon had endorsed it. On the other hand, the majority of the Egyptian Christians condemned Leo and his "Tome" and would not tolerate acceptance of the council that supported Leo and condemned their patriarch.

In the East the situation was quite different. Most Eastern Christians, even the Syrians, were increasingly dubious about the hint of Nestorianism in the two-natures-in-Christ formula of Chalcedon, and most may well have preferred communion with Egypt and Palestine and Syria to communion with Rome. But the Roman Pope held a strong hand, as Leo himself had shown when in 452 he led the successful diplomatic mission to turn away from Rome the apparently invincible Attila the Hun.

In retrospect it may seem strange that the Roman church could have been so important at a time when the Roman state in the West was in the throes of complete collapse—476 is a popular date for the "fall of the Roman Empire." But it turned out that the collapse of the state in the West actually enhanced the importance of the church and its top leadership, for now they had no strong ruler to contend with.

Also, Rome was the unchallenged leader of the Western churches; it was not only the capital city but the only church in the West that could boast apostolic leadership. Both Peter and Paul had been there and, indeed, had died as martyrs in Rome, thus hallowing the city forever for Christians. In contrast, there was always rivalry among the great Eastern churches for leadership. On the worldly level, Alexandria and Antioch rivaled one another for cultural and political leadership during the earlier Hellenistic and Roman periods, and then upstart Constantinople issued its claims on the basis of its becoming "new Rome" and the seat of the emperors. On the question of apostolic traditions, Ephesus claimed John and the Virgin Mary, Antioch claimed Peter and Paul, Alexandria claimed Mark, and late-comer Constantinople discovered traces of Andrew's apostolate in the region.

The great Christian churches of the Eastern Mediterranean all honored the heritage of the Roman church, but it was only when they needed Rome's help that they accepted the Roman pope's claims for authority in the East. As we have already seen, this help could be very important. Indeed it was particularly important for Alexandria until the fateful councils in Ephesus, 449, and Chalcedon, 451, which transformed Rome and Alexandria into apparently implacable enemies.

During much of the period we are considering in this chapter, the emperors and patriarchs of Constantinople were confronted with the difficult choice between seeking peace with the Eastern churches which rejected Chalcedon and maintaining communion with the Roman church, and therefore the other Western churches as well. We shall see that during much of the earlier decades, Constantinople preferred peace with the Christians of the East, but in the later decades the support of Rome and acceptance of the position of the Council of Chalcedon became the dominant considerations for emperor and patriarch.

Constantinople did end up as the dominant church in the East, but its fateful decision for Rome against the East also resulted in apparently endless schism among Eastern Christians. This weakened the Empire and contributed to the loss of the Eastern Mediterranean to the Arabs and Islam at the end of our period. *N.B. The Eastern churches and theologians who have rejected the Council of Chalcedon and its two-natures-after-the-union in the Incarnation have traditionally been called "monophysite," since they have recognized only one, divine-human, nature after the union. Their present-*

day successors reject the term because they confess that the incarnate Word of God is "from" or "out of" (ek) two natures and that they do believe that Jesus is perfect in his humanity (as over against Eutyches) as well as in his divinity. So we use the term "anti-Chalcedonian" instead of "monophysite."

Let us now see how the story unfolds. Developments in the two centuries after the Council of Chalcedon were critical in making Coptic Christianity what it became and what it is today. Patriarch Dioscorus went off to exile in 451 and died three years later. The *History of the Patriarchs of Alexandria* has surprisingly little about him. It reports that Mennas wrote of Dioscorus' "suffering at Chalcedon" but that "no biography of the holy patriarch Dioscorus after his banishment has been found."[1]

In the meanwhile, Proterius, Dioscorus' archpriest, who did accept Chalcedon, was selected to replace him by the only four Egyptian bishops who accepted the council. For being consecrated patriarch while Dioscorus was still alive and for his position on Chalcedon, Proterius was rejected by the Egyptian majority as their patriarch and needed the imperial authorities to protect him. Indeed, in the fateful year of 457 Roman Emperor Marcian died, Timothy, nicknamed "the cat," was selected and consecrated patriarch by the anti-Chalcedonian majority, and Proterius was lynched by the populace. "From now on, Chalcedon was a minority cause in Egypt."[2]

The new emperor sent his own patriarch for Alexandria, another Timothy, this one nicknamed "wobble-cap," from the pro-Chalcedonian monastery at Canopus, East of Alexandria. The counterpart of that monastery was the anti-Chalcedonian monastery called "Enaton" for being at milepost nine on the other side of Alexandria. Both monasteries were in the Pachomian tradition but for years remained the spiritual homes of the rival patriarchs, Enaton being the leader of monastic opposition to Chalcedon. Thus the christological issue was also dividing the Pachomian movement, and the Kellia (northwest of Wadi Natrun) anchorites as well, into sharp rivalries.[3]

On the Emperor's orders, Timothy the Cat[4] was sent off into exile for seven years, but he returned to Alexandria as patriarch when Emperor Leo died and Basiliscus briefly held the power. Timothy brought Dioscorus' remains with him, and died as unchallenged head of the Egyptian church. Peter Mongos, a strong supporter of the anti-Chalcedonian position, was selected and consecrated successor to Timothy the Cat by that party, but he had to go into hiding when the emperor Zeno, who had ousted Basiliscus, backed Timothy Wobble-Cap as patriarch for the five remaining years of Wobble-Cap's life.

Things began to change for the Egyptian church when Zeno and his patriarch in Constantinople, Acacius, decided in the early 480s that their need for communion with Rome was less beneficial for them than communion with Alexandria, and also with Antioch which was in a "gradual but irreversible shift away from Nestorian-oriented Christianity."[5]

482 turned out to be another crucial year for the Egyptian church: Wobble-Cap died (and Zeno backed for only two years the successor he chose for him), Acacius "entered into relations with Peter Mongos," and Zeno wrote his famous Henoticon to the Christians in the world of the Alexandrian patriarch.[6]

Each of these developments was conducive to the reunion of the great churches of the East. The Egyptians were especially happy, although some anti-Chalcedonians would have preferred for Zeno to have gone on to condemn Pope Leo's Tome and the Council of Chalcedon. Some of these diehards actually broke with the Alexandrian hierarchy, but since they had no bishops to lead them, they came to be called "acephali," i.e., "the headless."

The Empire for a while stopped trying to force an unwanted patriarch on Alexandria to replace the anti-Chalcedonian patriarch. And Zeno's Henoticon condemned both Eutyches and Nestorius and any heresy "whether advanced at Chalcedon or at any synod whatever," said nothing of "natures," and approved Cyril's Twelve Anathemas so beloved of the anti-Chalcedonians.

The "acephali" were not the only ones unhappy with the Henoticon. In 484, Zeno's intruded patriarch left Alexandria and went to Rome, and Roman Pope Felix got a Roman synod to excommunicate Acacius. Thus Constantinople's effort to reach out to the Egyptian Christians and other anti-Chalcedonian Easterners resulted in rupture with Rome in a schism that lasted thirty-five years (484-519).

While the Rome-Constantinople axis was not functioning during the "Acacian Schism," the Egyptian church was thriving, even though the ongoing Egyptian hostility to Leo I and his Tome and to the Council of Chalcedon boded ill for any restoration of communion with Rome. When Emperor Zeno was succeeded by Anastasius in 491, there remained twenty-seven more years of tolerance and prosperity for Egyptian and other Christians who wanted to leave the Christological issue where it had been when patriarch Cyril of Alexandria crushed Nestorius at the Council of Ephesus twenty years before Chalcedon.

A major actor in the Christian East during the reign of Anastasius was Patriarch Severus of Antioch. Born about 465, he became a monk in 488. Twenty years later he was a prominent figure in religious circles in Constantinople because of his acute intelligence, leadership ability, and monastic discipline. He was a sharp critic of the "two natures after the union"[7] doctrine of the Council of Chalcedon. In 512 he became patriarch of Antioch and also increased his influence in the Egyptian church and other churches that agreed with his cause. The *History of the Patriarchs of Alexandria*, for which "orthodox" meant anti-Chalcedonian, called him "Severus the excellent, clothed with light, occupant of the see of Antioch, who became a horn of salvation to the orthodox church."[8]

It is notable that Severus long opposed setting up a separate anti-Chalcedonian church. His desire was to reverse the two-natures victory of Chalcedon throughout the universal church, just as Chalcedon had reversed Dioscorus' victory at Ephesus in 449. But it turned out that Severus' leadership was soon hobbled by the death of the sympathetic Anastasius and the rise of Justinian's family to the office of emperor. Severus was exiled to Egypt in 518 and died there in 538 at the anti-Chalcedonian monastery Enaton.

Severus was an acute theologian, and part of the irony of the schism after Chalcedon is that historians of Christian theology now tend to agree that Severus' explanation of the one nature of the incarnate Word was quite compatible with what his equally acute opponents were saying about the two natures. The tag is: "it was a controversy over words."

Severus was not the only distinguished thinker in the anti-Chalcedonian East. John Philoponus became the first Christian head of the Platonic school in Alexandria. And a still unidentified "monophysite" writer, using the pseudonym of Dionysius the Areopagite (the name of Paul's convert in Athens, Acts 17:34), produced mystical writings which have been a major influence on Christian spirituality both East and West, Chalcedonian and anti-Chalcedonian. For centuries, readers simply assumed that the author was Paul's convert, so that he would be authoritative in depicting the nature, the methods, and the stages of spiritual development.

Severus died still hounded by Constantinople. He had even come to feel that he had to consent to the consecration of bishops for Christian communities in Egypt and in Syria who had rejected Chalcedon. This meant the institutionalization of schism, but something had to be done about replacing fifty-five bishops who had been sent into exile and about finding a home for many monks who had been sent from their monasteries.[9]

Under Emperor Justin, beginning in 518, his nephew and successor, Justinian, had become the dominant force in making religious decisions for the Empire and had opted for the enforcement of the Council of Chalcedon in the East. By the time Justin II died in 578, Egypt and Syria had their own anti-Chalcedonian hierarchies, which have been perpetuated until today in the Coptic Orthodox Church and the Syrian Orthodox Church.

Justinian's religious policy was: "Every conceivable effort. . .to conciliate the Monophysites, but in the last resort Chalcedon could not be abandoned. Even schism with the Monophysites was preferable."[10] This was ironic, for Justinian's own religious views seem to have been "monophysite." His famous wife, Theodora, was an open supporter of that cause, and Justinian himself actually died a believer in the extreme theory called "aphthartodocetism" which argued that Jesus' body was not really like ours but rather immune to any kind of decay. Severus had strongly countered this theory of Julian of Halicarnassus,[11] although Julian had a lot of support in Saint Macarius' and other Egyptian monasteries. The Julianist Archdeacon Gaianus was consecrated in 535 by admirers, and was accepted as Patriarch of Alexandria by powerful elements. He held the day there until Empress Theodora got Justinian to dislodge him in favor of Theodosius, who had been made patriarch by the majority element.

Justinian's support for Chalcedon virtually guaranteed schism. Why did he do it? It would seem to have been largely his determination to reconquer the rest of the old Roman Empire, which was then in the hands of the "barbarian" Vandals in North Africa and Goths in Italy. To do this he needed support in those regions, and he could not get it without the support of the popes in Rome, who were adamant on the issue of Pope Leo's two-natures-after-the-union and the Council of Chalcedon which supported Leo and his Tome.

It was Justinian's pro-Chalcedonian policies that had convinced even Severus that clergy must be provided for the "orthodox" (i.e., according to Severus) communities which rejected Chalcedon. At Empress Theodora's behest, the indefatigable Jacob Baradaeus was consecrated metropolitan of Edessa by Theodosius, the exiled anti-Chalcedonian patriarch of Alexandria. Jacob is said[12] to have left behind in the East twenty-seven metropolitans and 100,000 "monophysite" clergy. Because of this remarkable achievement of guaranteeing leadership for the anti-Chalcedonian Christians in the East, they are still often called "Jacobites," even the Copts in Egypt. Later, Theodosius' anti-Chalcedonian successor in Alexandria, Peter IV, reconstituted the hierarchy in Egypt by consecrating seventy bishops.

Justinian did not immediately intrude his own Chalcedonian patriarch in Alexandria, but he began to do so regularly, starting with the exiling of Theodosius only two years after he was consecrated in 535. Thus began "a long line of Chalcedonian patriarchs in Alexandria with a formidable combination of civil and ecclesiastical powers."[13]

Theodosius had been supported by Justinian against his rival, Gaianus, and probably could have remained at his post in Alexandria if he had been willing to subscribe to Chalcedon. According to the *History of the Patriarchs of Alexandria*, he repeatedly turned down promises that he would be granted the civil governorship as well as the patriarchate on the condition of accepting that council. Most Egyptians remained loyal to Theodosius during his long exile (537 until his death in 566) and Empress Theodora was his strong support until her death in 548. For a time, the Christians of the

Egyptian majority that opposed Chalcedon were known as "Theodosians."[14]

The intruded Chalcedonian patriarchs and their supporters came to be called "Melchites," i.e., "royal" Christians, since they survived with the backing of the Roman or Byzantine Empire. The Melchite church was Greek-speaking, and great men of the cities sometimes joined with the imperial officials and foreigners in supporting the Melchite patriarch in Egypt. The exiled Coptic patriarch Theodosius could function in prominent circles in Constantinople because he could speak Greek, but as an anti-Chalcedonian Coptic hierarchy was created for Egypt the importance of Greek declined. Theodosius' successors until the Arab invasion were generally harassed by the imperial government and often felt they had to reside outside of Alexandria, but none after Theodosius went to Constantinople or anywhere else outside Egypt. From the time of the exiling of Theodosius, there were two churches in Egypt: the Melchite, whose support hardly went beyond Alexandria and its neighborhood, and that of the Egyptian majority, which we shall henceforward call "Coptic."

It may be said that the first specifically Coptic churches were started in Alexandria in 539 when the anti-Chalcedonian Christians were driven by the imperial forces from the existing church buildings so that the anti-Chalcedonians had to build separate churches of their own. The churches of Angelion and of Cosmas and Damian became major centers for Coptic Christianity.

Separate hierarchies and separate buildings indicate separate churches. And even bloody persecutions were not out of the question; "early in 538. . .with [John of Tella] the roll of Monophysite martyrs opens."[15]

The history of Coptic Christianity in the period from the Council of Chalcedon to the Arab invasion is by no means simply the contest of wills between East Roman emperors and the Coptic Christian majority in Egypt. It includes the development of most of the special characteristics of Coptic Christianity, which made it so durable. Dominant Islam was to displace rather quickly the churches in the rest of North Africa, but despite its eventual rooting out of the Coptic language, it was never able to displace the Coptic Church in Egypt. This fact clearly shows the importance for Coptic church history of the two centuries before Egypt was conquered by the Arabs.

One prominent factor was the evangelization of Nubia and the spread of Christianity up the Nile. The Christianization of Nubia is a story comparable to the evangelization of Ethiopia we noted in Chapter Three. The Nobatae were still generally following their traditional religion in 541 when an anti-Chalcedonian named Julian, evangelist of Nubia, "persuaded the Empress Theodora that the conversion of the Nubians to Christianity was possible."[16] In fact, already there were Nubian Christians, and Bishop

Theodore of Philae had established a church on an island where a Nobatian temple was.

Emperor Justinian planned to make the mission to Nubia a Chalcedonian mission, but Theodora cleverly got instructions to the military commander of Upper Egypt to put the empire's wealth and prestige behind Julian as the one in charge of the mission. Julian arrived with Justinian's gifts and "a richly equipped caravan" in 542, and the king of Nobatia and other leaders were baptized. The nation became "orthodox" (anti-Chalcedonian) Christian, although Justinian's pro-Chalcedonian mission had some success from 570 in the kingdom of Makurrah to the south.

The exiled Patriarch Theodosius of Alexandria consecrated Longinus bishop for the Nubians, and this bishop's heroic efforts not only consolidated the church in Nobatia but also leapfrogged Makurrah to convert the kingdom of Alwah further to the south. A successor of king Silko of Nubia, the conqueror of the Blemmyes people of the East, was converted to Julian's Christianity; and by 700 the whole Nile valley conformed to the Christianity of the Coptic patriarchate. The Coptic language was not adopted, but Old Nubian used its alphabet and was supplemented by Greek. Having a Christian nation to the South was to be very important to the early medieval Coptic church, dominated as Egypt was by Muslim rulers.

Even more important to strengthening the Coptic Church for survival was the influence of the monasteries. Just as in the Coptic monasteries today, the Coptic monks were counted on by lay folk for advice and help of many kinds, mostly spiritual and personal. But Besa's *Life of Shenoute*[17] also shows us that his monastery could be a powerful advocate for the needs and rights of peasants or other workers and could be a refuge from raids.

It was also in the monastic movement that the Coptic language of the native Egyptians first became the standard Christian language. Greek had long continued to be the standard language of Alexandrian Christianity and of the theologians, and through this universal tongue of the Eastern Mediterranean, Egyptian Christianity had maintained immediate communication with other Eastern Christians. Indeed, Egyptian monasticism and Alexandrian theology had been able to lead the Christian world in the fourth century and part of the fifth because of the universality of the Greek language. But throughout the particular period of this chapter "the Coptic language and literature were gradually replacing Greek culture throughout the country"[18] and the future of Egyptian Christianity lay with the Coptic, especially after Emperor Justinian broke with the church of the Egyptian majority.

The *History of the Patriarchs of Alexandria* reported in its biography of Peter IV, 567-569, that there were "600 flourishing monasteries, like beehives in their populousness, all inhabited by the orthodox who were all monks and nuns, besides thirty-two farms called 'Sakatina,' where all the people held the true faith , and the father and patriarch Peter was the administrator of the affairs of all of them."[19]

In Chapter Three we saw what a tremendous establishment a Coptic monastery could be, as evidenced by the huge church still standing of Shenoute's White Monastery, out from present-day Suhag. We have also seen that monasteries functioned almost like industries, since they had to be self-sustaining on a scale grand enough to support hundreds or even thousands of monks or nuns. The Melchite Metanoia monastery in Canopus had its own boats, for example, which it sent out to collect the grain due the monastery.[20]

Also important to the crucial character of the two centuries covered in this chapter was the great wealth of the churches, coming from their extensive properties. "The emperors were occasionally generous;"[21] and, as to the Egyptians, "every will of the period yet found had some legacy to the church."[22] Indeed, the churches and the Apion family "may well have been the largest landowners in Egypt."[23] These extensive holdings caused monasteries and churches sometimes to resort to private armies of "brucellari" as watchmen who could enforce the rights of property and wealth.[24]

Edward R. Hardy, Jr., has written rather extensively about the family of Apion[25] of Oxyrhynchus, using the large quantity of papyri available. Apion himself "converted" to the Melchite church to become the Empire's praetorian prefect[26] about 518. It was probably one of his own descendants, however, who, back in the Coptic fold a century later, urged the end to the Alexandria-Antioch schism.[27]

Her wealth in properties tied the Coptic Church closely to the economy and society, for, inevitably, the clergy and lay people were very much involved in managing the church's property and the income from it.[28] It is interesting to note that the clergy could be drawn from the laboring classes. They could even be serfs, called "coloni," on condition that their patron gave permission.[29] Priests could be so caught up in the various aspects of the life of Egypt that one could be found even in a private prison.[30] Thus we see a variety of ways in which the Coptic Church was very intimately tied to the lives of the Egyptian people, even though the Empire was supporting a counter-church with close connections with the churches of the West and many churches of the East. The Roman Empire had given more opportunity for local economies to flourish on their own than had the Ptolemies, and even more encouragement for local political life. This is even truer in the period we are considering in this chapter: "in the Byzantine period Egypt was at last not directed by government policies but began to live its own national and social life."[31]

The Coptic Church was helped to survive and thrive because of the revival of national life, and it, in turn, served as an important agent in this revival. It was too late to reverse this trend toward a national church and a national life when Emperor Heraclius sent a Melchite patriarch, Cyrus, just before the end of our period with instruction and powers "to stamp out [the Copts'] organization all over Egypt."[32]

The progressive consolidation of the Coptic Church as the church of the majority and the increasing use of Coptic as the church language continued under the last five patriarchs before the Arab invasion in the seventh century. It was the Roman governor himself who had advised the anti-Chalcedonian "orthodox" to go out of the city to az-Zajaj or Enaton monastery where they elected Peter IV to become their patriarch in 567. He took up his residence there at the nine-mile post.[33] Peter's deacon and scribe, Damian, who had been a monk in a Wadi Natrun monastery sixteen years, succeeded Peter. Damian was a theologian and writer; but while he was patriarch, a schism opened between the anti-Chalcedonians of Alexandria and Antioch (which we have already referred to) as a result of the dispute Damian had with the patriarch of Antioch on "naming the Trinity."[34]

The next patriarch, Anastasius, had been a priest who had had charge of the two churches, Angelion and Cosmas and Damian, in Alexandria and had even been on the city council.[35] He was able to visit the city frequently and was also able to ordain clergy and to build churches. But he had trouble with one Melchite patriarch, Eulogius, who got the emperor Phocas to give him the Cosmas and Damian Church. Prompted by a prominent Coptic layman,[36] an Apion, patriarch Anastasius ended the schism with Antioch, whose patriarch paid him a month-long visit after the grand reconciliation.

One of the most attractive of the personalities of the period was the Melchite patriarch of Alexandria known as John the Almoner. He came from a leading family and had actually been married and a father, though wife and child had died. His broadmindedness and openhanded generosity to all were famous. His five-year ministry in Egypt ended when the Persians invaded in 617, but his memory was so revered that even the Copts kept him in their calendar of saints.

Andronicus, who succeeded Anastasius as Coptic patriarch, was also well-connected and "resided in his cell at the church of the Angelion all his days," a church he had served as deacon, a "virgin and scribe." In his time the Persians under Chosroes captured Egypt and ruled it 616-629. The monasteries near the city were wrecked, and initially, at least, there was a great loss of life among the Copts.[37] but this did not last long, and, since Egyptians had not governed their own country for many a century, they may have wondered if Persians would simply take over from the Byzantines, and if it would make much difference.

The long delay of Roman Emperor Heraclius before counterattacking against the Persians made a profound impression in Egypt. Could the Empire really defend Egypt? Did the future of Egypt lie with Byzantium or with some conqueror from the East? But Heraclius did finally reconquer Egypt for the Empire in 629. Benjamin had by then been the Coptic patriarch seven years. He had come from a rich family but had become a monk; Patriarch Andronicus ordained him and "kept him with himself."

In 631, Heraclius sent Cyrus "Mukaukus," his adviser at the outset of his counteroffensive against the Persians, to be Melchite patriarch of Alexandria with civil and military powers as governor of Egypt. Benjamin fled to Wadi Natrun and then on to Upper Egypt, until the Arab invasion.[38] Cyrus was commissioned and empowered to destroy the Coptic Church as a rival to the Chalcedonian church in Egypt. He also hoped that the Ecthesis, a formula of one "energy" in Jesus Christ, supported by Roman Pope Honorius and the patriarch of Constantinople, would unite the Coptic Church and the Melchites.[39] In all, Cyrus felt compelled to unite the Christians of Egypt to combat the Arab threat.

Cyrus launched his attack, killing even Patriarch Benjamin's brother. "This blessed people who were thus persecuted were the Theodosians."[40] The persecutions were beginning to have the desired results. "On account of the greatness of the trials and the straits and the afflictions which Mukaukus brought down upon the orthodox, in order that they might enter into the Chalcedonian faith, a countless number of them went astray."[41] Two straying bishops are named, and there seemed to have been other bishops as well who went over to the Melchite Church. After the Arabs conquered Egypt, Patriarch Benjamin was able to draw the strayers back to the "right faith by his gentleness, exhorting them with courtesy and consolation," including the bishops, some of whom "returned with abundant tears."[42]

The *History of the Patriarchs* tells us that there was one monastery, Deir Metras, ("which was the episcopal residence") which could not be forced to accept Chalcedon, the monks "being Egyptians by race and all of them natives, without a stranger."[43] This suggests that Egyptians, that is, the Copts, were essentially "orthodox" anti-Chalcedonians, whereas the Chalcedonians were normally foreigners.

We cannot overlook the successes of the brutal Cyrus Mukaukus in forcing the Melchite church on many if not most of the Egyptians by argument or force, even if Benjamin seems to have been able to win them back to the Coptic Church, after the resounding defeat of the Byzantine forces and the departure and death of Cyrus.

We shall never know the direction Egyptian Christianity would have taken if the Byzantine Empire had been able to maintain itself strongly in the Eastern Mediterranean. Why? Because the Arabs, fresh from their conversion to Islam and consequent unity, burst out of their peninsula in the seventh century to conquer Egypt and end Byzantine rule there forever. The beginnings of Islamic rule in Egypt, which was to have such a drastic impact on Coptic Christianity, will occupy our next chapter.

[1] *History of the Patriarchs of the Coptic Church of Alexandria (HPCC)*, ed. B. Evetts, Vol. 1 of *Patrologia Orientalis* (Paris: Firmin-Didot, 1948), p. 447.

[2] W. H. C. Frend, *The Rise of Christianity* (Philadelphia: Fortress Press, 1984), p. 791; Frend has a long list of important writings on early Christianity in Egypt; for the period under consideration, see especially *The Rise of the Monophysite Movement* (Cambridge: Cambridge Univ. Press, 1972.)

[3] D. J. Chitty, *The Desert a City: An Introduction to the Study of Egyptian and Palestinian Monasticism under the Christian Empire* (London: Mowbrays, 1966), pp. 74, 92 and A. Guillaumont, "Kellia," *Coptic Encyclopedia*, 1991.

[4] The *History of the Patriarchs* has almost nothing about him.

[5] Frend, *The Rise of Christianity*, p. 809.

[6] Frend, *The Rise of Christianity*, p. 809.

[7] That is, the divine and human in Jesus.

[8] *HPCC* 1, 449.

[9] W. H. C. Frend in an article reprinted as "The Mission to Nubia: an Episode in Struggle for Power in Sixth Century Byzantium" from *Travaux du Centre d'archéologie méditerranéenne de l'Académie Polonaise des Sciences*, Vol. 16 (Warsaw, 1975), 10-16.

[10] Frend, *The Rise of Christianity*, p. 830.

[11] Most of the biography of Timothy III in *HPCC* 1, 453-454, is about Severus, including his conflict over Julian's Christology.

[12] "Lives of James and Theodore" in John of Ephesus, *Lives of the Eastern Saints*, according to W. H. C. Frend, *The Rise of Christianity*, p. 848.

[13] Frend, *The Rise of Christianity*, p. 844.

[14] We now have four possible names for the Coptic Christians: Monophysites, anti-Chalcedonians, Jacobites, and Theodosians.

[15] Frend, *The Rise of Christianity*, p. 843.

[16] We are following the account of W. H. C. Frend's "The Mission to Nubia," pp. 10-16; he is drawing heavily on John of Ephesus' *Church History* III and IV.

[17] D. N. Bell, ed. and trans., *The Life of Shenoute* by Besa (Kalamazoo, Michigan: Cistercian Publications, 1983).

[18]E. R. Hardy, *The Large Estates of Byzantine Egypt* (New York: Columbia Univ. Press, 1931), p. 21.

[19]*HPCC* 1, 472.

[20]Hardy, p. 47.

[21]Hardy, p. 44.

[22]Hardy, p. 44, note 6.

[23]Hardy, p. 87.

[24]Hardy, p. 82.

[25]Hardy, chap. 2.

[26]Hardy, p. 27.

[27]Hardy, pp. 35, 36.

[28]Hardy, p. 47.

[29]Hardy, p. 78, and see p. 140.

[30]Hardy, p. 64.

[31]Hardy, p. 148.

[32]Hardy, p. 21.

[33]*HPCC* 1, 469.

[34]*HPCC* 1, 477-478.

[35]*HPCC* 1, 478-479.

[36]Hardy, p. 36.

[37]According to Andronicus' biography in *HPCC* 1, 484-486, 80,000 men were tricked into massing themselves in the city, where they were slaughtered. In A. J. Butler, *The Arab Conquest of Egypt and the Last Thirty Years of the Roman Dominion*, 2nd ed. (Oxford: Clarendon Press, 1978), pp. 75-76, the author dismisses this massacre as being quite impossible.

[38]*HPCC* 1, 487-490.

[39]Aziz S. Atiya, "Cyrus al-Muqawqus," *Coptic Encyclopedia*, 1991.

[40]*HPCC* 1, 492.

[41]*HPCC* 1, 491.

[42]*HPCC* 1, 497.

[43]*HPCC* 1, 498.

Chapter Five

First Centuries after the Arab Conquest

✠ ———————————————————————————————— ✠

640 to about 970

OR MORE THAN THIRTEEN HUNDRED YEARS before 642 A.D., Egypt was often conquered and normally incorporated into one empire or another. One wonders how Christian Egypt would have felt in 640 had it known that Egypt would now be ruled for a variety of Islamic empires for the ensuing thirteen hundred years? Would they have assumed that their Coptic Christian culture, with its strong Hellenistic elements, would survive intact? Why not? Coptic was a traditional and national language, and Christianity had firmly taken over as the Egyptian religion—and cultural conservatism was an Egyptian specialty.

For example, classic Egyptian culture was so firmly established in the pharaonic period that arts and religion stayed surprisingly stable for many centuries. Then, after Alexander's conquest of Egypt and the establishment of the Ptolemaic government in the 330s B.C., for a thousand years Hellenism was to have a profound impact in Egypt, largely in the Hellenistic cities of which Alexandria was chief, but also in Upper Egypt as well.

Yet, Hellenism itself did not replace traditional Egyptian language or religion. Written Coptic looked like Greek and used many loan words from Greek, but it was still the traditional Egyptian language. Even in the Greco-Roman era, the religious picture was not significantly altered until the Christian movement began to make large-scale conversions in the latter half of the third century. But before another century was completed, the combination of Roman government, Hellenistic civilization, and the Christian church had transformed urban Egypt. We have already seen that Alexandria remained the most prosperous and most cultured city of the world west of India for most of the 330 B.C. to 640 A.D. millennium.

Of all the successful invasions of Egypt, however, it was to be the Arab conquest which would make the most profound and lasting changes. After emphasizing the glories of Alexandria ("even in the seventh century the finest city in the world") and the Copts' ongoing loyalty to their faith, A. J. Butler goes on to say: "Nevertheless, few things are more remarkable in history than the manner in which a handful of victorious Arabs from the desert absorbed and destroyed in Egypt, broadly speaking, both the Christian religion and that older Byzantine culture, which owed at once its refinement and its frailty to the blending of the three great and ancient civilizations of Rome, Greece, and Egypt."[1]

Arabic was to replace Coptic, even as the spoken language of the Coptic Church, and Islam was to become the dominant religion, even though Christianity was to remain an important minority religion. Cairo was to become a great center of Islamic civilization and the capital of Egypt, so that even the Coptic patriarch of Alexandria was to change his residence to Cairo. That Christianity remained an important, if minority, religion is testimony to the hardihood of the Egyptian church, and along with their own survival as a community the Christians maintained a tenuous hold on the Coptic language, even when they stopped speaking it. In this chapter we begin to see the initial impact of the Arab conquest and the Copts' adjustment to it.

The rise of Islam and the eruption of the Arabs from the Arabian peninsula into the Fertile Crescent and into North Africa and Spain are also among the astonishing developments of human history because of how swiftly it all happened. The prophet Muhammad "fled" from Mecca with a small group of disciples in 622, returned in triumph in 630, and died in 632. Within ten more years, Iraq, Syria, and Palestine had been conquered, and the triumphant Arabs were in control of Egypt.

This rapid expansion of Arab conquests[2] was made without any master strategy or any plan for empire. It did take place in the full light of history with ample contemporary documentation, but it is still a challenge to explain how it could have happened, especially in view of its important results for all subsequent history, not just Egypt's.

Two factors stand out. On the one hand there was the exhaustion of the Byzantine and Persian empires from their long wars with one another. On the other hand was the bitter religious division among the Eastern Christians over the doctrine of Christ. The division, and the Empire's persecution of dissident Christians, badly eroded any loyalty Syrian and Coptic Christians might have had to Constantinople and its empire.

Now let us see how the story unfolds for the Coptic Christian community in Egypt. First, we recall that at the time of the invasion, the Coptic Church had been in disarray for almost a decade. Emperor Heraclius had sent Cyrus as Melchite patriarch and civil governor, and Cyrus used his vast powers and fierce determination to force many Coptic Christians, even bishops, to go over to his side. Coptic Patriarch Benjamin had to flee to Upper Egypt for at least ten years. Cyrus' activities constituted a reign of terror.[3]

But it seems that it was not only the Copts who had little incentive to perpetuate Byzantine rule in Egypt. The tens of thousands of Byzantines were routed by the thousands of Arabs under Amr al-As. The imperial forces not only vastly outnumbered the invaders, they had powerfully fortified cities, which the Arabs had neither the proper equipment nor the expert knowledge to attack. Did things turn out as they did simply because Cyrus, the patriarch-governor, was a traitor? It is more likely that with all his cruelty Cyrus was simply as cowardly and as inept as were his military commanders. There were occasions when the Byzantines fought bravely, but there was not to be found in Egypt any indomitable desire to keep Egypt for the Empire, even among the Byzantines.

Butler argues[4] in detail that there is no truth to the story that the Copts aided the Arab forces in the conquest of Egypt. But he also points out frequently that the Copts had little motivation to support the Byzantine efforts even if they had been in a position to do so. Their "Church lay weakened and almost lifeless. it seemed, from the blows rained upon it during the space of ten years by the relentless hand of Cyrus."[5]

Amr and his Arab forces fought determinedly and were well led and would not accept defeat. They entered Egypt by land at the end of 639 and at Heliopolis in 640 won the first great battle. The strategically important and powerfully fortified Babylon (in today's Cairo) fell to them in the spring of 641, and the great fortified port city of Alexandria capitulated in the late summer of the same year. It is easy to see why Amr's army, without any naval support or equipment to attack cities, believed that it must have been Allah who gave them their victory in Egypt.

As early as 640, when Amr and his forces were threatening the fortress of Babylon, he was asked for his terms. His response was: "Only one of three courses . . . 1) Islam with brotherhood and equality; 2) payment of tribute, and protection with an inferior status; 3) war till God decides between us."[6]

As it turned out, course 3) rather quickly ceased to be an option; so the choice of individuals and families came to be between 1) and 2). Choice 2) could be changed to 1) at any time, but once a person became a Muslim there would be no turning back, practically speaking. Conversion from Islam could be a capital offense. From the beginning there were Copts who chose equality with the conquerors over the inferiority and the special taxes to be suffered by loyal Christians. The loyal Christians were the perpetuators of Coptic Christianity, of course.

Three years after the capitulation of Alexandria to the Arab invaders,

Coptic Patriarch Benjamin was returned to the city in triumph. He was to head up the Christian church in Egypt and to rule the Copts. This signaled the beginning of a new relationship of the Coptic Church to society and government.

"The praises the *History of the Patriarchs* lavishes on the Arab conqueror (Amr) have doubtless less to do with his personality and the preeminence he gave to the Coptic patriarch Benjamin than with the unique position that the Arab domination at the beginning conferred on the Egyptian church and its heads. The country was Christian, the Muslim Arabs few, the church remained the only nationally accepted authority which could serve as a link between the government and the people."[7]

E. R. Hardy made the interesting observation that "with the Mohammedan conquest Egypt returned to a more effective centralized bureaucratic government than it had had since the days of the early Ptolemies."[8] The Copts played a central role in this, as they were the bureaucrats who ran the government for the victorious Arabs, especially in the early decades.

In the short run, at least, the Copts drew two benefits from the Arab conquest: reduced taxes and greater religious freedom. In comparison with the last decade of Byzantine rule, the Copts found that "now their civil bondage was lightened and their religious bondage removed."[9] They were no longer treated as heretics, for now they were "dhimmis," that is, a "protected" people. As such they were to be secure at home and protected from foreign invaders, but the cost of that protection could be quite high, as we shall be seeing.

Non-Arab converts to Islam were called "mawali," originally meaning clients of an Arab tribe. In theory, they should have been equal to their Arab fellow Muslims, but, in fact, at least until the Abbasid dynasty took over the caliphate in 750, the Arabs reserved many of the major privileges for themselves. The dominant element under Islamic rule before 750 was the Arab warrior aristocracy. After 750, in most Islamic lands, mawali scholars and mawali businessmen became dominant. The day of the warrior was passing, and the day of the governor had come.

The loyal Copts, as dhimmis, were to suffer higher taxation, second class citizenship, social disabilities, and sometimes even persecution. They were excluded from the military, for their conquerors were there to protect (as well as exploit) them. But Copts did have property rights and certain rights of religious observance, and they often prospered in the crafts, in business, and in government administration.[10]

The Copts were a subject people, obliged to pay an annual poll tax for the "protection" they received, and never free of social disabilities and

potential humiliation. Among the rules for the Copts were temporary hospitality to Muslims, submission to Muslim justice, riding donkeys only (or
sometimes, on horses backwards), special dress, and sharp limitations on
building churches. With such rules, Muslim ideologues planned to drill into
Muslim and Christian alike that dhimmis were a particular, separated group
whom Muslims needed to be able to identify and deal with properly, e.g.,
not to greet them first.[11] But Copts had their church, their community, and
opportunities in government and business that could lead to a level of wealth
and prestige which sometimes provoked the envy of Arabs and mawali.

During the first two centuries after the Arab conquest, " the vast majority of the people of Egypt were, of course, the Christian Copts, and whatever oppression existed was mainly borne by them. There is very little evidence, however, to show that they were grossly ill treated," according to
Lane-Poole's widely read history of medieval Egypt.[12]

In Egypt the Coptic Christians rivaled, and frequently outdid, the
"mawali" as merchants, craftsmen, and bureaucrats. The Arabs had neither
the preparation nor the desire to run the business of governing Egypt, which
became simply a Byzantine successor state,[13] administered in many cases by
officials who converted to Islam, but more and more by Copts as time went
along. A Muslim "hadith" (a traditional saying attributed to the Prophet) says
that the Copts "will help Muslims become pious, by discharging their temporal duties." Copts seem to have been more than glad to fulfill this role.

When Coptic Patriarch Benjamin returned at Amr's invitation to
Alexandria in 644 to lead the Coptic church and people for eighteen years,
the majority Copts began their long pilgrimage as dhimmis. They were on
their way to be a vigorous but frustrated minority in their own country where
their religion and its language had long been standard. The very Arabic word
for Copts is "qibti," the Arabic transliteration of the latinized Greek "aegyptus," suggesting that the Copts were the real Egyptians!

Amr, the conqueror of Egypt, seems to have treated the Egyptians fairly, but the Arab thirst for tribute was great and he was recalled in favor of
Abdullah ibn Sa'd, who exacted tribute beyond the treaty amount, enough
to place the Copts in great straits. Philip Hitti[14] argued that the Arab conquest had been, in fact, principally motivated by the search for tribute: "not
fanaticism but economic necessity drove the Bedouin hordes." (Bernard
Lewis rather emphasized overpopulation and a drive for living space as the
Arabs' principal motivations.[15]) Like the nineteenth-century imperialists, the
Arabs ran their empire to suit their own needs, not those of the subject peoples.

Benjamin had been back in Alexandria not much more than a year
when the Byzantines launched a powerful surprise effort to recapture
Alexandria and Egypt. After early Byzantine success, the Arab counterat-

tack, led once more by Amr (who was hastily recalled), again defeated the Byzantines, although the Arabs still lacked the same instruments of war they had lacked before. The Copts did not assist the Byzantine invaders this time, any more than they had helped the Arab invaders five years before.

Benjamin died in 662 and was succeeded as Coptic patriarch by Agatho, his biographer who had been "as his son in the administration of the holy church." During Cyrus' reign of terror, Agatho had taken communion to the faithful Copts in Alexandria in secret, disguising himself and his sacred vessels by posing as a carpenter.[16] Surprisingly little is known about his eighteen-year patriarchate, except that he spent a lot of funds charitably in ransoming Christians whom he considered to be heretics;[17] and he consecrated bishops for vacant sees.

Agatho was succeeded as patriarch by his saintly and charismatic protégé, the monk John, who became John III. By the late seventh century, bishops were largely drawn from the monasteries,[18] which also meant that the Coptic Church continued longer than many churches to recruit bishops from the common people, since most monks came from that class of Copts.[19]

In his eight or nine years as patriarch, John was an active leader, although the governor, Abdul Aziz, tried to squeeze a fortune (100,000 dinars) from him by throwing him in prison. The patriarchs of Alexandria had had enormous financial resources during most of the history of the Egyptian church, as we noted in Chapter Four. These funds were largely designated for support of the church establishment and for large-scale charity, usually, but not always, used for the needs of the faithful.

Such reserves, or even the rumor of their existence, inevitably interested the Muslim governors whose major function was to squeeze the maximum income from Egypt. Governors were even to argue that since the Arabs were the protectors of the Egyptians, the latter needed only food and clothing—not the money required for massive military expenditures.[20]

After John's "fine" was substantially reduced, the money was raised by church leaders and he was released. In fact he became a friend of the governor, rebuilt the church dedicated to Saint Mark, and constructed an oil press, a flour mill, and houses.[21] The latter represented important investments, but they also made food and housing available to church members, clearly an important continuing activity of the Coptic Church hierarchy. John also won many Melchites to the Coptic Church, and in a time of famine, he put his mill to work for the sufferers. John brought into his administration his successor and biographer, Isaac, from the monastery of Saint Macarius, once again a major center of preparation of church leadership.

George, a deacon, almost became John's successor but governor

Abdul Aziz decided for Isaac. George then occupied himself with preparing biographies of the patriarchs. Although the governor had become a friend of the patriarch, he did try to force the Christians to put on their churches the inscription, "Muhammad is the great Apostle of God and Jesus also the apostle of God, but verily God is not begotten and does not beget."[22] So much for the two central Christian doctrines of the Trinity and of Christ.

Abdul Aziz was also important in the selection of Simon I to succeed Isaac.[23] Simon was a Syrian by birth, a monk brought up in the Enaton monastery, having been dedicated by his mother to the Coptic Church. He was chosen over one John, the head of his monastery, whom he made administrator of church affairs. Simon appointed another John, bishop of the important and nearby diocese of Nikiu, to supervise the monasteries from 696 on. This latter John also chronicled much of the period covered in this chapter.[24]

The ascetic and studious Simon, thus freed, spent his time in solitude and Scripture study. Many Alexandrian church members hated him for his lack of patriarchal hospitality, to which they had become quite attached. We might note here that the mystique of the Coptic patriarchate allowed for, if it did not exactly encourage, selection of a solitary and extremely devout monk. Such a one could easily turn out, like Saint John Chrysostom, to lack the administrative and diplomatic abilities often admired in successful prelates.

Both Simon and Bishop John of Nikiu were rigid adherents to traditional Coptic antipathy to the Council of Chalcedon, to breakaway movements, and to lack of discipline. When "the amir rebuked their [opponents'] want of agreement in the doctrine of religion," Simon's excommunication of his rivals impressed the governor more than the broadminded approach of the other church leaders.

By the end of Simon's patriarchate about 700, King Mercurius of Makouria was also ruling the Lower Nubian kingdom of Nobatia so that "thenceforward . . . there was only a single northern Nubian kingdom, extending from Aswan at least as far south as the Fifth Cataract."[25] Nubia was becoming under Mercurius, "the new Constantine," a counter force to Arab pressure.

Simon's successor, Alexander II,[26] another learned monk from the same monastery, presided over the Coptic Church during almost all of the first quarter of the eighth century, a turbulent period for the Coptic Church, and a sort of turning point. Upon the death of Abdul Aziz, who had befriended the Coptic leadership, his nephew, Abdallah, the son of the caliph, succeeded him as amir and extorted 3000 dinars from Alexander. This inspired Abdallah's superior to demand 3000 dinars for himself. Arab rule had previously been broadly tolerant, for the Arabs wanted to rule and tax a productive society and economy. "The whole structure of the Arab state was based on the assumption that a minority of Arabs could rule a majority of tax-paying non-Muslims."[27]

Although extracting wealth and supplies remained the dominant goal of the Arabs, things were to change. Abdallah forbade the burnoose to Copts and ordered the use of Arabic in all public documents.[28] Thus began the long process of going "from a predominantly Christian province with a small Arab-Muslim governing minority . . . to a Muslim province with a relatively small Christian minority."[29]

During Alexander's patriarchate, the poll tax was extended to include even monks,[30] and conversions to Islam accelerated, an even more important part of the transformation of Egypt.[31] After 717, converts were welcomed into the Islamic community.[32] Caliph Omar II even tried excluding dhimmis from administrative activities, on which they had had almost a monopoly, and he enforced discriminatory financial and social laws.[33]

Taxes, like discrimination, were a large factor in the conversion of Copts to Islam,[34] for they were quite burdensome. Each Coptic male in a village paid the poll tax, the land tax, a proportional tax on the land's productivity, and sums to cover the needs of the Muslims and the support of public officials. There had been rather little conversion in the early Umayyad period (661-750). Indeed, the Arabs had rather discouraged conversion and often tried to deny to converts the Muslim's exemption from the poll tax on dhimmis. But that was now changing, especially as the "mawali" converts became more powerful and more demanding of privileges.

In the 720s many Copts lost patience and rebelled when an order from the caliph resulted in a destruction of their icons[35] and when the tax burden appeared to be unbearable. The result was the massacre of Copts, who had no military experience.

The successor of Alexander as Coptic patriarch was Cosmas, who distinguished himself by successfully praying for his early death! This may illustrate once again the possible result from electing a monk of dramatic sanctity to a post demanding great powers of organizational leadership.

W. Y. Adams questions[36] Abu Salih's report[37] that under King Cyracus, in 745, "a Nubian army of 100,000 men invaded Egypt and forced the Arab governor to release the Patriarch of Alexandria, whom he had imprisoned." But, Adams continues, "the threat of Nubian intervention gave the Egyptian Christians a certain political leverage."

The century of patriarchs Michael I through Joseph I (744-849) "is in every respect a period of accelerated transition in which the position of the community is to be thoroughly revolutionized, both internally and in its relation to the Muslim power."[38] The center of Islamic rule shifted from Syria to Iraq, the arabization of Egypt accelerated, the last and most violent of the

Coptic revolts was crushed, and the Christians became a minority in Egypt. We shall see these evolve one by one.

After a breathing space of eleven years under his predecessor, Michael I became patriarch, another monk from Saint Macarius' monastery. He was proposed by a gathering of bishops and lay leaders in Egypt's Babylon. His selection had raised the troubling question of who should choose the Patriarch of Alexandria. If he was to be bishop of Alexandria, should not the clergy there dominate the decision? But as leader of the whole Coptic Christian community (Amr had called them a "nation" when he recalled Benjamin to "govern" them[39]), should not the patriarch be chosen by the whole church—in particular, the bishops and the leading members?

Michael I[40] began a fourteen-year career as patriarch during a time of great challenge and change. During his time there was the crucial change from the Umayyad "Arab Kingdom" to the Abbasid "Islamic Empire",[41] another Coptic revolt, and the first mass conversion to Islam—in one case 24,000 Copts.[42]

As to the transition to Abbasid rule, Marwan II, the last Umayyad ruler, made his last stand in Egypt where he both hounded Patriarch Michael and pursued a drastic scorched-earth policy. The Copts may have hoped that Marwan's failure and the new Islamic empire of the Abbasids would improve their lot. Instead, it became worse, in large part because the pace of change of governors for Egypt now doubled. This meant that before they were replaced the Abbasid governors had only half the time that the Umayyad governors had had to squeeze their fortunes from the hapless Egyptians.

In fact, throughout the first two centuries of Islamic rule Egypt was governed for rulers in Arabia, in Syria, or in Iraq. Egypt provided a wonderful supply of food, a rich source of wealth created from its fertile fields and its skilled artisanry, and a market to sell and buy products from all over the Eurasian as well as the African trading area. It is not surprising that the medieval imperialists looked upon Egypt as a great prize. As in most of its long history, a large proportion of Egypt's wealth was confiscated for foreign rulers.

Egypt was trading her material wealth, it would seem, for a new language, Arabic, and the cultural changes that inevitably go with a language change. It is interesting to note that in the biography of Patriarch Michael, he could not understand his jailer, Kauzara.[43] A bilingual Egypt was not to last forever. We have seen that government administration was already conducted in the Arabic language.

The early eighth century was also a period when there were major migrations of Arabs into Egypt. And Egyptian resistance to political and cultural change was not strong. Egyptians, "long accustomed to alien domination, seem to have had no national feeling like that which sustained the national identity of the Persians even after their conversion to Islam. The Coptic revolts against Arab rule were occasional, spasmodic, and unorganized . . . and were not accompanied by any signs of religious or national revival or even awareness."[44]

Mennas I,[45] who succeeded Michael as patriarch, had been his disciple, a scribe, and a monk from Saint Macarius' monastery. He suffered from an imprisonment which was not uncommon during much of the Copts' existence under Islamic rule. He was being held for a large ransom. As we have seen, the church in general, and the patriarchate in particular, were believed to have very substantial financial resources, for many Coptic Christians characteristically positioned themselves to accumulate money, especially as tax-collectors; and they supported their church and its hierarchy. Mennas, however, argued that in his case the church was poor; even the chalices which they believed to hold the blood of Christ were of glass or wood.

More important, Mennas' imprisonment also illustrates how disappointed seekers of church office could, and sometimes did, threaten patriarchs and then proceed to denounce them to a Muslim government. A deacon named Peter did precisely this to Mennas. Such denunciations were another side of the tragic history of "simony" in the medieval Egyptian church. Consecrating bishops, or even priests, for a fee was a sore temptation—and may sometimes have seemed to be a necessity to prelates who were expected to pay outrageous exactions to a governor desperately trying to take advantage of his brief chance to enrich his family. Rejected aspirants to sacramental ministries could make the hierarchy's situation even worse.

The Abbasid dynasty of caliphs in Baghdad reached its peak of fame under the legendary Harun al-Rashid who reigned from 786 to 809. Then the civil war between his two sons foreshadowed the breakup of his empire. One of his sons, al-Ma'mun, had to come to Egypt himself to put down the 831 revolt, "the most difficult to suppress and . . . the cause of the most murderous expeditions . . . Al-Ma'mun thought it necessary to go to Egypt in person in order to clear up a situation which his lieutenants had been unable to control."[46] And yet Muslim expansionists from the West, called "Spaniards" by the *History of the Patriarchs*, controlled Alexandria during the latter part of the period!

The last four patriarchs before 844, not counting the short-lived Simon II, had varying careers, of course, but with much in common, e.g., they all came from Saint Macarius' monastery and most were builders and rebuilders. Mark II saw the destruction of the great monastic centers at Wadi Natrun by nomads but Joseph I rebuilt them. Joseph had created productive vineyards and mills and an olive press, and, when the opportune moment came, he restored Saint Macarius' and the other monasteries. The career of Joseph[47] shows us a great deal about the evolving Coptic Christianity that was to carry the Copts up to the nineteenth century. We are well acquainted with him, for his biography was written by an eyewitness.

Joseph had to be brought in chains to be consecrated patriarch. This indicated both the great danger there was in being patriarch and also the convention that ambition to be patriarch automatically disqualified the candidate. The principal rival to Joseph's accession was a rich layman who had been married! This able Copt, named Isaac, was later ordained deacon and then bishop of the important diocese of Wassim, with care over the Muslim capital city, Misr.[48]

It was early in Joseph's patriarchate that the terrible Bashmurite revolt, which both Joseph and Patriarch Dionysius of Antioch tried to stop, was put down. In this 831 revolt, it is interesting that Muslims joined in at first, for it was not only Christians who suffered from the brutal exactions of the Muslim rulers. After an initial defeat, the Copts, who had no military tradition, had to fight on alone, only to be more cruelly crushed.

As a result, reported Makrizi[49] the medieval Muslim historian, the despair led to a wave of conversions. Islamization "took a decisive step in the second half of the ninth century," beginning in the Delta.[50] The ninth century was, indeed, to see a great tide of conversion; financial hardships, social restrictions, legal inferiority, insecurity, and popular Muslim hostility[51] proved too much for many Christians, and they became a minority in Egypt for the first time since the fourth century.

Meanwhile, for the two centuries since the Arab conquest, "the bishops and lay notables are rapidly assuming power in the church; and the *History of the Patriarchs*, being focused on the patriarchs, becomes rather anecdotal—a book of signs rather than a tableau properly speaking, of the community's life."[52] Nevertheless, we are heavily dependent on the *History of the Patriarchs* for much of our knowledge of Coptic church life in that era.

Let us pause to consider the impact of conversion on the people involved. For the "mawali" who converted from the Coptic Church to the religion of the rulers of Egypt, there were vast religious changes, e.g., instead of the ecumenical Nicene Creed, the Holy Scriptures of the Old and New Testaments, and the theological heritage of the great church fathers of the fourth and fifth centuries, the converts now had the Holy Quran, the simple confession, "there is no God but Allah and Muhammad is his messenger," and a detailed pattern for right social and personal conduct.

The converts had their mosques; the Copts still had their churches, but it was normally hard to get permission to build or even to rebuild or repair their church buildings. Sunday ceased to be the weekly holiday in a country ruled by Muslims, so Sunday worship had to be before work or after work, unless one worked for oneself. The Copts had their seven sacraments and the daily offices of prayers and Psalms and Scripture readings, for which the converts now substituted the five times of daily prayer to which they were called by the muezzin. Copts continued to fast in seasons like Lent and Advent and on Wednesdays and Fridays, while the converts fasted from sun-up to sun-down during the holy month of Ramadan. The Copts looked to Jerusalem as their pilgrimage city, the converts to Mecca.

Even the calendar changed. The Copts still preferred to date the years "in the year of the martyrs" or possibly "in the year of the Lord", while converts used "in the year of the Hijra," using a year based on the moon. The Copts clung to Coptic as their language of worship, even after they began to use Arabic as their everyday language. For the converts to Islam on the other hand, Arabic was recognized as Allah's own language. He had dictated the Holy Quran to the Prophet word for word in Arabic, so that there can be no recognition of a translation of the Quran into another language—only an interpretation.

Family life changed for converts. A Muslim man is allowed up to four wives if he can treat them equally, and divorce was easy for a Muslim male, whereas Christians were allowed only one spouse, and divorce was not recognized by the Copts. This meant not only a lot of stability in Coptic marriages but it also discouraged intermarriage for Coptic women, who could easily be put aside by their Muslim husbands. Even the diet of converts was affected, for Islam forbade the consumption of pork or of alcohol.

Let us return to Pope Joseph. In addition to trying to forestall the fatal 831 revolt, he was called upon to help keep the peace between the Christian king of Nubia and Egypt's Muslim rulers, with the assistance of Bishop Isaac. King Zacharias of Nubia sent his son to Egypt and to the prince in Baghdad. He was received with honors in Baghdad and by Pope Joseph, who allowed the bishops from Nubia to celebrate the Liturgy for him. The bishops had been selected by the Coptic patriarch and were consecrated by him, and normally they were Egyptians. This was just one instance of Joseph's diplomatic service to his Muslim rulers in their relation to Nubia. He also acted as a mediator between Egypt and Ethiopia.

Joseph, like his Israelite patriarch namesake, knew how to forgive. After having to discipline two rebellious bishops, he later interceded for them; again, when a heretical Lazarus, who had despoiled churches for a Muslim prince, fell on hard times, Joseph helped him. This patriarch-diplomat (who could not even speak Arabic!) and builder was also noted for his piety—he was said to recite the entire Psalter every day. His biographer included this note along with the other history, for he was not trying to write an unbiased account of a patriarchate during this crucial period. Rather, he intended to show how important actions like building the economy and edifices of the church, mediating, forgiving, praying, and using the skills of rivals could be to Coptic survival.

We have now seen the beginnings of the process of the triumph of Islam and the Arabic language in Egypt. In the rest of the chapter, we see the continuation of the process of the Coptic Christians' becoming a minority and virtually losing their own Coptic language, along with much of the culture that accompanies a language. Ironically, it was not as if Egyptian Christians had never before been a minority or suffered persecution—or gone through a change of language, for that matter. Until 313 Egyptian Christians had been a minority and were subject to disabilities and active persecutions; we have already noted their problems with the Roman and Byzantine Empires; and Egyptians had already shifted their church language progressively from Greek to Coptic. But the Arab conquest and the Islamic governments of Egypt radically changed—as the Romans and Byzantines never could—the relation of the Coptic Christians to their native Egypt.

Egypt as a country was going through dramatic changes in government. The last, and best, Arab governor of Egypt,[53] who served during the latter part of the tenure of Pope Cosmas II (851-858), was Anbara (852-856). Then, for the first time since the Arab conquest, Egypt became no longer simply part of a foreign empire, or "a subject province . . . with its centre elsewhere."[54] Ibn Tulun from 869 and the "Ikhshid" from 935 created short-lived dynasties which ruled Egypt from Egypt, even if they were Turks supported by Turkish troops, and although they formally represented the Sunni caliphs in Baghdad.

> [T]he Tulunids and Ikhshidids inaugurate the separate history of Muslim Egypt, follow recognizably Egyptian policies, and win strong Egyptian support. First, they brought the country security and prosperity. . . . The size and good discipline of the Tulunid and Ikhshidid armies presuppose an efficient fiscal organization with a high yield. . .[It] is clear that the government was well supplied with money and the country prosperous . . . [Increased revenue] was not achieved by extortion—certain taxes were in fact remitted—but by wise agrarian policies, inducing a higher yield, and by elimination of abuses . . . A major factor in this prosperity was certainly the retention and expenditure in Egypt of great sums previously drained away to Baghdad."[55]

These summary arguments from a distinguished historian of Islam point up how during the century beginning with the 850s and 860s government became a positive force in the Egyptian economy. Although he squeezed what he could from the Coptic patriarch, ibn Tulun was generally tolerant of the Copts. But still in this period, the Coptic Christians were seeing their proportion of the population decline.

The Copts' sad fortunes are symbolized by the consecration of the learned and experienced but short-lived Pope Michael II[56] against his will. Such reluctance was later to become so frequent that it may have become conventional. The special burdens put on the Copts' higher clergy, however, may also have given them serious pause.

Michael's successor, Cosmas II,[57] had so much trouble with the governor in Alexandria that he actually felt he had to leave the historic seat of the patriarch and move to Damru, which was to have a history in the gradual move of the patriarchate from Alexandria to Cairo, the future capital of Egypt. Interestingly, the temporal affairs of the church were entrusted by Pope Cosmas to two Coptic laymen in the capital who were ranking bureaucrats in the government of Egypt. Already we see educated and capable lay Christians simultaneously exercising leadership in the Coptic Church and in the Muslim government.

Still, having Christians in high administrative offices did not keep the caliph in Baghdad, al-Mutawakkil, from afflicting the Christians by forbidding them white clothes, requiring them to deface their property, trying to drive Christians out of office, and actually ordering Christians to convert to Islam. Many did. The caliph's deputy forbade crosses, Christian prayer audible to Muslims, riding horses for Christians, or their using wine.

One notes with a certain wonder how easy it was for Coptic Christians to move from a subjugated and despised group into the dominant and prestigious group with all the accompanying advantages. The move was accomplished by simply "islamizing," i.e., converting to Islam. Why did not all of them convert? Islam did not have any effective way to block the move into the favored group, for it is a universal religion, open to everyone, and all Muslims are supposed to be brothers and sisters. It was not that Muslim rulers necessarily wanted conversion, for defections from Christianity cut into the revenue from the special tax on non-Muslim, "protected populations!" But government policies did have the effect of encouraging conversion.

Taxes were a major incentive to wavering Christians to convert,[58] however, as were also the kinds of disabilities noted above. Bloody persecution was quite rare, except, later, for the "new martyrs" under the (probably) insane caliph al-Hakim[59] between 1010 and 1020. More common was popular rioting against Christians,[60] perhaps encouraged by religious leaders.

Copts were excluded from the highest offices, not surprisingly, but there were also occasions when governors even tried to force them out of all the levels of government bureaucracy for which the Copts' administrative skills made them invaluable. The exclusion never lasted long, but it was enough to convince many to convert to Islam. Dismissal for being a Christian was always a threat to an ambitious official.

Specialized studies of the historic movement from Christianity to Islam in Egypt point to this period, especially the ninth century, as "the crucial epoch in the conversion of Christians to Islam," although "we cannot say the minority of Christians was anything less than very substantial in the ninth and tenth centuries."[61] Copts did not disappear into Islam as did their fellow Christians in the rest of North Africa—the home of Latin Christianity.

Again we wonder. Islam is one of the great "world religions," offering a monotheistic faith and a high standard of morality spelled out in careful and clear detail. Belief in Jesus—even his virgin birth—is actually encouraged in Islam, although he is represented as only a messenger from God. This may have been easier for some Egyptian Christians to believe than the brain-twisting theology of three divine persons in one godhead and two natures in one person. Also, in the centuries we are beginning to consider, Islamic Civilization was to offer Egyptians the best in philosophy and the sciences. Loyalty in the face of trials, however, was the Egyptian Christians' heritage. Jesus had founded and Paul had propagated a Christianity which abhorred defection and powerfully emphasized standing firm even when confronted with the most frightening threats. Indeed, the Christian Church was born as a rejected and persecuted minority.

In trying to understand how the Copts could come up with a religious explanation for their progressive losing out to Islam, Maurice Martin develops an interesting theory from the emphasis on the miraculous in the *History of the Patriarchs.*

The miraculous Christian is at one and the same time an expression of the aspirations of the [Coptic] community, a supernatural compensation for deprivation and impotence, a presence of secret help held in reserve. Miracles performed by a holy monk or holy icons nourish reports, endlessly reborn, passing quickly from mouth to mouth, which justify patience while maintaining the community's will to live, its hope.[62]

There were also less specifically religious reasons, of course. The Copts always continued to make a place for themselves in Egypt by their skills as bookkeepers, administrators, professionals like architects and physicians, or as craftsmen. Copts were (and are) achievers. In fact, their very successes sometimes made their wealth and standing so prominent that they provoked jealousy and persecution from Muslims. Coptic Christians also had a strong community spirit among themselves, which gave them a sense of identity and community support which conversion to Islam would destroy for them. Muslims have historically suspected that converts from the Coptic Church secretly retained their old faith and their family ties and personal friendships while they publicly professed Islam in order to enjoy the advantages of being in the dominant group.

In the period we are considering, there were some conversions from Islam to Christianity, even though conversion from Islam was quite dangerous. Syed Barakat Ahmad has argued that Islam does not punish recantation with death,[63] although there were such cases,[64] which we will consider when we get to the eleventh century.

Coptic Christians not only suffered problems from without. Under Cosmas II's successor, Shenouda I,[65] arose an ongoing problem of charging for ordaining clergy, known as simony or *cheirotonia* (laying on of hands). Shenouda was an experienced cleric, whose patriarchate from 858 to 879 saw many changes. The simony was normally related to the financial demands, sometimes staggeringly large, imposed by governors on the patriarchs and other clergy. One way to get money and to spread the cost around was simony. Some patriarchs tried to abolish it, some tried to control it, some frankly enriched themselves by it. It was to be a continuing problem, and, although the corrupting effect of simony is obvious, the desperation of prelates being coerced to pay exorbitant fines and extortions helps explain why simony was so hard to eradicate.

In more ways than one, times were hard for Christians in Shenouda's day. Taxes became increasingly harsh and conversions increased. Shenouda himself fled when the government threatened him. Within the church, old heresies were cropping up again, some associated with familiar names like Origen or Apollinaris, or Julian of Halicarnassus, plus a new one asserting that Jesus' divinity died.[66] Shenouda had to deal with these challenges in a church that put great emphasis on adherence to strictly orthodox belief.

Shenouda had an experience that illustrates rather well two important aspects of the Coptic Church under Islamic rule: the vulnerability of patriarchs to pressure from ambitious seekers of church offices, and emphasis on forgiveness (at least, of fellow Christians) as a principal Christian virtue. A "false deacon," disappointed by the patriarch's refusing his demand for consecration, denounced Shenouda before the Muslim governor, who proceeded quite unjustly to cast the patriarch in prison (where, incidentally, he did much good.) Once the matter was straightened out, Shenouda did not wreak vengeance on the cause of his suffering but rather forgave this "false deacon."

While all this was going on, there was civil strife and much chaos and destruction in Egypt. Coptic monasteries suffered especially, since virtually all of them were in isolated areas where they could not easily be protected. This turmoil was the occasion for the Turkish governor, ibn Tulun, to exert himself from 869 on to pacify Egypt and, in the process, shift control to his own governmental apparatus in Egypt, a government in which the Copts maintained themselves in many important bureaucratic posts.

This change did not save Pope Michael III,[67] 880-910, however, from being squeezed by the government. As we have seen, the patriarchate had long been looked upon by Muslim governments and people as a prime source of wealth, and not without reason. The success of Copts in government and in business put important wealth in the hands of Coptic leaders who supported the massive charitable and administrative work which had always been associated with the patriarch's office. What better way to get at this wealth than to hold the patriarch at ransom until large sums were extorted?

In the particular case Pope Michael did not have money, so he tried to meet his crisis by getting the church in Alexandria to sell properties to raise half the amount demanded of him and by obligating aspiring bishops to pay for the remainder. Pained cries of opposition were raised, for obvious reasons: the patriarch was going to have to pay 1000 dinars a year to the Alexandria church, and where else than from simony were he and the bishops to get the money? The arrangement did in fact proceed to befoul relationships among the prelates, and their relations with the jurisdictions they served. Michael's successor, Gabriel I, a monk from Saint Macarius' monastery, made patriarch against his will, did practice simony to pay the Alexandrians.[68]

Pope Gabriel essentially hid himself at Saint Macarius' monastery, far from the administrative apparatus of the patriarchate. His absence from the center of church activity shows again the sharp decline of the importance of the patriarch in church affairs. This decline[69] is further illustrated by the fact that the biographies in the *History of the Patriarchs*[70] of the next three patriarchs tell us very little about their work during the thirty-five years they served.

The first of the three, Cosmas III, did consecrate a metropolitan for the church in Ethiopia—which reminds us that that church, the biggest by far in Africa, had been tied to the Coptic Church from its earliest days and continued to receive its hierarchy from the Copts. Throughout the long history of Ethiopian Christianity from its beginnings in the fourth century to the 1950s, the Ethiopian church was dominated in its leadership by Egyptian Copts. The Coptic patriarch selected and consecrated the metropolitan for Ethiopia, and refused to consecrate enough bishops for that country to enable the Ethiopians to establish their own hierarchy. The Ethiopian Church has often been called "Coptic," although in fact the daughter church in Ethiopia soon surpassed the Coptic Church of Egypt in numbers and influence, since Ethiopia was never in the path of the conquering Arabs who took over the rest of Christian Africa.

The story of the new Metropolitan sent by Cosmas, Peter, was a sad one, for Peter was displaced by a clever impostor and was never able to function adequately in the post even after the impostor was exposed. The event illustrates the problems of unscrupulous ambition for high office in the church and of the slow communications between Egypt and Ethiopia.

While these things were going on, Arabic was becoming a literary language for Coptic writers. One of the early ones was Abu Ishak ibn Fadlallah, who wrote commentaries on the end of the world.[71] The biographies of the patriarchs, however, will still being written in Coptic.

Pope Macarius' biography tells us that he was consecrated three times, first in Alexandria, then at Saint Macarius' monastery, and then in the capital. After the first "consecration," of course, the others would be formal recognition of the new patriarch at what one might call a service of enthronement or institution. The sequence of consecrations shows both the dominance of Saint Macarius' monastery in the selection of leadership of the Coptic Church at that time and also the trend toward recognizing the importance for the church of the governmental capital.

In a pathetic story,[72] Pope Macarius' mother embarrassed him by showing herself totally unimpressed by his new office, describing it as no honor but only a burden. Poor Pope Theophanes, Macarius' successor, actually went crazy and died (murdered?) in 926 after the Alexandrians humiliated him when he could not come up with the annual 1000 dinars[73] due them.

During the thirty-five years of those three obscure patriarchs, the Turkish governor, the "Ikhshid," first restored effectiveness and probity to the government of Egypt and then left his young sons in the capable hands of the Sudanese Negro "tutor," Kafur. He was like a new Joseph in Egypt, who was also the principal patron of the brilliant cultural achievements of his time. Among the prominent Christians writing in Arabic in Egypt was a Syrian Jew converted by a Christian physician. Abd al-Masih al-Israili al-Raqqi was well versed in mathematics and in philosophy, one of his prominent works being a *Book of Dialectic.*[74] Christians were not being left out of the cultural flowering.

Kafur ruled well from 946 to 968—first as the regent for the Ikhshid's sons and then in his own name. The Tulunids and Ikhshidids had helped Egypt to return to prosperity and were not too harsh on the Christians. It was to be the incoming Fatimids (except for ten years under al-Hakim), however, who were to do even more for Egypt, and, on the whole, improve the lot of Coptic Christians. This story will unfold in the next chapter.

[1] *The Arab Conquest of Egypt and the Last Thirty Years of the Roman Dominion*, 2nd ed. (Oxford: Clarendon Press, 1978), pp. 291, 464.

[2] On Arab expansion and administration we draw largely on writings of Philip Hitti and Bernard Lewis, in particular the former's *The Arabs: a Short History*, 5th rev. ed. (Chicago: Regnery, 1949), and the latter's *The Arabs in History*, 2nd ed. (New York: Harper and Row, 1958-1966).

[3] so, Butler, especially in chapter 13.

[4] In the work cited. Stanley Lane-Poole disagrees in his *A History of Egypt in the Middle Ages,* 2nd ed. (London: Methuen, 1913), e.g., p. 15.

[5] Butler, p. 349.

[6] Butler, p. 256.

[7] M. P. Martin, "Une lecture de l'*Histoire des Patriarches d'Alexandrie*," *Proche-Orient Chrétien*, 25 (1985), 17.

[8] in *The Large Estates of Byzantine Egypt* (New York: Columbia Univ. Press, 1930), p. 193.

[9] Hardy, p. 446; also see Lewis, p. 58, and Hitti, p. 57.

[10] Lewis, p. 94.

[11] See Eliyahu Ashtor, "The Social Isolation of the Ahl al-Dhimma," in *Études Orientales à la Mémoire de Paul Hirschler*, ed. O. Komlos (Budapest: 1950), pp. 73-94.

[12] Lane-Poole, p. 26.

[13] Lewis, p. 66.

[14] Hitti, p. 59.

[15] Lewis, p. 56.

[16] *History of the Patriarchs of the Coptic Church of Alexandria (HPCC)*, ed. B. Evetts, Vol. 1 of *Patrologia Orientalis* (Paris: Firmin-Didot, 1948), 502.

[17] *History of the Patriarchs of the Coptic Church of Alexandria (HPCC)*, ed. B. Evetts, Vol. 5 of *Patrologia Orientalis* (Paris: Firmin-Didot, 1910), 5.

[18] see Ewa Wypszycka, *Les ressources et les activités économiques des églises en Égypte du 4ème au 6ème siècle* (Brussels: Fondation égyptologique Reine Elizabeth, 1972), p. 155.

[19] Wypszycka, p. 160.

[20] See, e.g., Vol. 2 of *History of the Patriarchs of the Egyptian Church (HPEC)*, ed. A. S. Atiya, Y. Abd al-Masih, and O. H. E. KHS-Burmester (Cairo: Société d'archéologie copte, 1948), p. 104.

[21] On John III see *HPCC* 5, 10-21.

[22] *HPCC* 5, 21-26. The quotation is from p. 25.

[23] *HPCC* 5, 27-48.

[24]See *The Chronicle of John, Bishop of Nikiu,* trans. R. H. Charles from Zotenberg's Ethiopic text (London: Williams and Norgate, 1916).

[25]W. Y. Adams, *Nubia: Corridor to Africa* (Princeton: Princeton Univ. Press, 1977), p. 454.

[26] *HPCC* 5, 49-52.

[27]Lewis, p. 72.

[28]Lane-Poole, p. 27.

[29]T. M. Lapidus, "The Conversion of Egypt to Islam," *Israel Oriental Studies,* 2 (1972), 248.

[30] *HPCC* 5, 51.

[31] *HPCC* 5, 52.

[32]Lapidus, p. 249.

[33]Lewis, pp. 76-77.

[34]The rest of this paragraph is drawn largely from D. C. Dennett, *Conversion and the Poll Tax in Early Islam* (Cambridge: Harvard Univ. Press, 1950), pp. 115-116.

[35]Lane-Poole, p. 27.

[36]W. Y. Adams, p. 454.

[37]Can be found in Abu Salih, *The Churches and Monasteries of Egypt and Some Neighboring Countries,* trans. B. Evetts and A. J. Butler (Oxford: Clarendon Press, 1895), pp. 267-268.

[38]Martin, p. 19.

[39]Butler, p. 440.

[40] *HPCC* 5, 88-215.

[41]For this terminology, see, e.g., the chapter headings in Lewis.

[42] *HPCC* 5, 116-117.

[43] *HPCC* 5, 172.

[44]B. Lewis, "Egypt and Syria," in *The Central Islamic Lands from Pre-Islamic Times to the First World War,* Vol. 1 of *The Cambridge History of Islam,* ed. P. M. Holt, A. K. S. Lambton, and B. Lewis (Cambridge: Cambridge Univ. Press, 1970), p. 176.

[45]His biography is found in *HPCC* 5, 360-382.

[46]D. Sourdel, "The Abbasid Caliphate," in *The Central Islamic Lands from Pre-Islamic Times to the First World War,* Vol. 1 of *The Cambridge History of Islam,* pp. 122-123.

[47]His biography is found in *History of the Patriarchs of the Coptic Church of Alexandria (HPCC)*, ed. B. Evetts, Vol. 10 of *Patrologia Orientalis* (Paris: Firmin-Didot, 1915), pp. 476-547.

[48]This is the Arabic name for Egypt but also was applied to the pre-Cairo Muslim capital of Egypt, and to what is today called "Old Cairo" in the tourist trade.

[49]According to Lapidus, p. 249.

[50]Sam I. Gellens, "Egypt, Islamization of," *Coptic Encyclopedia*, 1991.

[51]Lapidus, p. 260.

[52]Letter received from Maurice Martin, 9 June, 1992.

[53]Lane-Poole, p. 60.

[54]Lewis, "Egypt and Syria," p. 184.

[55]Lewis, p. 183.

[56]His story is found in *HPEC* 2, 1-3. Here and throughout, unless otherwise stated, the English translation used is found in this series, except that Arabic transliterations and most other parentheses are omitted.

[57]His story is in *HPEC* 2, 3-18.

[58]*HPEC* 2, 107.

[59]*HPEC* 2, 184 and following.

[60]*HPEC* 3, 165, or 4, 55-56.

[61]Lapidus, p. 260. R. W. Bulliett says one third of the conversions took place in the ninth century, in *Conversion to Islam in the Medieval Period* (Cambridge: Cambridge Univ. Press, 1975); M. Brett claims that Christians remained "a majority at least until the tenth century" in "The Spread of Islam in Egypt and North Africa" in *Northern Africa: Islam and Modernization*, ed. M. Brett (London: Frank Cass, 1973).

[62]Martin, p. 35.

[63]In "Conversions from Islam" in *The Islamic World from Classical to Modern Times: Essays in Honor of Bernard Lewis*, ed. C. E. Bosworth (Princeton: Darwin Press, 1989), especially pp. 6 and 7.

[64]*HPEC* 2, 151-163 and 257-260.

[65]His story is found in *HPEC* 2, 18-99.

[66]*HPEC* 2, 31-32 and 40-41.

[67]His story is found in *HPEC* 2, 103-115.

[68]*HPEC* 2, 117.

[69]Martin, p. 33.

[70]*HPEC* 2, 118-124.

[71]Khalil Samir, "Abu Ishak ibn Fadlallah," *Coptic Encyclopedia*, 1991.

[72]*HPEC* 2, 121-122.

[73]*HPEC* 2, 123-124.

[74]Khalil Samir, "Abd al-Masih al-Israili al-Raqqi," *Coptic Encyclopedia*, 1991.

Chapter Six

The Church in Fatimid and Ayyubid Egypt

✠ ——————————————————————————— ✠

from about 970 to 1260

EGINNING EARLY IN THE FOURTH CENTURY A.D.,[1] the Christian church was an important force in what was happening in Egypt, a significant determinant in the direction in which Egyptian society and culture were to develop. Even Roman emperor Diocletian's fierce attacks designed to destroy the church failed to curb the church's role and growing influence in Egypt.

Soon after, the Egyptian Christians successfully supported and protected their patriarch, Athanasius, in face of all the powerful efforts of Christian emperors Constantine and Constantius to get rid of him. Then, after 451, the Coptic Christians pursued their own way and refused to give in to the Christology of Rome and Constantinople, despite the various earnest efforts of the Byzantine Empire to force them to do so, including the intruding of its own "Melchite" patriarchs who represented the imperial church, with powerful economic and military support behind them.

When the Arab expansion had threatened Egypt, the Byzantine emperor Heraclius empowered Cyrus, called "Mukaukus," to defend Egypt by making him both the Melchite patriarch and the imperial governor in command of the military. The church was clearly a major factor in Egypt. So, when Cyrus failed to resist the Arabs successfully, the conquering Amr turned to the Coptic patriarch, Benjamin, to help establish a working relationship between victorious Arabs and vanquished Egyptians. No other Egyptian had the needed popular support and resources in personnel and, potentially, in finances to represent the conquered Egyptian people.

The biggest change for Christianity and the Coptic Church in Egypt came when Christians became a minority, whose church reacted to the society and culture of the majority instead of being a dynamic factor in determining the evolution of their country. Westerners will note with interest the contrast with Western Europe's development in the period of this chapter. After the overrunning of the West Roman Empire by the Germanic "barbarians," Latin Christianity was to be the leader in Western Civilization's gradual move from the primitive barbariansm of its Dark Ages into the splendid achievements of its High Middle Ages.

Throughout the early centuries after the Arab conquest, Egypt was always ruled by outsiders, who were sustained in power by armies manned by outsiders. That is, Egypt was an occupied country. The Arab governors commissioned by the caliphs had always been sent to Egypt, and their Arab troops were recruited from outside Egypt. This pattern was designed to block the emergence of any form of Egyptian nationalism. The Tulunids and Ikhshidids did little to change the pattern.

We turn now to the crucial period of the Fatimids. The end of the personal rule of the brilliant Sudanese Negro, Kafur, marked the end of the Tulunid-Ikhshidid governments which gave Egypt local rule, even though they formally recognized the caliph in Baghdad. It was to be the incoming Fatimid dynasty, however, which would make the biggest changes for Egypt and its Christians. Among other things, their rule of two centuries, which began at the end of the 960s, continued to increase the economic prosperity of Egypt through encouraging development of the traditional manufactures and increased exploitation of Egypt's strategic location for trade.

Of at least equal interest was the stimulation this Shiite Ismaili dynasty gave to cultural development. Sunnite Baghdad had earlier been a brilliant center of Islamic civilization, but now it was the Shiite Ismailis, the Fatimids, who sponsored the most brilliant era of that civilization; and Cairo, with its al-Azhar mosque, was its center. 1100 may have been still "dark ages" for Western Europe, but for Egypt it was a time when Egypt had the most advanced civilization of the world, except possibly in China. Its resident caliphate favored a brand of Islam particularly open to fresh ideas and artistic and scientific achievements, so that in philosophy and history, in physics and mathematics, geography, medicine and pharmacology Cairo became a wonder of the world.

Fatimid caliph al-Moizz, the fourth in the line in Tunisia, sent his capable general Jawhar to conquer Egypt in 969. For the caliph a new capital city, Cairo, was created near the old Arab tent city of Fustat, and Babylon, the site of the Roman fortress. The new mosque, al-Azhar, was built, and in 973 Caliph al-Moizz came to stay. Thus a new situation was created for Egypt, for the Fatimid era differed from the previous one in that now the caliph himself was to reside in Egypt. The Sunnite caliphs in Baghdad did not recognize the Fatimid caliphs, of course—there could be only one caliph—but for two hundred years Egypt now recognized no claims of any kind from beyond her own territories.

It was in the era of Pope Menas II, 956-976, that al-Moizz had sent Jawhar to conquer Egypt and to found Cairo. Again, we know little of Menas' works[2] but we do read in his biography[3] that the Fatimid régime retained Kafur's Coptic vizier and used other Copts as high officials and professionals. Prejudice erupted among Muslims when they saw that "both al-Moizz and Jawhar put aside all prejudices, whether of race or religion. . . . The Copts were as a rule far more efficient as clerks, accountants and scribes than their Muslim fellow countrymen . . . [They were] employed in all the subordinate branches of the administration and . . . some of the higher offices."[4]

The new and imposing Fatimid dynasty may have influenced the selection of Menas' successor as patriarch. The story of Pope Abraham[5] (or Ephraim), 976-979, has more than one point of interest. He was chosen[6] by a gathering in Cairo of bishops from all over Egypt, of Cairo "scribes" who were learned laymen, and of priests of Alexandria. Thus we see what three groups had power in the Coptic Church. Abraham was an elderly Syrian merchant in Cairo famous for his generosity, admired not only by the Christians but by the Muslim rulers who had done business with him, and much favored for the patriarchate by the "archons" (lay leaders in the church) among the Cairo Christians.

The wisdom of this selection was quickly shown. In his brief tenure before his death, Abraham abolished simony, reduced the patriarch's annual payment to Alexandria to 500 dinars, excommunicated the archons who had concubines (perhaps imitating their Muslim friends who were permitted up to four wives), and maintained a close relationship with Caliph al-Moizz, who was "favorably disposed towards Copts and other Christians."[7] Al-Moizz' successor, Caliph al-Aziz insisted that Abraham reside near Cairo.

This was the era when the great Bishop Severus of Ashmunein was writing influential theological treatises for the Copts and, possibly, gathering materials[8] for what was to become the first part of the invaluable *History of the Patriarchs of Alexandria*, which continued to bear his name long after his own day.

In Abraham's biography we also find an account of the miraculous raising of mountains by prayer. It is noteworthy that the miracle is not attributed to the admirable patriarch but rather to an unnamed poor ascetic whose hidden piety gave him the insight to encourage the patriarch and the power of faith that actually lifted and lowered the mountains. In another story about Abraham, the Coptic emphasis on forgiveness is again illustrated, this time the forgiving of a Muslim. The patriarch interceded with the ruler and saved the life of a Muslim sheikh who had physically opposed Abraham's rebuilding of a church with the ruler's express permission.

After Abraham, Pope Philotheus[9] served for fifteen years over the turn of the century (and the millennium). The "cell," or residence of the Coptic patriarch, was located at Damru from 975 to 1061.[10] In contrast to his admirable and generous predecessor, Philotheus practiced simony with gusto and led a luxurious life until his death, upon which his brothers quickly spent all the money before the church could reclaim it![11] Thus was shown how the good work of one patriarch could be undone by an unworthy successor.

During this same period of time, a devout Muslim youth, who had converted to Christianity, "asked [the priest answering his questions] to bring him the Gospels and the Books of the Church, the Old and the New, and to translate for him the Coptic into the Arabic tongue."[12] This suggests that such materials were still not readily available in Arabic, even the Bible. The bright young convert, whose Christianity almost cost him his life, ended up writing useful books in Arabic for the Coptic community, which was gradually moving into that language.

Caliph al-Aziz, 975-996, appointed late in his reign a Christian vizier, Abu al-Fadl Isa ibn Nasturus, who had been his financial secretary for twenty years. He was soon dismissed, along with other Christians, and then reinstated after paying a huge "fine." He became administrator of the young al-Hakim's personal possessions—but, for all his pains, he was executed as a Christian in 997.[13]

Al-Aziz had a Christian concubine, whose brother, Arsenius, was made Melchite patriarch of Alexandria, but who resided in Cairo.[14] Not surprisingly, that gave the Melchites a favored position there. In fact, another brother was made Melchite patriarch of Jerusalem, which was then within the Fatimid caliphate. At this period, Coptic physicians were very much admired. In 1003, a famous one, Abu al-Fath ibn Sahlan ibn Muqashir, interceded for the Christians serving in government.[15]

Pope Zacharias,[16] 1004-1032, was old before he was made patriarch and had been steward of all the Alexandrian churches. It had been Alexandria's "turn" to choose the patriarch, but its wealthy and well-connected candidate was rejected by the bishops—who may have preferred "poor, wretched, and pure" Zacharias because they assumed they could control him. The *History of the Patriarchs* reports that he was chosen because of an "opportune miracle": a vinegar jar he dropped as he fell from a ladder neither broke nor spilled![17]

Pope Zacharias saw seven years of peace before the notorious Caliph al-Hakim took charge from the regents, launched the slaughter of his own notables and of Christians, and imposed so many disabilities on Christians that many converted to Islam.[18] When a Copt who had been secretary to al-Hakim's tutor, Barjawan, refused to convert to Islam in 1013, the caliph had him decapitated. The *History of the Patriarchs*, now depending on a writer alive during these events, attributed the terrible sufferings of the Christians to God's punishment for the bishops' rapacity, their lording it over the priests, and their ordaining only the ignorant rich, rather than the learned and the continent.[19]

Zacharias himself was imprisoned after he was accused by a disappointed office-seeker, so that Zacharias fled for nine years to the community of monasteries in Wadi Natrun,[20] and the churches were closed for three of those years. But before al-Hakim's famous disappearance 1021 (the Druze still expect his reappearance), the persecution was halted, converts were permitted to re-convert, and churches were restored. Al-Zahir, who became caliph in 1021, issued a decree in 1024 in favor of the Coptic monks.[21] And yet in 1025 Abu Zakariya was beheaded.[22]

The selection of Zacharias' successor in 1032 had interesting aspects.[23] A method was suggested by a friendly vizier, a Muslim: a hundred monks should be selected and then narrowed down to three, from which the choice should be made by lot—unless the fourth name, "the Lord", was turned up in the drawing, in which case another three would go into the next drawing. The plan combined the reasonable principle of narrowing down to the most promising candidates with the more "spiritual" principle of the Biblical casting of the lot (the Greek term for which lies at the root of the English word "clergy.")

When the bishops and the superiors of the Wadi Natrun monasteries gathered, however, they rejected the plan and, along with the Alexandrians, simply negotiated a deal with one Shenouda and the office seeker who had denounced Zacharias. The result was the unfortunate fifteen-year patriarchate of Shenouda II,[24] 1032-1047, when, among other things, simony was the rule.

There was a more encouraging development in Asyut, a Christian stronghold in Upper Egypt, which showed the will of the majority of Christians in a diocese could not be overlooked. When Shenouda consecrated for Asyut a bishop who paid for the consecration, the people simply refused to receive him, citing the simony as the reason. The bishop finally gave up after three years of seeking to get possession of the see and tried, unsuccessfully, to get his money back from the patriarch.

Christodoulos' thirty-year patriarchate[25] after Shenouda's death in 1047 was a welcome change, at least at the top, and a time of important new directions for Coptic leadership. He had been a parish priest before becoming a monk but also a hermit without financial resources. So his consecration at Saint Macarius' monastery was described as "through God,"[26] that is, not through simony.

The major developments in the middle of the eleventh century were Christodoulos' definitively moving the patriarchate to Cairo and the publication of his canons.[27] The canons include rules about reverence at worship, the segregation and subordination of women, observing the sacred seasons, fasting, the proper conduct of deacons (e.g., the "assiduous in the ministry shall have precedence" over "the senior deacons [who] absent themselves from their churches"), baptism, and respect for priests.

In the biography of Christodoulos there is a touching story of a young man, Phoebammon, who re-converts from Islam to Christianity and is executed when he refuses to keep his reversion quiet. The account is designed to edify and to strengthen the loyalty of Christians; there is no evidence that the martyrdom of a convert from Islam was a typical experience, however.

Christodoulos' patriarchate brought him hardships, including some within the church. When he centralized the church's authority in his own office, a group of bishops tried to depose him when they could not get their own way; but that dispute was settled, with crucial help from a prominent layman. (Western Christians may be astonished at the leadership lay Christians often exerted in the Coptic Church.) Christodoulos also ran into sharp criticism from the monks at Saint Macarius' monastery when he forbade the reserving of any of the consecrated bread or wine of the Eucharist which was not consumed in the communion. He made this ruling stick, and reservation of the consecrated bread and wine is still forbidden in the Coptic Church.

It is worth a pause to analyze Christodoulos' financial problems and his efforts to resolve them, as recounted in the *History of the Patriarchs*.[28] The patriarch's announced policy was that bishops he appointed had to agree to send him and the patriarchate one-half the church revenue they collected. He collected a lot of money in this way, although he claimed that the method was designed to avoid simony, and "he firmly believed that he was absolved by God." In fact, at one time in his patriarchate, six thousand dinars were found at the patriarch's residence at Damru and confiscated for the government's treasury.

The troubles and trials for the church were attributed by the biographer of Christodoulos to the worldliness of Christian high officials in the government, with the resulting arrogance and gluttony, which inevitably led to envy and enmity. The very prosperity of the Coptic institutions in Damru excited an anti-Christian official to denounce the patriarch to the vizier, who proceeded to close the churches and demand money from the patriarch and the bishops. Seventy thousand dinars were demanded from them, creating an intolerable situation for the Christians, until, we are told, the Muslims began to notice the ill-fortune that befell the anti-Christian officials. The demand for seventy thousand was reduced to two by the friendly governor—and the Melchites paid one-half of that.

Christodoulos' troubles seemed to be endless. Once[29] he was falsely accused about his relations with the Ethiopian church. The accuser was quickly found out and officially condemned to death. When Christodoulos was asked about this sentence, he answered, "we have not (the right) according to our religion to kill nor to render evil for evil, but thou (art) the sultan, and authority (belongs) to God and to thee." It is noteworthy that the patriarch thus denied the death penalty and retributive justice to Christians but did recognize the sultan's authority to practice them. Christodoulos died poor in 1077, having been lauded by his counterpart in Antioch for his poverty, comparing it to the poverty of the apostles, but rather tactlessly pointing out that their poverty was voluntary.

The editor of this material was one Mawhub ibn Mansur ibn Mufarrig,[30] an Alexandrian deacon and a contemporary of Christodoulos. Mawhub, whose brother was a martyr in 1086, was in charge of the much revered skull of Saint Mark—a duty he took over from his father. Mawhub was a husband and father and rich enough to pay Christodoulos' ransom. He was always loyal to the Fatimids and to General Badr. Mawhub was probably the central figure in the putting together of the *History of the Patriarchs*. A specialist has recently argued[31] that Mawhub is not only the editor but also was from the first the one who "took the initiative to collect and have translated the Coptic sources." In the Christodoulos biography Mawhub identifies himself, and then goes on to speak of a deacon, Habib Michael of Damanhur, who was his "assistant in transcribing the biographies and rendering them from the Coptic into the Arabic."[32] At the conclusion of the preceding biography[33] Mawhub had fixed the year (1088) of his decision to compile the biographies of all the patriarchs. He then implied the completion of that project before he began the biography of Christodoulos.

When we consider historical sources for this period of history, mention must be made of the *Annals*[34] ascribed to one Sa'ad ibn Batriq, commonly called "Eutychius," who was Melchite patriarch in Egypt, 933-940. Although the *Annals* may have some historical utility,[35] their reliability has been sharply criticized, e.g., the pro-Melchite historian John Mason Neale says, "to the higher qualifications of a historian, Eutychius has not a single claim," even as Neale recognizes that "in advancing toward his own time, we are indebted to him for almost all we know of the [Melchite] Church in Egypt."[36] The question of ibn Batriq's relation to this material is unclear. Maybe there are parallels between ascribing the *Annals* to him and ascribing the *History of the Patriarchs* to Bishop Severus.

Christodoulos' thirty years as patriarch had seen much turmoil in Egypt. A virtual civil war raged under Caliph al-Mustansir between his Sudanese troops, favored by the caliph's Negro mother, and the Turkish component of his army, supported by the Turks' Berber allies from Northwest Africa. The rampaging Berbers were especially damaging to the rural churches and the monasteries of the Copts. In 1066-1067, sixty-three monks were assassinated near Ashmunein.[37]

At last, the Armenian soldier, Badr al-Jamali, was called over from Acre in 1074, and he quickly straightened things out. Not surprisingly, as a result he was appointed to be military and civil governor, which he continued to be for twenty years. (He was followed by his son, al-Afdal for twenty-five years.) Badr's action "brought peace and security to Egypt, and even some measure of prosperity . . . ; his military and administrative reorganization postponed the collapse of the Fatimid state for nearly a century."[38] The rule of the Armenians was beneficial to the Coptic Christians. Badr is always well spoken of in the *History of the Patriarchs* and is said to have greatly honored Pope Christodoulos.[39] Badr was born of Christian parents and was tolerant of all Christians, although he naturally favored the Armenian Orthodox, who were anti-Chalcedonian, like the Copts.[40]

The next patriarch was Cyril II,[41] 1078-1092, who could be referred to as "the saint."[42] He was a monk from Saint Macarius' monastery who had humbly tried to exclude himself from the office of patriarch by claiming he was "the son of a second wife" and thus ineligible. (A Copt could remarry after the first spouse died, but there were some disabilities for the new family.) When Cyril arrived in Cairo he was received by the caliph and by Badr with great honor. He took up residence on the small island of Roda, just across from the old fortress of Babylon on the outskirts of Cairo.

Cyril opposed all simony, and, like Christodoulos, rather arranged for the bishops to send one-half their church revenues to the patriarchate; but Cyril also dedicated this income from certain dioceses to particular institutions, like Saint Macarius' monastery; and careful documentation of the arrangements was made.[43]

Cyril was not a learned man, but he did set himself to study the Holy Scriptures. Even late in life "he did not relax his efforts in reading the Holy Scriptures, and the greatest part of his reading was in the explanation of the four Holy Gospels in Coptic."[44] Cyril was not wise in the ways of the world. He was soon challenged to defend himself from a group of Lower Egypt bishops who had hoped to control him. Badr summoned the patriarch and as many bishops as could make the trip to settle the matter. (The names of the forty-seven bishops who attended are listed.) Cyril came out well enough in the agreements established, of which an important part was the setting forth of a new set of church canons, which bears his name.[45] The churches of Upper Egypt did not accept the new rules at the time, however, preferring to stick with the old canons.

Many Armenian Christians came to Egypt in Badr's time and had their own churches there. They were welcomed as brothers by the Copts, and the Armenian patriarch visited Egypt and associated himself with them. As a result, "there was made known amongst all the people the genuineness of the agreement of the Copts and the Armenians and the Syrians and the

Abyssinians and the Nubians on the Orthodox, upright Faith on which the saintly, virtuous fathers agreed, and which Nestorius and Leo and the Council of Chalcedon disagreed."[46]

Not all the Copts' relations with Badr were perfect, however. At one point they were required to wear black girdles and to pay, without exception, the burdensome poll tax. The Christians also began finding Badr domineering, until a large gift arrived from the Christian king of Nubia, accompanied by his son who was to be made bishop for the Nubian church. Pope Cyril found himself in a complex relationship with Nubia and the Ethiopians. He was head of both churches, but in foreign policy he was an Egyptian. He could use his diplomatic and religious relationships to the benefit of the Copts in Egypt, but doing so was also a risk to his church position or his relationship with Muslim rulers.[47]

Cyril's successor as patriarch was Michael IV,[48] 1092-1102, a learned monk and hermit, a middle-aged priest considered virtuous and sound in doctrine. In his day the Crusaders from Western Europe captured Jerusalem and created a Christian monarchy in Palestine. Ironically, this did the Copts no good, as the Catholics from the West considered the Copts heretics and forbade them the Holy City. There is a brief reference at the conclusion of Michael's biography in the History of the Patriarchs to the First Crusade which states, "the Copts did not join in the pilgrimage to [Jerusalem], nor were we able to approach it, on account of what is known of [the Franks'] hatred of us, as also, their false belief concerning us and their charge against us of impiety."[49] The Christian Crusaders were to do great harm to the Christian Copts and almost no good. This may explain the surprising paucity of references to the Crusades in the History of the Patriarchs.

When Michael was chosen he was required to sign a statement foregoing simony and recognizing that as patriarch he would be "but the bishop of Alexandria . . . [with] the presidentship over the bishops of the sees of Egypt; he is not a sharer in those sees."[50] Michael assented, but he promptly renounced the agreements after his consecration and lorded it over the bishops. He was not able to prevail over Bishop Sanhut of Cairo, however, who was supported by his archons; and Michael had to give up on his efforts to oust him. Michael's purpose was to create a vacancy in Cairo so that he himself could act as bishop there and control the revenues of that important diocese.

Since the Fatimid caliphate in Cairo had controlled Palestine, it was from the Fatimids that the Crusaders won Jerusalem as well as other locations in the Holy Land. The Fatimids were unequal to the task of driving out the Crusaders. Al-Afdal himself suffered defeat at their hands near Askalon, and later efforts from Egypt to thwart the Crusaders were unsuccessful. In 1118, the crusader king of Jerusalem, Baldwin, captured and destroyed

Pelusium on Egypt's border with Palestine and threatened Tinnis, deeper in Egypt; but Baldwin's illness and death ended that threat of Crusader domination of Egypt proper.

To select Michael's successor, the Cairo churchmen and the monks of Saint Macarius' monastery invited the bishops and the Alexandrians to meet and advise with them. The selection was narrowed to two names. The more mature and superior debater, Macarius, was unanimously selected over one John, "a young man, a good priest, of comely countenance and eloquent in speech." Macarius tried to escape as son-of-a-second-wife and so not even a priest, but he was consecrated anyhow.[51]

By now al-Afdal had become *de facto* ruler and had installed the deceased al-Mustansir's son as caliph. Al-Afdal received Macarius II splendidly in the capital and also in Alexandria. But it was in the historic al-Muallakah church in Misr (not yet incorporated into Cairo) that his letter of undertaking (I prefer my translation here) was read, and in three languages: Greek, Coptic, and Arabic—the three languages the serious student of Coptic Christianity still has to study! It is striking that Greek still had a role to play.

Pope Macarius was away when the admirable Bishop Sanhut of Cairo died, so the Armenian patriarch presided at his funeral. Letters passing between the church in Cairo and Pope Macarius about selecting a new bishop for Cairo are notable for their remarkably flattering language but, more importantly, for their discussion of the qualities needed for a bishop: maturity, obedience to the monastic rule, leadership in worship, knowledge of church law, as well as devotion, learning, purity, asceticism, modesty, compassion, and manner of life. As to who should choose the bishop, Pope Macarius rejected the implied accusation that he was delaying his decision and the consecration of the new bishop, stating that the canon "says that the bishop shall be chosen by the people . . . [and] does not say that he shall be chosen by outside people or by a patriarch."[52]

The bishop for Cairo was chosen by lot from twelve worthy monks and was consecrated after he promised one-half his church's revenues to the patriarchate. More than one-half of Macarius' biography is devoted to getting this new bishop, and al-Afdal's assassination is described in detail—but Macarius' death is passed over in silence!

Pope Gabriel II was "from an old and noble Coptic family of scholars" in Cairo.[53] He was generous and virtuous and had had a lot of bureaucratic experience and knowledge of Coptic and Arabic. He had been in minor orders in a Cairo church where he was much admired. Perhaps the Copts hoped he would be another Abraham. After the bishop of Cairo died, however, Gabriel never consecrated a bishop for the capital, doubtless for the selfish reasons mentioned above.

Government became problematic in Gabriel's day, after the assassination of al-Afdal in 1121 and then of Caliph al-Amir in 1130. The new vizier proceeded to oppress the Christians: plundering churches, allowing the Armenian patriarch and his monks to be killed, doubling taxes on the dhimmis, driving Christians from administrative offices, and enforcing the humiliating social disabilities. Abu al-Barakat Yuhanna ibn Abi Layth, who had been head of the justice office until 1134, was executed by the new vizier.[54]

Pope Gabriel consecrated no fewer than fifty-three bishops, demonstrating thus that the church was still strong. He opposed simony, but he seems to have made some poor or, at least, strange decisions. He once refused pay to consecrate a candidate, but when he found out he was rich and might become a Muslim, he consecrated him for another see in order to keep him and his money (which was to be used to repair churches) "Christian." A layman did convert to Islam when Gabriel misjudged him, causing the patriarch "bitter repentance." Such stories illustrate the web of difficulties the Coptic Church found itself in as a result of being a despised minority which needed to function financially well away from public scrutiny.

The choice of the next patriarch, [55] Michael V, went to an illiterate but devout monk instead of an attractive and learned monk ibn Kadran, who sought the post, even though Michael was a layman when chosen. In his few months of service, he consecrated five bishops, and "no one left his religion." Ibn Kadran was passed over again for John V, a saintly monk and deacon, who served the twenty years until 1166. When the Muslim authorities tried to intervene in favor of the ambitious ibn Kadran, the Christians explained that a patriarch should be sought after and not an office-seeker and that he must qualify in "sanctity and learning and good-conduct and chastity and charity" before they "bind him with an iron fetter, lest he escape . . ."[56]

According to Abu Salih,[57] John practiced simony. His biography[58] is mainly about developments outside the church. A reforming monk and priest of this period, Murqus ibn Qanbar,[59] advocated private confession, frequent communions, reserving consecrated bread and wine of the Eucharist, and innovations in fasting and making the sign of the cross. He had many admirers and his reforms would not seem strange to Western Catholics, but the Coptic Church rejected these reforms.

The 1160s also saw much turmoil in Egypt with a series of moves and counter moves to gain or hold control of territory, including one deal between the Crusader King Amalric of Jerusalem and the adventurer Shawar to try to fend off the Syrian-backed Shirguh, the uncle of the famous Salah ad-Din. The final result of these struggles was the end of Fatimid rule in Egypt and, with the triumph of Salah ad-Din and his designation as vizier, the beginning of the ninety-year Ayyubid Sultanate.

The Ayyubid dynasty was based on a Turkish and Kurdish army so that Egypt's "ruling class was a military autocracy of Turkish praetorians, often able to control the Ayyubid Sultan himself."[60] The feudalizing of Egypt proceeded apace, but trade also increased—a paradoxical result of the Crusades—and was an important component of economic growth and prosperity. Under the Ayyubids, "the establishment of the feudal system . . . and the appropriation of landed estates by the leading aristocracy offered the Copts the opportunity to serve in the new field."[61] And yet it is true that "Egypt remained a strong united monarchy, the chief Muslim power in the Near East and the main bulwark of Islam against the West."[62] The dynasty recognized the Baghdad caliph and followed the Sunnite tradition. Sunnite madrasas[63] (religious schools) were introduced to spread Sunni Islam and "counter [Fatimid] revolutionary orthodoxy." Even al-Azhar mosque, founded as the university of Shiite Islam, came into the hands of the Sunnites.

Pope Mark III's biography[64] begins with a summary history of the Fatimid rulers but mainly praises Salah ad-Din and recites the history of his rule. Letters of Muslim officials are reproduced in which the Crusaders are usually referred to as "polytheists" and "godless." The author of the biography clearly sympathizes with the Muslims in their struggle against the Crusaders. Salah ad-Din's efforts to control Syria as well as Egypt made him the primary (as well as the most successful) opponent of the Crusaders, of course, and most notably after his recapture of Jerusalem in 1187—which once again made possible Coptic pilgrimages to Jerusalem.

In 1173, Salah ad-Din sent his brother on an expedition to Lower Nubia, probably wanting to create a secure hinterland from Crusaders or from Muslim rivals. Shams ad-Dawla captured Qasr Ibrim and then moved on upriver to Dongola, the Nubian capital. But the expedition was withdrawn and "peace reigned in Nubia for another one hundred years."[65]

In the early years of Salah ad-Din and Mark III, Christians were subjected to most of the worst disabilities in dress, riding animals, and church buildings. The sultan tried, though unsuccessfully, to do without Copts. Rioting against Christians in Cairo caused a number of conversions to Islam, including some well-known scribes. Not long after, however, Salah ad-Din reversed his anti-Christian policies, so that the Copts were better off than ever. The *History of the Patriarchs* attributed this change[66] to "the blessing of [Pope Mark's] prayers" and to the Christians' "patience, their return to God and to their obedience to their head," that is, their patriarch. A more worldly explanation might be Salah ad-Din's realization of the value of the Copts to his government, coupled with their obvious lack of motivation to side with their fellow-Christian Crusaders, who treated the Copts so badly. Many church buildings were restored and there took place rather an artistic renaissance in the churches.

Just five weeks after Mark's death in 1189, a devout and generous layman and virgin was consecrated patriarch as John VI, against his will, on the agreed opinion of elders and archons in Cairo and of the bishops available.[67] He had troubles, first, getting a suitable metropolitan for Ethiopia and then with two monks at Saint Macarius' monastery. The sultan's son and successor, al-Kamil, backed the patriarch in the latter disputes.

This al-Malik al-Kamil ruled Egypt from 1218 to 1238—during which time Saint Francis of Assisi visited him, with limited success. The Crusaders, realizing the importance of Egypt as the center of Muslim resistance in Palestine, turned to Egypt in 1218, but they were completely turned back in 1221 after very small, mostly early, successes. The last great achievement of the Ayyubid Sultanate was the frustration of the crusade of Saint Louis, King of France, to conquer Egypt in 1249-1250. A remarkable woman, Sharjar, maintained the government during the successful defense of Egypt in the name of her dead husband, the late sultan, until his son arrived from Iraq. But she ultimately lost out in the struggle for power between the factions of the Mamluks who were destined to end the dynasty and establish their own rule from 1260 (to 1517).

The confusion in these closing decades of the Ayyubids was paralleled in the Coptic Church, first by a two-decade interregnum in the patriarchate, largely caused by the machinations of one David ibn Laqlaq to become patriarch, then his eight year patriarchate, followed by a seven-year vacancy after him. The biographer of John VI, writing in 1221, appends a historical narrative[68] which begins with an account of David's early efforts, first to become metropolitan of Ethiopia and then to become patriarch (and concludes with the struggles between the sultan and the Crusaders centered on the 1218 seizure of Damietta.)

For the period of the ensuing twenty-five years a Paris manuscript gives the most detailed description we possess of what was happening with the Copts during the Middle Ages—one hundred and forty-five pages of Arabic.[69] Eighteen of the pages have to do with the three-year struggle of al-Kamil with the Crusaders, but also include accounts of the extortions from Copts and of consequent conversions to Islam to escape the seemingly endless disabilities Christians had to suffer.

In 1228 al-Kamil visited Saint Macarius' monastery. His generosity and sympathy with the monks renewed the generous attitude of the Fatimids. When they complained about not having a patriarch, al-Kamil offered to permit the consecration of their choice, without the payment of a fee. But the matter was complicated. David ibn Laqlaq had strong supporters and bitter opponents everywhere: among the bishops, among the monks, among the lay notables, in the government. A variety of officials offered themselves as brokers, for a fee, of course.

After twenty years of "falsity, division and contriving," David was finally consecrated patriarch as Cyril III in 1235. He practiced simony from the outset, explaining that he had no alternative because of the money he had to pay the government. His judgment was poor, e.g., when he consecrated a metropolitan for Jerusalem, he seriously alienated the patriarch of Antioch,[70] who should have been a natural ally as a fellow anti-Chalcedonian. Had Cyril forgotten that anti-Chalcedonian Jerusalem had long been subject to the patriarchal see of Antioch?

There was a massive effort to replace Cyril,[71] with major complaints of simony, consecrating the metropolitan for Jerusalem, ordaining ineligible candidates, luxurious dress, and alienating church revenues. Cyril was able to survive, but he had to agree to change his ways and to observe the canons, including some drawn up specifically to exclude some of his practices. In 1243, Cyril died wealthy, without the odor of sanctity, largely unmourned.[72] It may have appeared that the Coptic patriarchate was disintegrating along with the Ayyubid dynasty.

Our view of the Coptic Church from 970 to 1260 has focused largely on the patriarchs. This is principally because of the major source we have, the *History of the Patriarchs,* but also because the Muslim rulers found it convenient to deal with the Copts through their patriarch, even bringing him with them to their new capital of Cairo. The selection process for patriarchs varied, and into the office paraded illiterates and scholars, ascetics and money-lovers, monks and merchants, priests and deacons and laymen, the humble and the arrogant. Some were selected prudently, a few through cynical deals, but most were chosen for their manifest sanctity and some because of mysterious signs that they were destined for the office. In general, the popes were charismatic persons, as they were supposed to be, for there was always a mystique about the patriarchate—which gave an intensity and a focus to the Coptic Church, even in its worst days but which also made the office vulnerable to many problems, as we have seen.

Although the monasteries saw much destruction and sometimes massacre, they never disappeared and they powerfully linked Coptic Christianity to its Golden Age of devotion and commitment. Most monks were laymen, but monasteries usually supplied the bishops; and they kept most of the few records we have of the medieval Coptic Church.

Unfortunately, we know little about the bishops. We have some lists of names and some statistics, all of which show that the Egyptian episcopate continued to be substantial. The saintly and tough Bishop Sanhut of Cairo and the learned Bishop Severus of Ashmunein are among the very few who are more than names for us. "The bishops belong to the families of the rich notables—a kind of feudal system, willy-nilly linked to power."[73] But we do see groups of bishops trying to make their patriarch shape up as they think he should, and we have seen evidence that the church membership in a diocese could be decisive in the choice or acceptance of their bishop.

It is about the parish priests that we know the least. Their responsibilities were local and they stayed in the same place, so they were hardly worth noting beyond their own community. They had to know by heart their parts in presiding at the sacraments whose administration defined their order. Thus the demise of Coptic as a non-liturgical language and the Copts' prejudice against the intruder language of Arabic could only lead to the parish clergy's low level of literacy reported by the earliest visitors to Egypt in the modern world.

Lay members actually became increasingly important by maintaining the financing of church activities and by making themselves indispensable to government after government. Their literacy and the leadership talent they developed in governmental and business administration were invaluable to their church. Furthermore, since Copts never imagined that holiness or acts of devotion or the practice of charity were the specialty of clergy, lay men and women often provided the models for the most dramatic and the most unselfish ideals of Christianity. Cyril II's canons, however, suggest that "the customs of Christian notables became assimilated to those of the Muslims: harem, slaves . . ."[74]

Paradoxically, the thirteenth century, which was so hard and so turbulent for the Copts in so many ways, turned out to be the great century of Copto-Arabic literature.[75] Bishop Butrus Sawirus al-Jamil began the compilation of the first Coptic Synaxary early in the century, or perhaps even before.[76] Abu al-Mufaddal ibn al-'Assal, who bore the title "Fakhr al-Dawlah" (pride of the state), was the "father of the Coptic writers of the beginning of the thirteenth century." He was from a rich Cairo family, twice-married, with children, among whom were four sons who "were effective agents in the Coptic Renaissance in the thirteenth century."[77]

The sons, called in Arabic "awlad al-'Assal," were a scholarly group of writers in the Beni Suef province and master linguists. "Their legacy appears to represent the consummation of the Coptic culture in the Islamic Middle Ages."[78] Al-Safi ibn al-'Assal compiled canon law under the unfortunate ibn Laqlaq (Cyril III) in the *Great Nomocanon* which became the "basis of ecclesiastical law for the Coptic Church of Egypt" and continues to have that same role in the Ethiopian Church.[79] He composed doctrinal expositions of Christianity so persuasive that they were still being responded to by Muslims in the eighteenth century. Indeed, Khalil Samir has called him the "greatest Coptic apologist of the Middle Ages and one of the greatest Christian apologists in the Arabic language."

At the same time, Bishop Yuhanna of Sammanud was writing a Coptic grammar and a glossary of church books (including the Bible),[80] physician and priest Abu al-Khayr al-Rashid ibn al-Tayyib was writing a *Summa of the Beliefs* and other defenses of the faith,[81] physician Abu Hulayqah (originally from Edessa) was writing poetry,[82] and ibn al-'Amid al-Makir was writing a universal history,[83] and al-As'ad Abu al-Faraj Hibat Allah ibn al-'Assal, an important administrator, was making a new translation of the Gospels into Arabic and writing an introduction to the Apostle Paul and a Coptic grammar.[84] All this literary activity was going on as the Ayyubid dynasty begun by Salah ad-Din was collapsing. And Coptic scholarship and creativity were to carry over into the Mamluk era which followed.

The hard times for the government of Egypt and the low estate of the Coptic patriarchate in the middle of the thirteenth century must have been discouraging for Coptic Christians, now clearly a minority. In fact, however, the Coptic Church was about to enter the trying centuries of Mamluk rule quite strong enough to survive as an important minority throughout their worst times. The era we have covered in this chapter turned out to be a time of testing and a time of discovery by the Copts of how to succeed as a minority church.

[1] Here and throughout this book we employ the widely used and almost universally understood dating, A.D. (anno Domini), being the solar year since the conventional time of the birth of Jesus. Coptic sources for their history often use A.M. (anno martyrum), being the solar year since the accession of Roman Emperor Diocletian under whom was initiated the bloodiest of all persecutions against Christians. Muslim sources usually employ A.H. (anno hegirae), being the lunar year since the "flight" of the Prophet Muhammad to Medina in 622 A.D. To add to the complexity of calculating dates, the *History of the Patriarchs* sometimes uses the government's tax year. To simplify, we translate all years into A.D.

[2] *The History of the Patriarchs of the Egyptian Church (HPEC)* (Cairo: Publications de la société d'archéologie copte, 1941 et seq.), 2, 124-135.

[3] *HPEC* 2, 130.

[4] This paragraph depends on De Lacy O'Leary, *A Short History of the Fatimid Khalifate* (London: Kegan Paul, 1923), pp. 105 and 114; the quotation is from p. 113.

[5] *HPEC* 2, 135-150.

[6] *HPEC* 2, 135-136.

[7] *HPEC* 2, 116.

[8] This has become the classic theory; see, e.g., G. Graf, *Geschichte der christlichen arabischen Literatur* (Vatican City: Bibliotheca Apostolica Vaticana, 1947), 2, 300-301.

[9] His story is found in *HPEC* 2, 150-174.

[10]O. F. A. Meinardus, "Damru," *Coptic Encyclopedia,* 1991.

[11]*HPEC* 2, 169-170, and 174.

[12]*HPEC* 2, 157.

[13]André Ferré, "Abu al-Fadl Isa ibn Nasturus," *Coptic Encyclopedia,* 1991.

[14]*HPEC* 2, 170-171.

[15]Khalil Samir, "Abu al-Fath ibn Sahlan ibn Muqashir," *Coptic Encyclopedia,* 1991.

[16]His story is found in *HPEC* 2, 174-228.

[17]*HPEC* 2, 176. His rival, another Abraham, was to be consoled with the next open bishopric, pp. 176-177.

[18]*HPEC* 2, 183-196.

[19]*HPEC* 2, 177, 180.

[20]*HPEC* 2, 199-200.

[21]Found in S. M. Stern, *Fatimid Decrees: Original Documents from the Fatimid Chancery* (London: Faber and Faber, 1964), pp. 15-22.

[22]André Ferré, "Fatimids and the Copts," *Coptic Encyclopedia,* 1991.

[23]*HPEC* 2, 229-231.

[24]His story is found in *HPEC* 2, 228-239.

[25]Recounted in *HPEC* 2, 245-321.

[26]*HPEC* 2, 248.

[27]These are summarized in *HPEC* 2, 250-255; and see O. H. E. KHS-Burmester, "Canons of Christodoulos, LXVI Patriarch of Alexandria," in *Le Muséon,* 45 (1942), 71-84.

[28]*HPEC* 2, 268-273.

[29]The story is in *HPEC* 2, 316-317.

[30]J. den Heijer, "Mawhub," *Coptic Encyclopedia,* 1991.

[31]J. den Heijer, "L'*Histoire des patriarches d'Alexandrie*: Recension primitive et vulgate," *Bulletin de la Société d'Archéologie Copte,* 27, (1985), 1-29; see pp. 23-24 for a summary of his conclusions.

[32]*HPEC* 2, 279 and 284.

[33]*HPEC* 2, 242-244.

[34]Found in *Corpus Scriptorum Christianorum Orientalium,* ser. 3, Vol. 7, ed. L. Cheiko (Beirut, 1909).

[35]cf. S. F. Griffith, "Eutychius of Alexandria on the Emperor Theophilus and Iconoclasm in Byzantium: a Tenth Century Moment in Christian Apologetic in Arabic,"

Byzantion, 52 (1982), 154-190.

[36]*A History of the Holy Eastern Church* (London: Joseph Masters, 1847), Vol. 2 of *The Patriarchate of Alexandria,* p. 182.

[37]André Ferré, "Fatimids and the Copts," *Coptic Encyclopedia,* 1991.

[38]B. Lewis, "Egypt and Syria," in *The Central Islamic Lands from Pre-Islamic Times to the First World War,* Vol. 1 of *The Cambridge History of Islam,* ed. P. M. Holt, A. K. S. Lambton, and B. Lewis (Cambridge: Cambridge Univ. Press, 1970), p. 189.

[39]E.g., *HPEC* 2, 318.

[40]Subhi Labib, "Badr al-Jamali," *Coptic Encyclopedia,* 1991.

[41]His story is found in *HPEC* 2, 321-370.

[42]*HPEC* 2, 247; on p. 365, he is called "a saintly monk, spiritual, lowly, meek, very ascetic, a hater of possessions, giving alms to all."

[43]*HPEC* 2, 331.

[44]*HPEC* 2, 365.

[45]O. H. E. Burmester, ed. and trans., "The Canons of Cyril II, LXVII Patriarch of Alexandria," *Le Muséon,* 40 (1927), 245-288.

[46]*HPEC* 2, 346.

[47]Subhi Labib, "Cyril II," *Coptic Encyclopedia,* 1991.

[48]His story is in *HPEC* 2, 370-399.

[49]*HPEC* 2, 399.

[50]*HPEC* 2, 383.

[51]Macarius' story is found in *HPEC* 3, 1-39. The quotation is from p. 3.

[52]*HPEC* 3, 22.

[53]His biography is in *HPEC* 3, 39-59; the quotation, however, is from Subhi Labib, "Gabriel II," *Coptic Encyclopedia,* 1991.

[54]André Ferré, "Fatimids and the Copts," *Coptic Encyclopedia,* 1991.

[55]His story is in *HPEC* 3, 59-66.

[56]*HPEC* 3, 67.

[57]*The Churches and Monasteries of Egypt and Some Neighboring Countries,* ed. and trans. B. Evetts (Oxford: Clarendon Press, 1895), pp. 106-107.

[58]*HPEC* 3, 66-69 and 90-96.

[59]Vincent Frederick, "Murqus ibn Qanbar," *Coptic Encyclopedia,* 1991.

[60]B. Lewis, *The Arabs in History* (New York: Harper and Row, 1967), pp. 154-155.

[61]Subhi Labib in "Mark III," *Coptic Encyclopedia,* 1991.

[62]Lewis, p. 153.

[63]Lewis, p. 149.

[64]*HPEC* 3, 97-166.

[65]W. Y. Adams, *Nubia: Corridor to Africa* (Princeton: Princeton Univ. Press, 1977), p. 456.

[66]*HPEC* 3, 165.

[67]His biography is found in *HPEC* 3, 166-168 and 183-203.

[68]*HPEC* 205-225.

[69]Reproduced, along with an English translation, from ms. arabe 302, Bibliothèque nationale (Paris), folios 287 verso to 355 recto, as *History of the Patriarchs of the Egyptian Church (HPEC),* Vol. 4 (Cairo: Publications de la société d'archéologie copte, 1974).

[70]*HPEC* 4, 158-160.

[71]*HPEC* 4, 168-180.

[72]*HPEC* 4, 276-279 and 284.

[73]Letter from Maurice Martin, 9 June, 1992.

[74]Letter from Maurice Martin, 9 June, 1992.

[75]Aziz Atiya, "Copto-Arabic Literature," *Coptic Encyclopedia,* 1991.

[76]Vincent Frederick, "Butrus Sawirus al-Jamil," *Coptic Encyclopedia,* 1991.

[77]Khalid Samir, "Fakhr al-Dawlah," *Coptic Encyclopedia,* 1991.

[78]Aziz Atiya, "Awlad al-'Assal," *Coptic Encyclopedia,* 1991.

[79]Khalil Samir, "Al-Safi ibn al-'Assal," *Coptic Encyclopedia,* 1991.

[80]Vincent Frederick, "Yuhanna of Sammanud," *Coptic Encyclopedia,* 1991.

[81]Vincent Frederick, "Abu al-Khayr al-Rashid ibn al-Tayyib," *Coptic Encyclopedia,* 1991.

[82]Penelope Johnstone, "Abu Halayqah," *Coptic Encyclopedia,* 1991.

[83]Aziz Atiya, "Makir, ibn al-'Amid al-," *Coptic Encyclopedia,* 1991.

[84]Aziz Atiya, "al-As'ad Abu al-Faraj Hibat Allah ibn al-'Assal," *Coptic Encyclopedia,* 1991.

Chapter Seven

Surviving Mamluk Rule

✠ ———————————————————————————————— ✠

1260 to 1517

COPTIC CHRISTIANITY HAD TWELVE CENTURIES of experiences behind it when in 1260 it began more than five centuries which should logically have seen it expire with a whimper. It did survive, however, and surviving the first half of those five hundred years is the story of this chapter.

After obscure beginnings in the first century and a half, Egyptian Christianity had become so intellectually and spiritually strong in its third century that it led the entire Christian movement until 451. From that year, however, the official churches of the Eastern and Western Roman Empires broke with the leaders of the Egyptian church. Egyptian Christianity, no longer a leader in the world church, became a national church, a Coptic-speaking church, a popular church. These may well have been the very characteristics which provided the necessary qualities for a long and successful survival in Egypt.

For almost two centuries more, Egypt remained part of the Byzantine Empire, when the Coptic Church had to adjust to living under a government that refused to recognize its legitimacy and set up a rival to it—an imperial (Melchite) church, backed up by coercion. Actually, when the Arabs wrested Egypt from the Byzantines in the 640s, many Copts hoped for a better day, now that a hostile Christian government was replaced by an Islamic government with orders to "protect" the conquered Egyptians. Egypt always seemed to be ruled by outsiders, after all, and the dominant Arabs needed the Copts' knowledge and skills.

Although by 833 the Arab element had yielded rule in Egypt to foreign mercenaries,[1] the Arabs' language and Islamic religion had made such strides in their two centuries of rule that most Egyptians were well on their way to becoming Arabic-speaking Muslims. The Coptic Christians continued to be a prominent and useful minority, however, for several centuries, and a force to be reckoned with.

The first of these "foreign mercenaries" were the Turkish Tulunids and Ikhshidids whose dynasties ruled Egypt for a century. Then after the two centuries of the Fatimid caliphate (969-1171), the Ayyubids reasserted Turkish power in Egypt—which the Turkish Mamluk sultans and the Turkish Ottoman Empire were then to reinforce for the five hundred and thirty-eight years before the French invasion in 1798. In his grand survey, *The Rise of the West*, William H. McNeill ranks the "steppe conquerors" (above all, the Turks) with the "European Far West" as the driving forces in world history from 1000-1500 A.D.[2] Specifically, he points out that throughout the Eastern Hemisphere "Turks provided the majority of the Muslim rulers and soldiers from the eleventh century onward and constituted the cutting edge of the Islamic expansion . . ."[3] Turkish domination may have meant stagnation for the Coptic Church, but it did not put Egypt or the Copts outside the sweep of world history.

As a prelude to our examination of Coptic Church development in our period, let us look at what was happening in the governing of Egypt. We begin, of course with the Mamluks who were taking over from the Ayyubids by the middle of the thirteenth century. In many ways the Mamluks created in Egypt, and beyond, a remarkable system of rule until the nineteenth century.

McNeill reports[4] that one historian has argued that the "Mameluke regime was in reality an overseas colonial empire of Circassian and Turkish merchants and warriors based north of the Black Sea." This theory has not attracted much support, however, for Egypt does seem to have been the center of Mamluk rule; but it does underline the roots of the great majority of the Mamluks.

Mamluks[5] were slaves of a special kind. They were overwhelmingly Turks and Circassians from the steppe country north of the Caspian and Black Seas. They were sold as boys and resold until they came into the hands of successful Mamluks, who had become ambitious officers, vying for position and power in Egypt (and southwest Asia). Young Mamluks were trained in riding and archery, but also in governing, and in some cases even in liberal arts. They were made strict Muslims. Although some had secondary loyalties, e.g., to their fellow Mamluks who had been emancipated at the same time, the Mamluk's real loyalty was to his purchaser, in whose family he became a son—who might actually become the principal heir of the family. Most often a Mamluk would be legally emancipated when his training was finished, but, paradoxically, this did not significantly change his role in the system.

The Mamluk system[7] had similarities to the European feudal system.[8] Mamluks were warriors, and they received the income from an *iqta*,[9] which functioned like a fief. But an *iqta* could not be inherited. Indeed, one could never become a Mamluk by inheritance—a Mamluk was a man who was bought as a slave. Patently, the Mamluk system had no place for legitimacy in the usual sense, and was a strange kind of meritocracy. Government was by those who had the power to take control of it and the ability to rule. It was also a military government ("a military oligarchy in an alien land"[10]), and a dictatorship by the Mamluk at the top of the pyramid. Thus the Mamluks were slaves bought to be made into warriors who could rise by some luck and much force to rule. They might learn Arabic, or even be Arabic scholars, but they spoke Turkish, for Turkish was the language of rulers in Egypt.

Baybars is accounted the first Mamluk ruler of Egypt. He was a Kipchak Turk, i.e., from a Mongol khanate ruled by the "Golden Horde." His rise to power was a signal of what was to come: first, he murdered the last of the Ayyubid rulers and then he assassinated Qutuz, who had been his fellow Mamluk leader in a crucial victory in Palestine over the Mongols in 1260. With much ceremony, including in the procession the Coptic patriarch,[11] Baybars installed in Cairo a caliph of the Abbasid family. This was intended to lend a certain legitimacy to Baybars' rule, but when the caliph went out on a military expedition on his own, Baybars allowed the expedition and the caliph to be destroyed, and a more pliant member of the Abbasid family was substituted.

Baybars' policy towards Christians seems to have been largely practical. He intimidated Christian Nazareth by destroying its church, and he depopulated a Christian village north of Damascus to make it an example. On the other hand, he admitted a Melchite patriarch to his realm in a deal in which Byzantine Emperor Michael Paleologus restored a mosque to the Muslims in Constantinople. Baybars once executed a Coptic Christian (who had also been charged with "oppressing and harming the people"[12]) who had "islamized" and then returned to Christianity.

Most of the Mamluk rulers' foreign policies had ill effects on Coptic Christians. From the outset of their rule, they determined to unite Syria with Egypt under Mamluk control as part of their policy to block the potentially friendly (to Christians) Mongols' control of southwest Asia. Then they crushed the remaining outposts of the Crusaders from the Christian West. An ally was lost to the Copts when the Mamluks were able to subdue Christian Nubia to the south. Of less interest to the Coptic Christians was the Mamluks' extending their control over the Hejaz (the section of Arabia in which Islam's holiest cities are located) and as much of the Red Sea as they could.

Virtually all these Mamluk objectives brought them face to face with Christian powers. Christians were prominent among the Mongol leaders and many of their allies, when they were first contesting southwest Asia with the Mamluks. Christian Nubia was led by bishops from the Coptic Church and was a Christian outpost, whose kings had intervened on behalf of the Egyptian Christians. The Crusaders were Christians, of course, and Catholic cities like Venice and Genoa competed with Mamluk Egypt for control of the markets of west Asia. Finally, it was Christian Portugal which was to win control of the Red Sea from the Mamluks in the last decades of their rule in Egypt.

Except for the brave Nubians, however, and the Christian Ethiopians, who could threaten to retaliate against their Muslim population (or to dam the Nile!), seldom did any of the other Christians do the Copts any good, even when Mamluks made temporary treaties with Christian powers. The Christian kingdoms of Nubia were ceasing to be a threat to Muslim Egypt. The centralized monarchy in Lower Nubia was seriously weakened by bedouin raids, and with the progressive feudalization accompanying "dynastic and factional warfare", the monarchy "disintegrated into a collection of warring principalities."[13] The Nubian church "had lost much of its popular appeal," and support from the Egyptian Copts "was weakened by the persecutions launched against the church in Egypt under the Mameluke régime."[14]

The Copts' Christian faith often made them look like potential spies, even if Crusaders, Italians, and Portuguese, all Catholics, considered the Copts to be heretics. Indeed, the interest the Catholic leadership in Rome took in the Copts was only to bring the Coptic Church under Rome's control—apparently a real possibility more than once when things looked desperate for the Coptic cause (but a possibility in each case frustrated by Copts generally who had always thought of Rome and its Catholic Church as their ecclesiastical nemesis). It should be said, however, that Christian powers, above all Aragon and Byzantium, and even commercial cities of Catholic Italy, did on occasion use their leverage to relieve some of the Copts' suffering at the hands of their rulers.[15]

The Mamluks were able to finish off the Crusaders in Asia by 1291; and the Mongols' final threat to west Asia, under Timur (Tamerlane), was stopped in the early fifteenth century. As for Nubia, after paying tribute (according to the *bakt*, three hundred and sixty slaves a year) to the Mamluks for many years, northern Nubians found themselves annexed outright, according to the medieval historian al-Makrizi.[16] So much for help the Copts might have gotten from the Mamluks' Christian rivals. Mamluk relations with the Christian traders were more complex. It turned out that it was more profitable for the Mamluk economy to foster trade with the Christian powers than to fight them. The Mamluks' control of Syria, Egypt, and the Red

Sea situated them perfectly to prosper from the rich East-West trade which did so much to finance the creation of the modern world.

The Mamluks themselves were not trained to be artists, scholars, or scientists, of course, but "though on the whole uncultured and bloodthirsty, their keen appreciation of art and architecture would have been a credit to any civilized dynasty and makes Cairo even now one of the beauty spots of the Moslem world," in part, at least, because "thirteenth-century Egypt became a haven of refuge for Moslem artists and artisans who fled from Mosul, Baghdad and Damascus before the Mongol invasions."[17] The Mamluks did encourage learning and the arts; and the disintegration of Iraq as a center of Arabic culture had resulted in Mamluk Egypt's and Syria's becoming "the main centres of Arabic culture."[18]

Coptic Christian culture could survive the enveloping Islamic civilization of Mamluk Egypt, however, for it is also true that Islamic civilization was eventually to decline during the Mamluk era. One scholar gives the opinion[19] that "this brilliant Islamic culture, which shone so brightly in contrast to the darkness of the Latin West and the stagnation of Byzantium, began to fade from the thirteenth century onwards. Arabic philosophy was dead by 1200, Arabic science by 1500." The reasons offered for this decline of Islamic civilization were the unceasing waves of nomadic invasions of the Islamic lands, the decay of urban life, the loss of the linguistic unity Arabic had provided, and the triumph of religious authoritarianism over open inquiry. These four factors did not help Coptic culture but neither were they fatal to it.

In fact, the Copts' scholarship described in the last chapter continued unabated in the early Mamluk period. Abu Shakir ibn al-Rahib was the son of an eminent scribe who became a monk after his wife's death. Abu Shakir was a deacon at the important al-Muallaqah church in 1260 and "in perfect command of both Coptic and Arabic." He wrote on the doctrine of Christ, on laws, on universal history in his *Book of Histories* (a source for dating the patriarchs), and a Coptic vocabulary and a Coptic grammar.[20] Abu al-Fakhr al-Masihi was a convert from Judaism who developed "the chronology for the oldest history of the Chronicon Orientale."[21]

Ibn Kabar was from a wealthy family of Old Cairo who was also well versed in Arabic and Coptic. He was "a great scholar at the end of the golden age of Coptic literary accomplishment." He compiled a Coptic dictionary, served as chief scribe of Prince Baybars al-Mansur, but retired from government in 1293. He became presbyter-in-charge at al-Muallaqah church.[22]

Bulus al-Habis was less important as a writer but perhaps the most important to the life of his fellow Christians. A scribe from a family of scribes, he served in the state chancellery in Syria but the Mamluk sultan transferred him to Cairo. He became a monk and a solitary, living in a cave near Helwan south of Cairo. He traveled about, however, used wealth at his command to pay fines and thus redeem Christians, and "saved communities of Copts and Jews" in 1265. He became a martyr when he was finally executed, never revealing the source of his wealth.[23] Still, his patriarch, John VII, presided over the Coptic Church when it reached its lowest number of members.[24]

One student of Mamluk Syria and Egypt has observed[25] that, by the beginning of the fourteenth century, news about the treatment of Muslims in the parts of Spain conquered by Christians and the fear of a Mongol-Christian alliance in the East meant that "inevitably the . . . [Copts] felt the repercussions of these contemporary currents of Muslim feeling . . . whipped up by popular preachers . . . and by books and tracts from scholars," so that peaks of violence against Coptic Christians were reached in 1301, 1321, and 1354. Al-Makrizi's account[26] of the 1321 destruction of churches and monasteries is startling to read. There were also concerted efforts to get the Copts out of the government bureaus and to close Coptic churches and monasteries.

It has been argued[27] that, in fact, the fourteenth century was "the real ruin of Coptic Christianity as a force in the mainstream of Egyptian life. Conversions to Islam, always a steady trickle, now became a flood, and even regions like Upper Egypt . . . became in majority Muslim." It has also been said[28] that the Mamluks "gave the coup de grace to Christianity in Egypt, which ceased to mean anything but a number of individuals."

On the other hand, a distinguished historian of Islam can say[29] that "the . . . fourteenth century was on the whole a period of tranquillity and peace. No major foreign enemy threatened the Mamluk realms, and the flourishing trade with both East and West brought great wealth to Egypt and ample revenues to the treasury." Even though the writer here is focusing on the state, his calling the fourteenth century "a period of tranquillity and peace" starkly underlines the marginalizing of the Copts who were being ruined in the very land they looked upon as their own.

The Mamluks themselves, though they were strong Muslims,[30] seemed to have little argument with the Copts, for they needed their skills as well as those of the converts to Islam;[31] and the Copts were never a threat to Mamluk dominance. In fact, a Copt was appointed vizier for the first time in the Mamluk state, during the patriarchate of Athanasius III (1250-1261).[32] It was largely popular pressure, then, especially in Cairo, that forced the rulers to take action against the Christians. Many Muslim religious leaders and intellectuals used their influence to move the masses and to justify prejudicial actions against the Copts. Crowded housing in Cairo did not help, and Muslims resented the wealth of some Copts, and, above all, "the overwhelming Coptic presence in the financial bureaus of the sultans and the emirs and in related commercial ventures."[33]

There were interesting features of the large proportion of financial administrators' being Copts—much larger than the proportion in the chancery. (This was equally true of converts.[34]) For example, the special nature of the feudal, or *iqta*, system required a fairly frequent "survey and redistribution of agricultural lands and the revenues that they yielded," called a *rawk*.[35] These redistributions naturally enraged those who lost out in the reshuffle, and they took out their anger, not so much on the Mamluks who ordered and set the standards for the *rawk* as on the Coptic bureaucrats who actually drew up the plans and put them in place.

Ibn Khaldun, the greatest of the medieval Islamic historical thinkers, said,[36] "It is a custom of [the Turks] that the wazir be appointed from among the Copts in charge of the office of bookkeeping and tax collection, because in Egypt they have been familiar with these matters since ancient times." To get to the top in financial administration required that the Copt "islamize," and many did. They were called "musalima." Many of these conversions were clearly *pro forma* (one top official was on the list of converts in 1293 and then again in 1301!); Muslims characteristically wondered if any of the conversions were genuine. The "musalima," in fact, frequently did defend Copts individually and as a group. High position and group favoritism by Copts may have provoked Muslim resentment, but they were also essential to the Copts' capacity to survive. Powerful physician-converts were in a particularly good position to cushion blows to their Coptic friends and kin.[37]

Copts were excluded from the orthodox "ulama" class which supplied religious leadership and were concentrated in fiscal and administrative bureaus. Law was also closed to them because of its religious basis in Islam.[38] But there was still Muslim resentment. There was a saying about a government leader: "his *qadi* (judicial officer) is a Muslim of recent date, his 'sheikh' is a Christian, and his 'pilgrim' is a spy."[39] Cries of "Coptic domination!" were frequently heard.

There is an interesting fourteenth-century pamphlet,[40] "An Earnest Appeal on the Employment of Dimmis," on the subject by a certain Asnawi, who came to Cairo as a youth and became highly respected for his probity and his religious, legal, and literary attainments. According to Asnawi, "The Copts declare that this country still belongs to them" and that therefore they steal what is theirs! Copts are accused of excessive wine-drinking, of seducing Muslim women, of incendiarism, and specifically of plotting to blow up the mosque in Medina. Asnawi doubted the genuineness of any conversion of a Copt to Islam, especially when it was of only one member of a family. He ruefully noted that ejecting Copts from administrative offices never seemed to last, but, of course, he strongly advocated excluding Coptic Christians from government. Somewhat earlier, a famous jurist, ibn Tammiya, sharply opposed the "influence of Christians and Jews in Mamluk politics and the economy, and the lax enforcement of discriminatory legislation aimed at them."[41]

As if pogroms were not enough, the Copts always had to come up with their special taxes, through which, in the words of ibn Khaldun, "God has strengthened and exalted Islam, helped and protected the Muslims, confounded and annoyed the enemies of Islam and the Muslims, and humbled and humiliated the unbelievers who are their subjects."[42]

The 1340s were hard for everyone—Christians were hounded and the "times . . . [were] marked by corruption and bribery, in addition to profligacy within the sultan's court."[43] But it may have been the outburst in 1354 that was decisive in setting the stage for exactly five hundred years of a special wilderness for the Copts. (1854 saw the consecration of the reforming Pope Cyril IV.) There was a renewal of the "sumptuary" (discriminatory) laws about special dress and travel and maintaining church property, rigid efforts to prevent *pro forma* conversions, and the widespread confiscation of the church's *waqfs* (inalienable endowments for the church's charities).The Muslim historian al-Makrizi reported a half-century after these events that Copts were losing their jobs and their property, and their churches were being destroyed, all of which led to mass conversions to Islam. Thus 1354 has been regarded "as a turning point in Egyptian religious history, as the point in time when the second great transformation of Egyptian religion became virtually complete,"[44] the first transformation being, of course, the conversion of Egypt to Christianity.

In his fourteenth-century work on "hierarchy, titulature, and appointment," the Muslim scholar, al-Qashandi, specifies the duties of the Coptic patriarch: supervising the lower ranks of the clergy and controlling the congregations, especially in "observing the covenant," overseeing inheritances, offering prayers for the Muslim state, giving hospitality for Muslims and travelers, and avoiding of spying or making alliances with any foreign state.[45] It is notable that these duties were prescribed by the Mamluk state rather than the Coptic Church. One of our authorities observes,[46] "It is surprising that, in the face of legal and social disabilities . . . and in the face of a relentless social and cultural Islamic pressure, if not of sustained persecution, the non-Muslim communities survived as well as they did in Medieval Islam." As if to demonstrate how dismal the centuries of Mamluk rule were for the Copts, the on-going *History of the Patriarchs of Alexandria*, so crucial for providing us with insights into Coptic history, gives us scarcely more than the names and dates of all but one of the Coptic patriarchs for the four centuries beginning with Mamluk rule.

In turning back to historical developments, we find that after the death of Baybars in 1277 and months of infighting for the succession, Qalawun and then his son al-Nazir were able to maintain themselves as sultans for most of the ensuing sixty-two years. Although they and their descendants came the closest to establishing a dynasty during the Mamluk period, the forty years after the death of al-Nazir were a time of steady decline.

The dominant Mamluks from 1260 to 1382 were called "Bahri" (river, because their barracks were on a river island opposite Cairo). The Bahri Mamluk era was a terrible time for the Copts. Not only were Christians subjected to job loss, confiscations, special discriminations, destruction of their churches, and bloody pogroms during the 1301, 1321, and 1354 persecutions we have referred to above; the Black Death, which broke out in 1347-48 and again in 1375, brought suffering to all Egyptians, and in 1365 a concerted attack on Alexandria by Christian foreigners provoked a reaction against the Christian Copts, whom the Mamluk government forced to pay the cost of throwing back that "Crusade."

Things could have been worse for the Copts, however. At the time of Pope Benjamin II, 1327-1339, the king of Ethiopia threatened retaliation against the governers of Egypt for their persecution of the Copts, with some success in moderating the persecution. Repairs to churches were permitted and the pope could resume some of his better known priestly activities, like preparing the chrism (the blessed oil to be used in the churches).[47] Also, it should be noted that the Coptic and the Nubian churches were alive and active enough to consecrate a bishop for Faras and Qasr Ibrim in 1372. (The documents recording this event were recently recovered.[48])

Shortly before the total collapse of the Bahri Mamluk regime, in 1378, Matthew I[49] became the Coptic patriarch. In the tradition, he was a village boy in Upper Egypt who had been a brave shepherd and early showed spiritual powers so that he was ordained priest at the age of eighteen. He spent time in Saint Anthony's monastery in the Eastern Desert and in Jerusalem, where he became famous for his miracles and his modesty. When he was back at Saint Anthony's, Matthew suffered at the hands of the soldiers trying to enforce on all Copts the fine for the 1365 "Crusade." Matthew did his best to redeem the Copts who were being fined.[50]

After some time at the al-Muharraq monastery in Upper Egypt, Matthew was forced in 1378 to accept consecration as patriarch. It is notable that Matthew insisted on having twelve bishops consecrate him in Alexandria, at the cost of some considerable inconvenience and delay. That number reflected the long Alexandrian tradition of having twelve elders or bishops consecrate the bishop for that city.

Matthew was famous both for his modest way of life and for his care for the poor, especially the Coptic nuns, but also for Jews and Muslims as well as Christians. Thus he was known as Matthew the Poor, or Matta el-Mesqin. He also became famous as a mediator or judge, even in state matters and among the Melchite and Catholic Christians. He was also said to have engendered "love and friendship . . . between the kings of Christendom,"[51] the Ethiopian and the "Frank" (i.e., Western European) kings in particular. The *History of the Patriarchs* biography suggests that Barquq, the first of the Burji Mamluk sultans, not only loved and protected Matthew but even waited for Matthew's approval of his being "seated as king" in 1382.[52]

Matthew was ready to forgive and be humble before the Christians who plotted against him, but they usually came to a violent end. He was a formidable opponent: on one occasion, he successfully threatened an official who was enforcing dress laws on Coptic women by reminding him that "the Christians are not without kings on the earth,"[53] and in general Matthew's prayers seem to have had a fatal effect on officials who opposed him. Another anomaly was that Matthew "the poor" could come up with 500,000 dirhams to try to forestall the attacks of one of these officials.[54]

At Matthew's death at the age of seventy-two, in 1408, Jews as well as Christian of all denominations were represented at his funeral. His patriarchate had not been an easy period for Christians—we are told that forty-nine suffered martyrdom in his time,[55] and all Egypt had suffered plague and famine. Matthew's gifts were, thus, particularly needed for such a time.

Amba Ruweiss, a contemporary of Matthew, was best remembered for his remarkable asceticism and his charismatic gifts over his long life, but he is also memorialized in the twentieth century by the location of the Coptic Cathedral and Patriarchate at the site of the small church in Cairo dedicated to him.[56] He was from Lower Egypt but he spent his adult life as a monk at a Cairo monastery.

Barquq had made himself sultan as a result of a process beginning with his part in the 1377 assassination of the Bahri sultan, Sha'ban, whose service he was in. After a period of violently eliminating rivals and trying to rule through Sha'ban's infant sons, Barquq formally assumed the sultanate in 1382. Thus began the sultanate called "Burji" (castle) since their focus was the Citadel, or "Circassian," since Barquq and most of the subsequent rulers until the Ottoman Empire took over in 1517 were of that ethnic group. Barquq built Muslim colleges but tolerated the Christians, and even lowered taxes. He and his son, Faraj, ruled for thirty years, rather a record in view of the years of violence and turmoil in changes of government which were to follow.

Barquq's bloody and treacherous path to the sultanate was matched by a "drunkard . . . [who] committed some of the worst excesses,"[57] called al-Muayyad Shaykh,[58] who ruled until 1421, after which the important Barsbay won out in the struggle for dominance. Under Barsbay, Cyprus was defeated, and Egypt's Red Sea trade became more developed than ever. Government monopolies were created to increase revenues, a practice that in the long run was to hurt the trade significantly. Indeed, the feudalization of productive land and the monopolizing of trade by government were to become major factors in the economic decline of Mamluk Egypt.

During the patriarchate of Gabriel V, 1409-1427, there were frequent revolts in Egypt. Christians in good positions were expelled from government employment and were squeezed financially; and all Christians suffered from the sumptuary laws. The Ethiopian "negus Yeshak attacked the Muslims of Ethiopia in 1423 and ravaged the Islamic kingdom of Jabart" for not letting Christians go to Jerusalem. For this, Barsbay took cruel vengeance. These were hard days for the Copts, the patriarch was impoverished, and the Abyssinian kings ceased trying to help. In spite of all this, Pope Gabriel did find time to reorganize the Coptic liturgy.[59]

Coptic Pope John XI, 1427-1452, saw some turbulent times. This may help explain how in 1442 Coptic representatives signed a Bull of Unity with the Roman Catholics,[60] though as in other cases, no final result came from this act. Earlier, we are told,[61] John had received the visit of prelates from Antioch and Jerusalem; but then he ran into serious trouble over a governmental decree disallowing repairs to churches. When the king of Ethiopia announced he was going to intervene on John's behalf, things got worse. John suffered beatings and imprisonment, and new rules were issued forbidding Copts to treat Muslim patients or to own female Muslim slaves. When one Copt who islamized and became vizier angered the sultan, he confiscated the vizier's wealth and had him beaten to death.

Later in the century, Coptic Pope John XII, patriarch from 1479 to 1482, corresponded with Rome about possible reunion. In John's response to Rome, "the matter of the discussion included the abandonment of obstinacy, and reconciliation and peace among all the denominations of the Christians." Neither did this correspondence have permanent effect.[62] The *History of the Patriarchs* tells us nothing else about any of the patriarchs of the last Mamluk century (1409-1517) except the name of their monastery, the date of their consecration, and the date of their death.[63]

The internal causes of Mamluk decline which led to Egypt's incorporation into the Ottoman Empire have been summarized[64] as "recurring drought, plague and famine, financial malpractice and economic dislocation, the depletion of the army through falling recruitment, the disruption of the Mamluk order and discipline by Barquq and his descendants." These, combined with the "devastations of Timur" early in the fifteenth century and the victory of the Portuguese traders in the Indian Ocean trade competition towards its end, plus the rise of Ottoman power, were to prove fatal to the Mamluk sultanate, even though the Mamluks continued to be a powerful element in society, finances, and government.

Copts may have felt in 1517 that things could hardly get worse and that incorporation into an empire which competed well with the European powers might help Egypt and them. In the next chapter we will see what being part of the Ottoman Empire was really going to mean for Egypt and the Coptic Church.

[1]David Samuel Margoliouth et al. in "Egypt," *Encyclopedia Britannica*, 1957 ed.

[2]W. H. McNeill, *The Rise of the West* (Chicago: Univ. of Chicago Press, 1963), chap. 10.

[3]McNeill, p. 357.

[4]McNeill, p. 540, note 12, referring to A. N. Poliak, "Le charactère colonial de l'état Mamelouke dans ses rapports avec la Horde d'Or," *Revue des Études Islamiques*, 9 (1935), 231-248.

[5]David Ayalon gives a detailed description of how Mamluks were secured and trained, how their careers unfolded, and how the system worked in *L'Esclavage du Mamelouk* (Jerusalem: Israel Oriental Society, 1951).

[6]See B. Lewis, "Egypt and Syria," in *The Central Islamic Lands from Pre-Islamic Times to the First World War*, Vol. 1 of *The Cambridge History of Islam*, ed. P. M. Holt, A. K. S. Lambton, and B. Lewis (Cambridge: Cambridge Univ. Press, 1970), pp. 226-228.

[7]A. N. Poliak, *Feudalism in Egypt, Syria, Palestine, and the Lebanon, 1250-1900* (London: The Royal Asiatic Society, 1939).

[8]"the allocation of tax revenues in money or in kind from a designated area of land or other revenue source for a limited period in return for administrative or military service." R. Irwin, *The Middle East in the Middle Ages: The Early Mamluk Sultanate 1250-1382* (Carbondale: Southern Illinois Univ. Press, 1986), p. 11.

[9]See P. Hitti, *The Arabs: A Short History*, 5th rev. ed. (Princeton: Princeton Univ. Press, 1943), p. 238.

[10]Hitti, p. 243.

[11]This quotation and the other information in this paragraph, with one exception, are taken from a thirteenth-century biography of Baybars as found in S. F. Sadeque, *Baybars I of Egypt* (Karachi: Oxford Univ. Press, 1956), pp. 202 and 148.

[12]W. Y. Adams, *Nubia: Corridor to Africa* (Princeton: Princeton Univ. Press, 1977), p. 508.

[13]W. Y. Adams, p. 509.

[14]D. P. Little, "Coptic Conversion to Islam under the Bahri Mamluks 692-755/1293-1354," *Bulletin of the School of Oriental and African Studies*, 39 (1976), 557-559.

[15]C. E. Bosworth, "The 'Protected Peoples' (Christians and Jews) in Medieval Egypt and Syria," *Bulletin of John Rylands Library*, 62 (1979-80), 12.

[16]Hitti, pp. 239 and 245; R. Irwin, p. 53, calls Mamluk Syria and Egypt "a sort of

Noah's Ark for an older Eastern Islamic culture."

[17]B. Lewis, *The Arabs in History,* 4th rev. ed. (New York: Harper and Row, 1966), p. 159; J. J. Saunders calls Mamluk Egypt "the home of what was left of Arabic culture" in *A History of Medieval Islam* (London: Routledge and Kegan Paul, 1965), p. 183.

[18]Saunders, pp. 195-198; the quotation is from p. 195.

[19]Aziz Atiya, "Abu Shakir ibn al-Rahib," *Coptic Encyclopedia,* 1991.

[20]V. Frederick, "Abu al-Fakhr al-Masihi," *Coptic Encyclopedia,* 1991.

[21]Aziz Atiya, "ibn Kabar," *Coptic Encyclopedia,* 1991.

[22]S. Labib, "Bulus al-Habis," *Coptic Encyclopedia,* 1991.

[23]S. Labib, "John VII," *Coptic Encyclopedia,* 1991.

[24]C. E. Bosworth, "Christian and Jewish Religious Dignitaries in Mamluk Egypt and Syria: Qalqashandi's Information on their Hierarchy, Titulature, and Appointment," *International Journal of Middle East Studies,* 3 (1972), 65.

[25]in Abu Salih, *The Churches and Monasteries of Egypt: and Some Neighboring Countries* ed. and trans. B. Evetts and A. J. Butler (Oxford: Clarendon Press, 1895), pp. 328-340.

[26]Bosworth, "Christian and Jewish Religious Dignitaries," pp. 65-66, quoting H. Laoust, *Essais sur les doctrines sociales et politiques d'ibn Taimiya* (Cairo, 1937), pp. 60-62.

[27]G. Wiet, *Encyclopédie de l'Islam,* 2, 996, according to D. P. Little, p. 552.

[28]Lewis, "Egypt and Syria," p. 219.

[29]D. P. Little, "Religion under the Mamluks," *Muslim World,* 73 (1983), 165-181.

[30]C. Petry, *The Civilian Elite of Cairo in the Later Middle Ages* (Princeton: Princeton Univ. Press, 1981), p. 273.

[31]Al-As'ad Sharaf al-Din Hibat Allah ibn Sa'id al-Fa'izi. He had become famous for reorganizing the tax system. See S. Labib, "Athanasius III," *Coptic Encyclopedia,* 1991.

[32]The quotation and the rest of the sentence are from Irwin, p. 98.

[33]Petry, p. 274.

[34]Irwin, pp. 81-82.

[35]*The Muqaddimah: An Introduction to History,* 2, 19.

[36]Linda S. Northrup, "Muslim-Christian Relations during the Reign of the Muslim Sultan al-Mansur Qalawun," in *Conversion and Continuity: Indigenous Christian Communities in Islamic Lands Eighth to Eighteenth Centuries* (Toronto: Pontifical Institute of Medieval Studies, 1990), p. 256.

[37]C. Petry, "Copts in Late Medieval Egypt," *Coptic Encyclopedia,* 1991.

[38]According to G. Wiet in *L'Égypte arabe: de la conquête arabe à la conquête ottomane 642-1517 de l'ère chrétienne*, Vol. 4 of *Histoire de la nation égyptienne* ed. G. Hanotaux (Paris, 1926), p. 570.

[39]The manuscript is in the British Museum (Or. 11581, fol. 6-14). I owe information about this writing to M. Perlmann, "Notes on Anti-Christian Propaganda in the Mamluk Empire," *Bulletin of the School of Oriental and African Studies*, 10 (1940-41), 843-861.

[40]Irwin, p. 97.

[41]*The Muqaddimah* 2, 137.

[42]S. Labib, "Peter V," *Coptic Encyclopedia*, 1991.

[43]D. P. Little, "Coptic Conversion to Islam," pp. 567-569.

[44]Bosworth, "Christian and Jewish Religious Dignitaries," pp. 205-206.

[45]Bosworth, "The 'Protected Peoples' (Christians and Jews)," p. 18.

[46]S. Labib, "Benjamin II," *Coptic Encyclopedia*, 1991.

[47]W. Y. Adams, p. 540.

[48]His story is found in *History of the Patriarchs of the Egyptian Church: Known as the History of the Holy Church by Sawirus ibn Mukaffa (HPEC)* Vol. 3, ed. and trans. A. Khater and O. H. E. KHS-Burmester (Cairo: Société d'archéologie copte, 1970), 235-271.

[49]S. Labib, "Crusades," *Coptic Encyclopedia*, 1991.

[50]*HPEC* 3, 249.

[51]*HPEC* 3, 252.

[52]*HPEC* 3, 257.

[53]*HPEC* 3, 268.

[54]*HPEC* 3, 271.

[55]The traditions about him are summarized in I. Habib el-Masri, *The Story of the Copts* (Cairo: Middle East Council of Churches, 1978), pp. 439-445.

[56]Hitti, p. 246.

[57]See, e.g., chapter 13 of W. Muir, *The Mameluke or Slave Dynasty of Egypt: A History of Egypt from the Fall of the Ayyubid Dynasties to the Conquest of the Osmanlis A.D. 1260-1517* (London: 1930; rpt. Amsterdam: Oriental Press, 1968).

[58]Khalil Samir, "Gabriel V," *Coptic Encyclopedia*, 1991.

[59]J. Gill, *The Council of Florence* (Cambridge: Cambridge Univ. Press, 1959), pp. 321-326. And see P. B. T. Bilanuik, "Florence, Copts at the Council of (1439-1442)," *Coptic Encyclopedia*, 1991.

[60]Habib el-Masri, pp. 429-432, citing as her authority a work in Arabic entitled *at-Tibr ul-Masbak fi dhail is-sulik* by the Muslim historian, Muhammad ibn Abdir-Rahman as-Sakhawi.

[61] *HPEC* 3, 274.

[62] *HPEC* 3, 272-274.

[63] Lewis, "Egypt and Syria," p. 228.

Chapter Eight

Under the Ottoman Empire

✠ ────────────────────────────────────── ✠

1517 to 1798

THE COPTIC CHURCH HAD SURVIVED eight and a half centuries of Muslim rule before Egypt was incorporated into the Ottoman Turkish Empire in 1517. During that era the Christian Copts had become a minority and their language had lost out to the Arabic language of their Muslim conquerors, but their talents and resourcefulness had made a succession of governments dependent on them. The loyalty to their faith and the strong sense of community of the Coptic Christians rivaled these qualities of the Jews in Egypt and other countries. Thus there was no reason to expect that the Ottoman Turks would be able to abolish Christianity in Egypt any more than their Islamic predecessors could.

After the decline of the Abbasid Empire in the ninth century A.D., most of Egypt's rulers had not paid much more than lip service to an external empire, but the situation was expected to change with the coming of the Ottoman Turks, for they were forming an empire which was to be a worthy competitor on the world scene. The Ottoman Empire, however, apparently wanted not much more from Egypt than to milk it for talent and treasure.The surprise for Egyptians was how little things would change for them, for the Mamluks still dominated the country.

The Mamluks first came into conflict with the Ottoman Empire because of Mamluk interests to the north and west of Mamluk Syria. The "first Mamluk war" between them was fought 1485-1490, inconclusively. The new Safavid dynasty in Persia complicated matters by challenging the expanding Ottoman Empire under the vigorous Selim I, "the Grim," who set out in the spring of 1516 to show his power in the East. Selim chose first to show his power against the Mamluks, largely because they were already on the move towards him. Mamluk sultan al-Ghawri died in the first battle, near Aleppo in Northern Syria; and the Mamluks were never able to halt the Ottoman advance, which moved steadily to capture Cairo, put down regional opposition in Egypt, and execute the new sultan Tuman Bey by the spring of 1517. Mamluk internal struggles, combined with inferior infantry and firepower, would seem to have made the outcome inevitable. The Mamluks had considered the use of guns to be unmanly and began using them too late against the well-armed Ottoman forces.

Thus ended the Mamluk sultanate and thus began Ottoman rule in Egypt, which lasted, in theory at least, until the abolition of the Ottoman Empire after World War I. This chapter deals with the Ottoman period until the French invasion in 1798. A French historian[1] has said of this Ottoman era, "during the two hundred and eighty-one years the real or nominal government of the Turkish pashas lasted, Egypt remained obscure, sleeping, forgotten;" concerning Selim's arrangements for governing Egypt, "he made no social revolution."[2] Selim intended simply to build on top of the Mamluk system.

It is hard to see how anyone in Egypt was going to benefit from Ottoman rule there, which seems to have been purely exploitive. Symbolic of this was Selim's prompt transporting from Egypt to Istanbul of the Mamluks' token caliph "and some 2000 leading Egyptian merchants, artisans, and religious leaders," and the building up of the Ottoman navy, using booty from Egypt and the head of the Mamluk Red Sea fleet.[3] Selim's son, Suleyman "the Magnificent," allowed artisans and intellectuals to return to Egypt, but offered them "liberal incentives [which] ultimately induced most to remain,"[4] incentives which had the same effect as deportation in denying their skills to Egypt.

Selim appointed as his vassal in Egypt the Mamluk governor of Aleppo, Khair Bey, who had collaborated with him against his own sultan in 1516. After the death of Khair Bey in 1522 (Selim had died two years earlier), Egypt was placed under a governor answerable to Istanbul, a "pasha;" and yet Suleyman had to deal early in his reign with a rebellion by his own pasha. A year later, in 1525, Suleyman's grand vizier issued the famous *qanun-name* which spelled out the organization and administration of Ottoman Egypt. With this "stabilization of Ottoman authority by Ibrahim Pasha, there ensued a time of quiescence, lasting about sixty years, during which Egypt had very little recorded history . . . and lay passive."[5] In fact, it was Suleyman, rather than Selim, who fastened Ottoman rule on Egypt.

The gap in general knowledge of the history of Egypt is more than matched in the *History of the Patriarchs*. Of the forty-year (the only other fact reported, except a date) patriarchate of John XIII we read only: "during the time of this father there was the conquest of Egypt at the hand of Sultan

Selim, a descendant of the house of Othman, and this was from the Sultan al-Ghuri [i.e., al-Ghawri], the last of the Circassian kings."[6] The patriarchs of the next century and a half are named and the dates of their consecration are given, but otherwise the only single fact reported about any of them was that a letter from and a reply to the Pope of Rome were sent—but without a word about their contents![7]

As the Ottoman system evolved, there were to be twenty-four "beys," who corresponded in most ways to the earlier amirs who came to function as local governors. They were "the institutional successors of the grandees of the Mamluk sultanate"[8] and were, in fact, predominantly Mamluks. In theory, the beys were responsible to the pasha, who was a kind of viceroy and ruled by decree (firman). The beys, however, were constantly trying to enhance their own power and limit that of the pashas. They had much success in this project, sometimes simply rejecting the pasha sent by the Istanbul government, the "Sublime Porte." We see the problems of the pashas when we consider that there were 110 pashas during the 281 years from Selim the Grim to Napoleon.

The rule of the closed corporation of the Mamluk beys, whose only legitimacy lay in their armed might, was only slightly modified by "religious leaders, judges and teachers who exercised spiritual and moral control over the other classes and were considered by them as their political leaders."[9] The Muslim "ulama [religious leaders] in particular acted throughout the eighteenth century as political middlemen between the Mamluk Beys and the Egyptian masses."[10]

The new element in the struggles for power were the "Janissaries," who were the infantry core of Ottoman military power. These men were forcibly converted to Christianity as slave (or captive) boys, well educated in languages and Islam, and trained in military tactics. They were considered, along with the mounted "sipahis," slaves of the Porte. Thus, in Egypt they acted as a counterweight to Mamluk power, though they could never match the Mamluks when they were united.

As for Christians, under the Ottoman "millet" system,[11] they, like other religious communities, were led by their principal religious official. Thus the Coptic patriarch held a wide range of powers over the Copts in managing church property and enforcing church law, e.g., laws respecting marriage and divorce, legitimacy of children, inheritance of property, church organization, and dispute settlement.

All Egyptians lived under the rule of foreigners, but different classes fared differently, and there were Copts in every class. The wealth of administrators (who were in a position to enrich themselves) and of merchants and landowners and tax farmers bought for these classes the security and influence they needed. Guilds of tradesmen could provide their members some protection as well as a system in which they could survive and even thrive. But the fellahin (farm workers), on whom the economic pyramid of Egypt rested, had neither power nor protection, other than the good will of the village headman or of a provincial "notable" (an influential person of property or family in a position to act as patron).

Fiscally, Egypt was dealt with as a tax farm,[12] and a whole class of tax farmers (called "multezim") was created. We are not surprised that Coptic Christians found their way prominently in the system. Although "they exercised the professions of architects, of masons, their preference was to be scribes or bureaucrats."[13] Coptic multezims also profited from the Janissaries' licensing them to manufacture and sell alcoholic beverages.[14]

A Coptic layman and an indefatigable visitor have left us with interesting observations on Coptic Church life late in the seventeenth century. Abu Dakn, known in the West as Josephus Abudacnus, described[15] Coptic economic, social, and religious life. He reported on the Copts' skills in the arts and crafts, their ability to get along with their rulers, their close and strict family life, and their asceticism. Concerning the worship, he described the Copts' canonical offices, hymnody and use of the Psalms, and the two to three hour Mass with its prominent use of incense, the Scripture readings, the prayers and litanies, the consecration of the bread and the wine, and the communion of the people.[16] It sounds remarkably like Coptic worship in the late twentieth century.

Father J. M. Wansleben (or Vansleb) spent 1672 and 1673 in Egypt, visiting numerous monasteries and churches. In 1677 he published in Paris a history of the Coptic Church,[17] in which some notes are of special interest: in Part I he states that the power of the patriarch did not include authority to change or introduce anything new, and that there were seventeen bishoprics; in Part II he mentions among many other things the modesty of Mary and child in Coptic iconography, the Copts' rejection of the notion of a purgatory after death, the limiting of musical accompaniment in worship to cymbals and the triangle, a list of liturgical books and the numerous and extended fasts, the priests' saying Mass by heart in Coptic, lessons being read in Coptic and then Arabic, Copts' not kneeling (which they see as a sign of humiliation or defeat), the consecrated bread and wine being always consumed at the service. (A Coptic historian has pointed out, however, that Patriarch John XVI "began the tradition—still followed today—of having the Holy Eucharist taken by the priest to the sick, the infirm, and the aged who were unable to attend the church services."[18])

Simultaneously with these publications, the Coptic patriarchs begin to reappear in the *History of the Patriarchs*, beginning with John XVI,[19] who served the forty-two years from 1676 to 1718. Interestingly, he was "in his youth a collector engaged in the reception of money,"[20] a typical Copt occupation, but one he had fled in disgust, going to Saint Anthony's monastery in the Eastern Desert. After becoming patriarch, John transferred the financial administration of the Cairo churches to the archons, who managed to keep the churches up and also to meet the needs of the poor. Indeed, there was a striking amount of rebuilding of churches and monasteries under John.

The 1692-93 famine drove many Copts from Upper Egypt into Cairo, where heroic efforts were made by the church leaders to assist them. An apt illustration of the leadership and the dedication of lay Copts throughout the period covered in this chapter was Muallim George,[21] a remarkable layman who lost his only son, and then proceeded to dedicate the rest of his life and his wealth to serving the clergy and the poor, rebuilding churches, organizing the bishops to provide the oil for Holy Chrism (called "myron") for the churches, and taking Pope John on pilgrimage to Jerusalem.

We are given[22] two more facts of John's time that tell us important things about the Copts of the era: in one, a governor intended measures against the Christians but "no harm happened by reason of the presence of the teachers, the archons, who were undertaking the service of the great of Egypt;" in the other, the patriarch celebrated the Divine Liturgy every day. Thus is seen in the one case how important well-placed lay leaders were in protecting the church, and in the other the intense piety that could be hoped for (if not always found) in a patriarch.

In 1711, "a schism ran through the whole complex of the ruling and military groups of Egypt,"[23] called "the Great Insurrection." It is described in John's biography in some detail, as well as another "sedition" of lesser consequence four years later. By now it was the beys who were dominant in Egypt, and this fact did not at all guarantee freedom from these "seditions" and changes in government.

It has been estimated that at the end of the seventeenth century there were 150,000 Coptic Christians.[24] If true, it would require an accelerating subsequent growth in the Coptic community. Accurate numbers are notoriously difficult to come up with for the Coptic population, but it has been also estimated that there were 200,000 in 1832, 600,000 in the early 1900s[25] and at least 3,000,000 by 1978.

One scholar specializing in this period has characterized the conditions of the Copts at the turn of the eighteenth century thus: intellectual life almost extinct, great ignorance among the clergy, but popular reverence for the patriarch. He cites statistics from visitors to Coptic monasteries that indicate that in the half-century after 1661 Saint Anthony's monastery declined from fifty monks to fifteen, Saint Macarius' from twenty to four, Amba Bishoi from twenty-five to four.[26]

Pope John had ordained to the priesthood the head monk of Saint Paul's monastery, who was to succeed him as Peter VI,[27] who served to 1726. He was brought to consecration in Cairo in fetters (by then an established convention). When the king of Ethiopia requested a metropolitan for the church there, Peter consecrated and sent along the former bishop of Jerusalem, an unusual action in the Coptic Church, which resisted transferring bishops from one jurisdiction to another. We are told little else about Peter's patriarchate, except about a prominent and generous lay leader, Muallim Lutf-Allah, who was able by paying large bribes to escape punishment for repairing a church, but was later murdered. This is a reminder of three important facts for the medieval Coptic Church: it was generally a crime to repair a church, there was always a Copt who could amass a fortune, but even rich Copts were extremely vulnerable.

Peter's successor, also from Saint Paul's monastery, was Coptic Pope John XVII,[28] who governed the church to 1745 and was said to have "merited being a priest." (Does this mean others did not merit priesthood or was John being damned with faint praise?) The special tax on Christians (and on Jews) was increased, and not even the monks were exempted. Foreigners were sent by the Sublime Porte to collect these taxes. As if this were not enough, there was a severe famine in 1739-40 and an important insurrection two years later. Some poor Christians were sold into slavery for non-payment of the tax, but were then redeemed by wealthy lay leaders in the church.

John's biography in the *History of the Patriarchs* does not mention an interesting correspondence he had in 1735-38 with Roman Pope Clement XII and a profession of faith John made during that time.[29] In this correspondence, the flattering adjectives John applies to Clement are standard for that kind of correspondence in Egypt and do not hide the fact that John sees Clement as his "brother," not his superior. At first John had been "hostile to Catholicism," but in September of 1736 the Catholic Custodian of the Holy Land not only received John's profession of faith but "absolved" him and reconciled him with the "Holy Catholic Church." The confession is striking in three ways: in accepting against the almost unanimous tradition of Eastern Christianity that the Holy Spirit proceeds from the Son as well as from the Father, in focusing on the oneness of Jesus Christ without using the controversial word "nature," and in professing the "holy verities" of the "holy councils" without specifying which councils—thus bypassing the controversial issue of the Council of Chalcedon which the Copts rejected. As it turned out, Rome's Propaganda office rejected the profession and by 1740 relations between the churches had completely soured and were broken off.

In 1739, Shaykh Damanhuri wrote a book[30] in which he argued that the strictest adherence should be made to the rules limiting Christian worship and the buildings in which it took place. It is clear that the noted Islamic jurist could see no real justification for the persistence of Egyptian Christians in resisting the truth of Islam; and therefore discriminations of all kinds against Christians were necessary to safeguard the honor of Islam. Thus another learned Muslim was giving an intellectual and spiritual justification for discriminating against Christians.

In 1741, Athanasius, the former Coptic archbishop of Jerusalem, now converted to Roman Catholicism, was appointed by the Roman Pope to head up the Roman Catholic faithful in Egypt, although he could not actually reside there.[31] The Coptic Church must have seemed moribund to those who wanted to bring Copts into their own ranks and to some Copts who questioned the future and even the validity of their own church.

Coptic Pope John XVII was succeeded by Mark VII,[32] until 1769. Like his predecessor he was from Saint Paul's monastery and "merited to be a priest." A 1748 insurrection is recounted in some detail in his biography, with even more detail on Mark's obsequies. He was subjected to certain "intimidations," some of which came from his own circle, perhaps too embarrassing to be specified in the *History of the Patriarchs*. In his day there were only ten dioceses in the Coptic Church in Egypt, according to a 1747 report[33] to the Propaganda office of the Catholic Church in Rome.

Even before Pope Mark's death, the notorious Ali Bey had begun his rise to dominance over the government of Egypt, via the usual route of violence and treachery. By late 1768, he had deposed the viceroy and made himself acting viceroy, as well as being already "shaykh al-balad," the most powerful position a Mamluk could hold. When another viceroy was sent the following summer, he was also deposed by Ali, and the following year Ali's intervention in the control of the most holy Islamic centers, in the Hejaz, resulted in his effective control of that region also.

Ali Bey was virtually sovereign until his defeat and death in 1773.[34] He favored the Copts as administrators, which was hardly unusual, and he appointed his favorite scribe, the "famous Copt Muallem Rizq controller of revenues and finances."[35] In addition to his administrative skills, Muallim Rizq seems to have been successful in astrology "and exercised by it a great influence on the bey."[36]

Coptic Pope John XVIII,[37] 1769-1796, served almost to the time of Napoleon's invasion. We know little about his activities, but the constant struggles among the Mamluk beys were bearing down hard on the Coptic Christians, for they were subjected to extra taxes needed to finance the hostilities from every side. Then when Hasan Pasha was sent by the Ottoman government to reassert its authority in Egypt against the apparently triumphant Ibrahim Bey and Murad Bey, things became even worse for the Christians, who were subjected to a wide variety of confiscations and humiliations. The 1791 plague killed many, including the Sublime Porte's designated representative. When the Mamluk leaders, Ibrahim and Murad, subsequently regained power in 1791, things got no better for the Christians, or the rest of the population for that matter, so that the French intervention would have hardly appeared to be a terrible tragedy for Egypt.

One visitor to Egypt in the 1780s, M. C.-F. Volney, wrote of the Copts of that day:

> both history and tradition attest their descent from the people who were conquered by the Arabs, that is, from the mixture of Egyptians, Persians, and above all, Greeks, who, under the Ptolemies and the Constantines, were so long in possession of Egypt. . . . [A]s they have always been intimately acquainted with the interior of the country, they are become the depositories of the registers of the lands and tribes. Under the name of writers [scribes], they are at Cairo the intendants, secretaries, and collectors of government. These writers, despised by the Turks, whom they serve, and hated by the peasants, whom they oppress, form a kind of separate class, the head of which is the writer to the principal chief. He disposes of all the employments in that department, which according to the spirit of the Turkish government, he bestows on the best bidder.[38]

The expertise of many Copts was legend and helped them to high position. A French consul wrote of Ibrahim Bey and Murad Bey that "they act only in appearance, and the one and the other depend on Muallem Ibrahim Giaoury [i.e., Gawhari, a Copt], who is their chief scribe and, one may add, even their prime minister."[39]

Why were Copts often hated? A French general wrote of one, an intendant who "insolently dominated the fellahin, when in his [master's] absence no one can guarantee them from his tyranny;" and a French interpreter speaks of enormous fortunes Copts accumulated, so that, for example, "some of this class are served in their harem by sixty or eighty slaves, white, Abyssinian or Negro. Valets, scattered around the outer apartments, were even more numerous."[40] Lording it over farm workers was certainly designed to provoke hatred, especially if religious prejudice was already at work. And resentment of riches had much of the same effect, especially in light of the desperate conditions, which took Volney four pages to describe,[41] under which the great majority of Egyptians lived.

A final note about the Coptic Christians of this era could be taken from another visitor, in 1778, an Italian nobleman, probably acting as a French spy. He hated most Copts, especially the monks (whose manuscripts he loved to steal), but he observed of the Copts that they were "numerous, as they constitute the true Egyptian race, and powerful, as they enjoy the confidence of the great, whose affairs they superintend."[42]

As he wrestled with the question of what it meant to be an Egyptian, one historian of modern Egypt has argued[43] that "by the time Napoleon arrived [the Egyptians] had ceased to be a nation . . . but they never lost their consciousness of 'separateness' from all other and of self-identification." He theorizes that this consciousness of being Egyptian came from a sense of being victims (even victims of the native Copts who collected the taxes and acted as money-lenders). If it is true that in 1798 being an Egyptian was thought of as being a victim, a lot of history would have to take place before Egyptians could assume control of their own government and destiny. In fact, much of that history was to begin in the nineteenth century when education and military service convinced many Egyptians that they did not need foreigners to rule them.

Egyptians may have wondered in the late eighteenth century if even nature as well as history had turned against them. Plagues and pestilence, famine from low Niles some years and devastation by floods in others, went hand in hand with high cost of living[44] and maladministration to make life miserable for most Egyptians.

Since 451, Coptic Christians had been ruled by a series of foreign governments, under severe disabilities, sometimes actively persecuted. They survived by intense loyalty to their faith and community and by making their services so valuable that the economy and government could scarcely function without them. The most successful supported their spiritual hierarchy, managed the affairs of their church, and saw that their poor sisters and brothers survived. "Both charitable and showy, they helped their indigent fellow Christians; in the court of the residences of the rich Copts the poor Copts gathered twice a day for a food ration."[45] The late eighteenth century was a bad time for Egyptians in general and Copts in particular, but the nearby "modern world" was too dynamic and too expansionist to leave so strategic an area as Egypt to stagnate in isolation. When Napoleon led a remarkable expedition of soldiers and scholars and artists into Egypt in 1798, he certainly had ambitious plans, but could he have possibly known how his invasion would help bring in a nineteenth century of such great consequence for Egypt and the Copts? That century is the subject of our next chapter.

[1]H. Dehérain, *L'Égypte turque: Pachas et mameluks du XVIème au XVIIIème siècle: L'Expédition du général Bonaparte*, Vol. 5 of *Histoire d'Égypte* ed. G. Hanotaux (Paris: Librairie Plon, 1931), p. 2.

[2]Dehérain, p. 3.

[3]S. Shaw, *Empire of the Gazis: The Rise and Decline of the Ottoman Empire, 1280-1808*, Vol. 1 of *History of the Ottoman Empire and Modern Turkey* (Cambridge: Cambridge Univ. Press, 1976), pp. 85-86.

[4]Shaw, p. 87.

[5]P. M. Holt, *Egypt and the Fertile Crescent 1516-1922* (Ithaca, New York: Cornell Univ. Press, 1966), p. 52.

[6]*History of the Patriarchs of the Egyptian Church: Known as the History of the Holy Church by Sawirus ibn Mukaffa (HPEC)* Vol. 3 ed. and trans. A. Khater and O. H. E. KHS-Burmester (Cairo: Société d'archéologie copte, 1970), p. 274.

[7]*HPEC* 3, 275-277.

[8]Holt, p. 73.

[9]P. J. Vatikiotis, *The History of Egypt*, 3rd ed. (Baltimore: Johns Hopkins Univ. Press, 1985), p. 36.

[10]Vatikiotis, p. 35.

[11]For a description of the millet system in Egypt, see B. L. Carter, *The Copts in Egyptian Politics* (London: Croom Helm, 1986), p. 3.

[12]Shaw, p. 122.

[13]Dehérain, p. 80.

[14]S. Shaw, *The Financial and Administrative Organization and Development of Ottoman Egypt 1517-1798* (Princeton: Princeton Univ. Press, 1962), p. 140.

[15]The 1675 Latin is in the Bodleian Library; an English translation of it was published by E. Sadleir, *The History of the Copts commonly called Jacobites under the Dominion of the Turk and Abyssinian Emperors with some geographical Notes or Descriptions of the several Places in which they live in those Dominions,* 2nd ed. (London: R. Baldwin, 1693.)

[16]I was able to read this book in the British Library in 1982, but I am also dependent here on the summary in I. Habib el-Masri, *The Story of the Copts* (Cairo: Middle East Council of Churches, 1978), pp. 470-471.

[17]*Histoire de l'Église d'Alexandrie fondée par S. Marc que nous appelons celle des Jacobites-Coptes d'Égypte, écrite au Caire même en 1672 et 1673* (Paris: Veuve Clousier et Pierre Prome).

[18]Habib el-Masri, pp. 476-477.

[19]*HPEC* 3, 277-285.

[20]*HPEC* 3, 278, correcting the translators' "perception" to "reception."

[21]*HPEC* 3, 281-284.

[22]*HPEC* 3, 282.

[23]Holt, p. 88.

[24]This figure is from J.-P. Trossen, *Les Relations du patriarche copte Jean XVI avec Rome (1676-1718)* (Luxembourg: Imprimerie Hermann, 1948), p. 5, based on notices in

Anba Isidorus' *Book of the Precious Pearl.*

[25]The first figure is reported in S. Lieder, *Church Missionary Review,* 3 (1832), 105; the second from D. M. Thornton, *The Church Missionary Intelligencer,* 57 (1906), 689. These reports were written for the Church Missionary Society in these publications of the Society by veteran workers in Egypt.

[26]Trossen, p. 9; the visitors were Fr. Marc de Lucques and Fr. C. Sicard.

[27]*HPEC* 3, 285-289.

[28]*HPEC* 3, 289-292. The quotation is from p. 290.

[29]J. M. Détré, "Contribution à l'étude des relations du patriarche Jean XVII avec Rome de 1735 à 1738," *Studia Orientalia Christiana collecteana* No. 5, (1960), 123-169; the profession is given in Arabic, with an English translation, pp. 162-168. The background is covered in pp. 135-147.

[30]A recent English translation is found in *Shaykh Damanhuri on the Churches of Egypt (1739)* ed. and trans. M. Perlmann (Berkeley: Univ. of California Press, 1975).

[31]See O. F. A. Meinardus, *Christian Egypt: Ancient and Modern* (Cahiers d'histoire égyptienne: Cairo, 1965), p. 405.

[32]*HPEC* 3, 292-295.

[33]Trossen, p. 9.

[34]Holt, pp. 92-98, explains the "shaykh al-balad" and recounts Ali Bey's history.

[35]Vatikiotis, p. 32.

[36]Dehérain, p. 81.

[37]*HPEC* 3, 295-298.

[38]M. C.-F. Volney, *Travels through Syria and Egypt in the Years 1783, 1784, and 1785,* 2 vols. (London: G. G. J. and J. Robinson, 1787), 1, 78-79. I have not seen a French original for this work.

[39]Quoted in Dehérain, p. 81.

[40]Dehérain, p. 81.

[41]Volney, 1, 187-190.

[42]C. N. Sonnini de Manoncourt, *Travels in Upper and Lower Egypt,* trans. Henry Hunter (London: J. Stockdale, 1807), p. 632; his descriptions of the monasteries are found, e.g., on pp. 340-370.

[43]T. Little, *Modern Egypt* (London: Ernest Benn, 1958), pp. 27-28.

[44]Vatikiotis cites the Egyptian historian of eighteenth century Egypt, al-Jabarti, and the Frenchman Savary's *Letters on Egypt,* English version in two volumes (London: 1786), as major sources of such information, pp. 33-38.

[45]Dehérain, p. 81.

Chapter Nine

The Nineteenth Century

✠ ———————————————————————————————— ✠

1798 to 1882

B Y 1798, THE COPTIC CHRISTIANS of Egypt had been a minority in their own country much longer than they had been a majority. After all, Egypt's long "Middle Ages" were for the Copts more than five centuries of being progressively marginalized by a religion and a language they still considered foreign to Egypt. It is estimated that in 1798 there were hardly more than 150,000 Copts in a population of about two and a half million. Islamic law and tradition called for protection of Jewish and Christian minorities. Nevertheless, their daily bread was discrimination and humiliation for being too stubborn to accept Islam.

And yet Copts were not powerless. They had continued to make themselves useful in administration, especially in financial administration, in government and for private interests as well. Rulers often favored Christian officials because they would never be in a position to challenge their rule, whereas Muslims might do so, and in fact often did. The factors that made it possible for Copts to survive, however, did not in any way keep them from being harassed, despised, exploited, vulnerable. Modern secular thinking can only marvel at the doggedness of Egyptian Christians who insisted on staying Christian. Although Muslims generally suspected converts to Islam of being insincere and self-serving, still one could move from the inferior minority to the ruling majority by simply converting to Islam, an honored religion, which had been the cultural base of a brilliant civilization and of governments that were still considered dynamic political and military forces in world affairs as late as 1798.

The Copts' fortunes were not to change completely during the nineteenth century, but even before its end, as we shall see, Copts had become far more than a weak and disappearing minority. In fact, it is hard to over-estimate the importance of the nineteenth century for the Coptic Orthodox Church in Egypt.

What we call the "nineteenth century" begins with the French invasion of 1798 and ends with the British invasion of 1882. The French invasion was frustrated militarily by Lord Nelson and Britain's Royal Navy and by Egyptian opposition, so the French appeared to fail, for their forces lasted only three years in Egypt. But the French intervention and subsequent influence in Egypt wrenched the depleted forces of both the Egyptian nation and the Coptic Church into contact with the most powerful dynamics of the modern world, whether economic, technological, cultural, or political. The results were amazing.

One result was a Coptic Renaissance which seemed to reach its peak just beyond mid-century during the brief career of the charismatic patriarch Cyril IV; but reform forces released in his time proved to have irrepressibly revolutionary consequences, even after they came to be opposed by the most powerful and respected elements of the Coptic hierarchy. Indeed, the 1800s ended while the intense conflict was still going on in the Coptic Church over who was best qualified to conduct the affairs of the awakened church: an apparently immortal and immovable patriarch, or an educated and devout lay leadership uncowed by reverence for the man and his office. The lively struggle did not by any means lead to stagnation in the church.

We will bring to an end our consideration of the nineteenth century with the economic and political collapse of Egypt that provoked the British invasion, which in contrast to the French invasion, was to result in a British military and political occupation which lasted for decades. The Occupation was for Egypt both a humiliation and a handicap to its political, social, and economic development; but it marked a change in Egypt's history so definite that it is clearly the place to end the "century" in Egypt.

Ending the nineteenth century in a history of the Coptic Church is not as simple as it is for a general history of Egypt, for the important fifty-three year patriarchate of Cyril V is divided almost equally between the nineteenth and the twentieth centuries. Thus, we shall be following the division marked by national events for Egypt rather than any really new internal church developments—although, in fact, the coming of the British was to have significant effects on religion in Egypt, not least upon the Coptic Church, as we shall see in our next chapter.

In considering conditions in Egypt when the French invaded in 1798,[1] we find that it was still ruled by foreigners, largely Turks and Circassians, who displayed no interest in Egypt other than exploiting its wealth and strategic location. The Ottoman Empire, of which Egypt was a part, exercised little authority in Egypt and was largely satisfied by whatever tribute the

Sublime Porte could get from the Mamluk beys who were the real rulers of Egypt. What central government there was was dominated by two of the beys, Ibrahim and Murad, who fought each other except on those occasions when it served both of their interests to cooperate.

The political chaos and the social and political stagnation of late eighteenth century Egypt made it a ripe target for expansionist powers in Western Europe, especially France and Britain, which were in commercial and strategic competition in the Eastern Mediterranean as well as on almost every continent of the world. Napoleon turned out to have the most pressing interest in expanding a French empire into the Eastern Mediterranean. It may have been that Napoleon's "real purpose was to use Egypt as a battlefield from which he might rebound to an empire of the West, or failing that, as a base on which to build an empire of the East."[2] At any rate, in 1798, after careful planning for a wide range of activities in Egypt, he and his troops invaded.

Along with his 40,000 veteran troops, Napoleon brought an impressive team of one hundred and twenty-two experts and Egyptologists. Earlier, the extraordinary number of eighteenth-century European visitors to Egypt, many of whom seemed to be reporting to France, had shown the way for those who might want to make a systematic study of the country, its culture and its resources—and how it might be governed. Napoleon's experts launched this kind of investigation and their studies were to have a significant influence. Still in the late twentieth century, this influence is strong on Egyptian culture and technique and on the way historical Egypt is perceived by historians and their readers.

Napoleon's invasion not only discredited the Mamluk Beys; it also essentially severed Egypt from the Ottoman Empire. Furthermore, it "introduced educated Egyptians to the ideas of the French Revolution" which "generated a gnawing and uncomfortable feeling among them that the *umma* (the Islamic community) of Egypt at least was not as perfect or as strong as they had imagined. Such uncertainty was the basis of new ideas and conceptions."[3] These factors showed how Egypt was in for substantial changes, for they eroded the basic assumptions Egyptians had held about government.

The Copts should have had few if any hopes about the coming of the French. Article 4 of the order of the day of the 10th of Vendôme of year X (according to the revolutionary calendar) organizing the administration of Egypt stated: "The Copts are only a minority in Egypt, hated by the Muslims; and they apply themselves to earning that hatred. They are owed justice and liberty, but it would be impolitic and dangerous to choose them as allies and grant them any privileges."[4]

In most ways the "justice and liberty" owed to the Copts were over-looked as much by the French as by Egypt's earlier rulers during the pre-ceding thousand years. Of course, the French deemed it politic to choose the Muslims of Egypt as allies and to grant them privileges. Napoleon and his officials "represented themselves as being the liberators of Egypt from the alien rule of Circassian Mamelukes and of Turkish Pashas"[5] and rather hypocritically claimed to be Muslims, although General Menou and a few other French officers did, in fact, convert.

The *History of the Patriarchs* tells a sad story of the Copts' experience of the French invasion.[6] Life had been already bitter enough. Then, in spite of the governor's efforts to protect them, when the invasion came, the Cairo rabble rioted against the Copts—presumably because the French were Christians and the Copts might be expected to defect to them.

Copts did hope that the French victory over the Mamluks would improve their situation; but the sheikhs of the al-Azhar mosque rallied the people against the Christians of Cairo, and the Mamluks who escaped to Upper Egypt pillaged the Christians there. When General Menou took command of the French forces after the assassination of General Kléber (whom Napoleon had left in charge), the Coptic officials were dismissed from the government diwans (administrative councils.)

The French occupation was short-lived. The British wanted no French army threatening their route to India. Their naval victory in the Battle of the Nile was decisive. The Ottoman Turks wanted their Egyptian province back, and the British aided the Mamluk beys in the effort to push the French out. Napoleon had already left Egypt in August of 1799. It was General Menou who surrendered, "and the last French soldier left Egypt at the end of September, 1801. With this, the sultan of Turkey reasserted his sovereignty over Egypt, and a chaotic Egypt it was. From this chaos arose the modern Egypt under Muhammad Ali."[7]

Before passing to the crucially important rule of Muhammad Ali, we shall consider a trio of rich and powerful Copts who illustrate some impor-tant things about the role of Coptic laymen in the early part of the nineteenth century. In the *History of the Patriarchs*,[8] the biography of Mark VIII, who served from 1796 to 1809, tells us little about him (other than his poor health) but much about two laymen who were brothers.

In the days of Ibrahim Bey and Murad Bey, the Copt Ibrahim Gawhari had risen to become chief scribe for all Egypt, virtually a prime minister. A very wealthy man, he was famous for his openhandedness to the poor. When his only son died, "he overcame his grief by intensifying his ser-vices to the Church to which he donated most of his wealth,"[9] for example, in making valuable property available for a cathedral and a patriarchal resi-dence, in making repairs on many ecclesiastical buildings, and in having old manuscripts copied. Ibrahim Gawhari died on the eve of the French invasion and his brother Girgis followed in his footsteps in reaching the top in public administration and in lending powerful support to church activities, completing some of the projects his brother had initiated,[10] above all in getting Saint Mark's Cathedral and the Patriarchate established in the Ezbekiah, near central Cairo in a fine residential area.

Girgis Gawhari was the consummate government minister,[11] serving in the highest government finance positions under Ibrahim Bey and Murad Bey and then under the French rulers (whom he seemed to favor most of all, provisioning their army, organizing nationwide intelligence, and raising loans from rich Copts); he regained his finance position under the restored Ottoman administration. Even Muhammad Ali kept him on but did finally turn against Girgis, who spent four years in exile in Upper Egypt with his Mamluk friends before returning to Cairo to die.

Even more interesting was Muallim Yaqub Hanna.[12] Before the French invasion he had become a force in Upper Egypt as a strongman, well versed in the methods of fighting and administration used by the Mamluks, with whom he closely collaborated. He concluded, however, that Ottoman Turk and Mamluk bey alike were bad for Egypt, so he threw in his lot with the French, to whom he was able to render a great deal of help in Upper Egypt.

Yaqub got permission from General Kléber to form a Coptic Legion and was commissioned colonel to lead it. Not long after, the French withdrew from Egypt. Yaqub left too, with an English captain through whom he tried to send a message to the British government urging them to support independence for Egypt. It seems that the dying Yaqub still hoped the European Powers would help free Egypt of the foreign rule fastened on her by Mamluks or Ottomans.

Turning back to the governing of Egypt, we find that the departure of the French was followed by considerable infighting among groups like the Mamluk beys, the Ottoman imperial officials, Egyptian religious leaders, notables who under the French had gotten a taste of sharing in governmental consultations, and generals like Muhammad Ali. This last, an Albanian adventurer, was able through the traditional tactics of shifting alliances, treachery, and sheer brutality to gain control of Egypt by 1805. The French and the British did not, however, cease their meddling in Egyptian affairs, as each continued its goals in Egypt.

The triumph of Muhammad Ali was a fateful development in Egyptian history, and historians tend to agree that he was "the founder of modern Egypt."[13] Once settled in, he "proceeded to impose a New Order in Egypt in the first three decades of the nineteenth century. The New Order became the basic framework for that country's drive towards modernity for the next one hundred years."[14]

Modernization of Egypt was to be achieved through improvements in administration, agricultural reform, industrialization, education, establishing a truly Egyptian army, and providing Egypt for the first time in many years with an environment of law and order in the country. French officers and experts made signal contributions to the whole process. It has been observed that "Muhammad Ali's schemes of reorganization by French officers and technicians . . . began that gallicization of Egyptian culture and institutions which continued . . . [and] has left an enduring mark."[15]

The human cost of consolidating power for enforcing "law and order" was high: the Muslim religious leaders, i.e., the *ulama,* were cowed by 1809, and in 1811 Muhammad Ali invited four hundred Mamluks to a banquet and proceeded to massacre them, the major step in the destruction of Mamluk power. By the time he had neutralized the power of his own Albanian troops, the potential for challenging centralized government in Egypt was sharply curtailed.

In agriculture, Muhammad Ali improved production, largely through land reform, and made the highly profitable cotton a major crop. Muhammad Ali was able to concentrate much land under the control of his family, and tax-farming was effectively ended. The subsequent opening of opportunity for private investment was to have a greater socio-economic effect. The fellahin were still exploited; but investors, including Copts, were able to build strong positions for themselves through the new patterns of land ownership.

The French technocrats who had come with Napoleon had developed ambitious plans for industrialization in Egypt, many of which served as blueprints for Muhammad Ali's model projects; and the suppression of the guilds aided in modernizing the industry.[16] The problem remained, however, that the European Powers, which were well ahead in industrialization, wanted only raw materials from Egypt—and no competition from Egyptian manufactures. This factor, rather than poor planning, was to be the principal cause of the ultimate failure of Egypt's grand plans for industrialization in the nineteenth century.[17]

Equally ambitious were Muhammad Ali's educational efforts, here again drawing heavily on French expertise and leadership. He realized that "modernization" called for a practical and widespread system of education if reform in government, industry, and even commerce and agriculture were to take root and bear fruit. His preference for a state system of education over the "traditional [Muslim] institutions,"[18] however, created a cultural chasm that has been a problem for Egyptian Islam ever since. Should a conscientious Muslim parent send his child to a school devoted to Islamic tradition or to a school trying to prepare pupils to compete successfully in a modernizing society?

As for the army, it has been argued[19] that Muhammad Ali's Egyptian army was the major force in creating Egyptian nationalism, although he was not himself a nationalist.[20] After all, he was a foreigner too, and he had many foreign advisers. But he knew the dangers of the Mamluk system and saw the threat to his own rule of depending on his Albanian troops. Albanian and Mamluk alike were foreign mercenaries easily tempted to change sides to a paymaster who could offer them more than they were getting. After failing in his effort to develop a satisfactory army of Sudanese, Muhammad Ali decided to try recruiting the Egyptian fellah. This decision made possible an authentically Egyptian force. "When finally six smart regiments of Egyptian regulars . . . marched one day into Cairo, the Albanian chiefs saw their day was ended, and abandoned Egypt for pastures new."[21] After all, General Yaqub and his Coptic Legion had demonstrated that Egyptians could indeed fight.

The career of Coptic patriarch Peter VII, 1809-1852, closely coincided with Muhammad Ali's rule, 1805-1848. According to a Coptic writer, "A cordial relationship developed between the two personalities which made it possible for the patriarch to carry out many of his constructive projects."[22] The *History of the Patriarchs* records[23] events that might explain why. First there was a healing by a Coptic bishop of a daughter of the Pasha, for which the bishop only requested "Your Excellency to extend your good-will towards the sons of the Coptic people, and to employ its sons who have been dismissed." Second, the patriarch's prayers may have been considered the crucial element in getting the Nile to rise.

Peter had been a monk at Saint Anthony's monastery, was almost consecrated metropolitan for Ethiopia, but then was consecrated "general metropolitan for the Preaching of Mark," i.e., the see of Alexandria, and raised to the patriarchal office three days after his predecessor, Mark VIII, died. When "Muhammad Ali Pasha conquered the Sudan, and many of its inhabitants returned to the Christian religion . . . [Peter] consecrated for them two bishops in succession."[24]

Roman Catholics were able to maintain their efforts in Egypt, but bringing the Coptic Church in line with Rome was as remote a possibility as ever. Under the influence of a group of French advisers to his government, "Muhammad Ali Pasha endeavored to unite the Church of Egypt with the Church of Rome."[25] He even went so far as to command his head of finances, Muallim Ghali and his son, both Copts, to convert. They and a small group "went over to the papalists, in appearance," but planned to return to the Coptic Orthodox at an opportune time. Actually, Muallim Ghali was assassinated on order of the Pasha, who may have resented Ghali's candor in reporting the true condition of Egypt's finances.[26]

One window through which some features of the Coptic Christians can be seen is the records of the relatively young Church Missionary Society of the Church of England. It began to take an interest in the Middle East in general and Egypt in particular in the second decade of the nineteenth century, the two clearly specified objectives being to "revive the Eastern Churches . . . and evangelize the Mohammedans."[27] Detailed reports to the Society contain much interesting information about the conditions of the Copts and their institutions. Like their imperialist contemporaries, the missionaries portrayed what they found as uniformly dismal, perhaps at least subconsciously justifying their presence and their projects and also proving the desperate need for their backers to support their work. But a careful reading can be instructive. Generally the Anglican missionaries and visitors pictured the Copts as poor (except for a few rich laymen), sometimes numerous, generally ignorant and superstitious.[28]

The Reverend William Jowett was the first Anglican to make an official visit to Egypt. His mission to the Eastern Mediterranean was stated to be to influence the Eastern patriarchs, communicate "our systems of education," and help establish Bible Societies.[29] The Coptic Pope refused Jowett a list of convents and churches but did give him a letter of introduction. Patriarch Peter also stated that he himself should carry out the work of the Bible Society, for, reported Jowett, he was "jealous of foreign influence." Later reports, in 1831 and 1839, indicate that the patriarch took a positive attitude toward the efforts of the two Swiss ministers from Basel who were sent out by the Church Missionary Society to distribute Christian literature and begin Anglican work in Egypt.[30]

The missionaries reported that, unlike the Greeks and the Catholics, the Copts were encouraged by their clergy to secure and read the Bible. One recounted a cordial reception he had from the Patriarch and other bishops.[31] The same missionary had earlier filed the following descriptions[32] by no means untypical of the missionaries' evaluations of what they found: in February of 1828 in Beni Suef "I entered a miserable schoolroom; in which, in our country, we should scarcely place an ass. I found in it a poor, blind, decrepit *areef* (schoolmaster) sitting on the floor, in the midst of about twenty-five children: besides the *areef* there is a *shammas* (deacon), a boy of about ten years, who teaches the children to read."

The missionaries' first effort in education was to start in 1833 a "seminary" to train schoolmasters. In an early 1840 letter a plan is set forth for an Institution for the Education of Coptic Priests.[33] The patriarch sanctioned the plan, which made him Patron of the Institution and designated a committee of one bishop, six priests and six well-informed laymen, all Coptic Orthodox, to oversee the institution. Two deacons from each of the twelve Coptic churches in and around Cairo would be the students, and they would study the Bible, the Coptic and Arabic languages, general literature, and church history. In 1842 the "Coptic Institution" opened. Three years later three of their graduates were ordained by the Coptic patriarch, but after another three years the Institution was closed, they reported, "for 'only the scum of the Church' were sent to it."[34] The Coptic theological students were suspect, and were also tempted by their education to go into government service. Perhaps Pope Peter never lost his suspicions of the Anglican missionaries or had heard about the quite negative reports they had been sending their readers back home about the Copts.

In fact, Peter developed the reputation of being anti-missionary. In his day he turned back two efforts of the Russian Orthodox to get the Coptic Church to accept their protection: in 1845 a Russian archimandrite went to Jerusalem to "realize the union between the Orthodox Church and the Jacobite Copts;"[35] he failed. On another occasion[36] the Russian ambassador to Egypt visited the patriarch himself and offered the Tsar's protection; Peter thanked him but said that no other protection was needed than God's. When Muhammad Ali heard of this, his esteem for Peter increased.

In turning to Egypt's general history before mid-century, we must mention Muhammad Ali's expansionist efforts in the Middle East, although they do not seem to have affected the Copts very much. Not only did he conquer the Sudan and succeed in the traditional desire of the rulers of Egypt to annex Syria and Palestine and the Hejaz to their empire. He even aspired to replace the Ottoman Empire as the dominant power in the Middle East and essentially did so. The Ottoman forces could not resist the Egyptian armies; but by 1839, the "Powers," i.e., Britain and France, whose goal was to preserve the status quo in the Eastern Mediterranean, indicated that they would tolerate no further expansion of Muhammad's dominance and no more humiliation of the Ottoman Empire. Though frustrated in his goals of domination, Muhammad Ali remained a major factor in the region.

Indeed, most of Muhammad's grand plans fell short of realization, but we can summarize his special importance in Egypt's history with these words of a recent specialist:[37] "Thus Muhammad Ali and his new administration inevitably put Egypt on the path of independent statehood and self-recognition as having a separate identity from other Muslims and Ottomans; . . . without his efforts it might have taken Egyptians much longer to be able to call Egypt their own."

It has been said of Muhammad Ali that he "detested the Arabs as a race as much as he despised the Copts for their religion" but under his 1826 constitution in fact "the working officials were, as before, the harmless, necessary Copts."[38] William Jowett made the point early in the century that " the despised race of Copts has been found, at all times, too useful to be extinguished."[39] And in 1838 the two Church Missionary Society missionaries wrote flatteringly of Muhammad Ali's achievements, and they reported that Christians were now getting along better.[40] Still, it was the Armenians whom Muhammad Ali favored, not the Copts.[41]

Egypt as a nation emerged[42] from lethargy with Muhammad Ali; the "awakening" of the Coptic Church came somewhat later. Coptic notables were able to get hold of land when private property became available. Thus the Copts were able to preserve solid links with their rural and provincial origins. Nevertheless, they suffered severe handicaps in their broader relation to the nation still in 1850: they were cut off from the memory of their own past by the lack of Christian literature in Arabic; they were overwhelmingly rural and outside the orbit of Cairo and Alexandria; many villages had no church; only the clergy knew the liturgy; monasticism was almost extinct; their culture was scarcely more than popular piety. It was largely their sense of being different that saved the Copts as a group from the various pressures of the majority. They had no links with a universal church nor with their country, and they had no access to sources of real power or of high culture.

Copts were able, however, to take advantage of the new educational opportunities and turn this to their advantage.[43] Traditionally, their education had been in the village school like the one described above, the *kuttab*, where they were taught "religion, good manners, to read and write Arabic and Coptic," also geometry and arithmetic, and Peter's and Paul's Epistles by heart. All boys were supposed to attend and girls if their mothers wanted them to. The boys were preparing to be land-surveyors, land agents, accountants, clerks, and tax-collectors. After the *kuttab* they went to learn from their fathers and uncles. When Muhammad Ali opened civil schools, they were probably open to all. We have already mentioned Anglican efforts, especially in the preparation of schoolmasters. The chance to buy property and become active in industry and commerce was of at least equal importance to Copts. Education and wealth, combined with religious loyalty, were destined to produce a powerful Coptic laity who were to have a tremendous impact on their church.

If it was Muhammad Ali who did the most to wrestle Egypt into the modern world, it was probably Coptic Pope Cyril IV, 1854-1861, who tried to do the same for the Coptic Church: a reform that would be the turning point in the history of modern Egyptian Christianity. David (his name) entered Saint Anthony's monastery in 1838 at the age of twenty-two. Only two years later he was made head of the monastery and soon after began at Bush, where the monastery had property, a school for children and educational activities for monks.

David was sent by Pope Peter on a mission to Ethiopia[44] which lasted sixteen months, during which time the patriarch died, in 1852. David was a favorite to succeed Peter, but there was serious conservative opposition, probably for his youth and also for his advanced ideas about what direction the church should be taking. An agreement was entered into to consecrate David as a general metropolitan bishop, as Peter had been consecrated before him. In this position David "continued a year and two months, and he displayed a good conduct which made him worthy to be a patriarch," so he was raised to that post as Cyril IV, in 1854.

Education continued to be one of Cyril's primary interests. He founded schools at the patriarchate and at Harat as-Sakkayin, with emphasis on language study, above all Coptic itself which had long been a dead language, but also Arabic and European languages as well. Schools for girls were also opened. The upper classes did not hesitate to send their children to the schools, which helped to prepare much of the lay leadership later in the century. As part of his educational efforts, Cyril bought a printing press from Austria and had it paraded from the railway station to the patriarchate with great ceremony.

Cyril was also concerned with the education of the clergy, meeting with them weekly and "conducting systematic readings and theological discussions for the education of his clergymen."[45] He may have been influenced in this by one of the Church Missionary Society missionaries. Douglas Thornton observed that a Coptic notable "attributed to the patient work of Lieder the fact of the possibility of the present reform," and it seems that Cyril had attended Lieder's Bible class, along with some priests of Upper Egypt.[46]

Churches were repaired and the cathedral was replaced with a fine new building, but Cyril was an iconoclast, refusing to have the traditional icons in his new cathedral or other Cairo churches. He is reported to have said: "Behold, those wooden pictures you used to honor and even worship can neither avail nor harm, God alone should be adored."[47] Cyril "was also rigorous in requiring the priests to practice church discipline, and more especially in regard to traditional sacred music and vestments."[48] He reorganized the management of church property and instituted strict bookkeeping for records of births, marriages, and deaths as well as for church finances.

Khedive Said, Egypt's ruler since the beginning of Cyril's patriarchate, sent him, as patriarch of Ethiopia as well as Egypt, back to Ethiopia on a delicate but dangerous mission to frustrate British encroachments. It took him away for a year and a half, and his very success may have sealed his doom. Also, Cyril "was on friendly terms with all the denominations,"[49] and this was especially true of the Orthodox. Cyril may thus have seemed to the Khedive to be a potential rival for national leadership.[50] At any rate, the patriarch was called away from a meeting with the Greek and Armenian patriarchs by the Khedive, and Cyril died very shortly thereafter, in 1861. Copts have suspected government complicity in his death. O. F. A. Meinardus says with great tact: "His dynamic character and his efficient thoroughness soon attracted the attention of the authorities, who had him quietly removed."[51] Cyril was only forty-six years old. The reforms could not be stopped, but the Coptic Church had to wait almost another century to find another patriarch, Cyril VI, quite so progressive and dynamic.

Turning the clock back to the death of the now senile Muhammad Ali in 1848, we find that his oldest son, Ibrahim, had predeceased him by a few months and that their successor was a grandson, Abbas. Abbas tried to reverse his grandfather's modernizing efforts and was only tolerated for six years, during which he "swept away all the foreign advisers of Mohammed Aly and Ibrahim, closed the secular schools and eliminated French influence," and "gave the British the Cairo-Alexandria railway concession, which Mohammed Aly had resolutely opposed."[52]

Abbas was succeeded by his uncle Said, who in turn reversed the anti-European policy of Abbas but who equally disregarded Muhammad Ali's economic experiments. Said's Suez Canal concession was "impossibly generous to the concessionnaires" and cost Egypt more in transit trade than canal profits could earn.[53] It was only the worst of Said's policies, however, which began to build up the gigantic debt which was practically to stop Egypt's industrial development, deliver the small farmers into the hands of the money-lenders and foreign traders in raw materials, and eventually cost Egypt its independence. In the end, Said's modernizing efforts did more harm than Abbas' reactionary policies. Said's efforts resulted in the colonization of Egypt rather than the modernization he intended.

Said's rule from 1854 to 1863 closely paralleled the patriarchate of Cyril IV with whom, as we have seen, he had an ambiguous relationship. In 1855, Said gave Copts more equality by ordering their young men to do military service along with all other Egyptians, while also canceling the traditional discriminatory *jizya* tax on Christians and Jews. Ironically, the removal of the tax meant the loss by religious leaders of their "most important administrative functions, although they continued to administer to their people in such matters as inheritance, adoption, and marriage which relate to personal status."[54] Unfortunately for the Copts, Said's moves toward equality for them backfired, as conscription came to be used as a tool against them, e.g., every male in Asyut, a largely Christian city, was drafted. Cyril was able to intervene, with the aid of pressure "through influential Englishmen," and get Said to restore exemption for the Copts from military service.[55]

Said was succeeded in 1863 by his nephew Ismail, who continued Said's extravagant efforts to modernize and liberate Egypt. They were counterproductive for Egypt's independence, for the foreign debt became impossibly swollen by unjustified payments to finish the Suez Canal, by the ruinous interest rates charged by foreign investors, and by bribes to Constantinople to get the Sultan to recognize in 1873 Egypt's complete independence—an independence which was quite nullified by the debts assumed. Because of them Egypt "came under European financial control first, and direct British occupation later."[56]

Not long before Said died, Pope Demetrius II[57] succeeded Cyril IV as patriarch and held the post until 1870. He is said to have "followed in the trace of his predecessor, . . . completed the building of the [cathedral], [and] stimulated the schools and the elementary schools." He did not abandon reform in the Coptic Church, but he may well have been warned by Said not to assume too much active leadership.[58] Cyril's good relations with other Christians were not continued under Demetrius, perhaps partly for that reason. At any rate, Demetrius was troubled by American Presbyterian missionaries' success in attracting many Copts, especially in areas like Asyut and Minya which had large Coptic populations, who felt that their church was too backward. Presbyterian schools, like the Catholic schools, were well run, and many Copts were drawn into Protestant and Catholic congregations.

O. F. A. Meinardus, a German pastor for years in Cairo and an accomplished student of the Coptic Orthodox Church, has written: "Dissatisfied with the spiritual laxity and the political intrigues within the Coptic Church, many educated Copts joined the Protestant Mission Churches."[59] Salama Musa, a Coptic intellectual and man of letters of the twentieth century, after stating that "the Copts had inherited their ecclesiastical lore as it had become fossilized under the Byzantine Empire," went on to say that the Protestants had "stimulated a more genuinely Christian consciousness . . . [and without it] our Orthodox Church would not yet have risen from its medieval slumber."[60]

A young Englishwoman in poor health, Lady Lucie Duff Gordon, wrote a series of letters during Pope Demetrius' time with interesting, though seldom charitable, observations on her part. In the latter portion of her stay she criticized Pope Demetrius for his anger against the Protestants, his rudeness (lack of subservience?) to her, his money-collecting, his support from the Pasha. "The brute of a Patriarch is resolved to continue his persecution of the converts . . . They are backed by the government, and they know that the Europeans will always side with them."[61]

Depending on the intercession of foreign consulates put the Protestants more than once in an ambiguous situation: they welcomed the help but suffered from depending on foreign support.[62] Ismail, for example, was pressured by consuls of the United States and Britain to block interference with the work of the Protestant missionaries. But there was another side of the story: in the first graduating class of the Protestants' theological school in 1864 there were four Coptic priests![63]

Earlier, Lucie had written, "I can't describe the kindness of the Copts"—the high class Copts, it seems, for she found poor Copts dirty and unpleasant. She was quite pleased, though, that the Copts allowed their children to act freely in church instead of intimidating them into unnatural stillness, as Western Protestants did. Finally, she noted the dissatisfaction of young Coptic men with their priests and the old customs.

After the death of Pope Demetrius, in 1870, "on account of the tardiness of the government to issue the order to consecrate a patriarch for the denomination, the Throne remained vacant after him for four years."[64] This interim was the period when communal reform began in the Coptic Church.[65] The economic policies of the house of Muhammad Ali and the educational opportunities opened up by government and church had produced for the Copts by 1870 a significant number of powerful lay notables ready to challenge the conservative and generally poorly educated hierarchy for leadership in many aspects of church life. It must be remembered that Copts had never believed that clergy were more devout or more saintly or more church-centered than lay people.

The reforming Pope Cyril IV had been critical of bishops who were ignorant, avaricious, or "lowborn." He had found the priests more admirable but still ill-educated. Coptic laymen saw that the bishops and monks controlled the church *waqfs* (endowments for charitable purposes),[66] and questioned their competence for this kind of administration.

After Demetrius' death, Bishop Mark, metropolitan of Alexandria and the administrator of the Preaching of Mark, administered the affairs of the patriarchate until a new patriarch was consecrated.[67] Also, five lay members, two from Cyril's school, including the historian Yaqub Nakhla Rufila, founded a Reform Society to call for church assistance to the poor and the formation of a *majlis al-milli* (a religious council).[68]

"Bishop Mark selected some Coptic notables to help him in fulfilling his task and requested them to concern themselves especially with the financial affairs of the Church. The Coptic community, on finding that this system was effective, decided to obtain permission of the government to organize a maglis al-milli to assist the patriarch." Some lay persons were dissatisfied with the educational level of the clergy and the use the bishops and monks made of *waqf* income. Laymen felt that their education and experience fitted them better than the clergy for the job of managing the *waqf* income—and also to decide matters of family law. The government accepted the idea of such a council, under the chairmanship of the patriarch. Butrus Ghali Pasha, one of those educated at the patriarchal college, obtained the Khedival decree for the council, and the first was elected in 1874—in time to greet the newly elected patriarch, who could hardly be expected to be pleased by the encroachments on his traditional responsibilities.[69]

That patriarch, Cyril V[70] named Hanna, had been educated by an older brother and had loved solitude. He got away from his family to become a monk on a second try, when he was still nineteen, at Baramus monastery in Wadi Natrun, then the poorest and the smallest of the monasteries there. Quickly famous for his asceticism, he was ordained priest before he was twenty-one, and did much to support the monks by copying manuscripts. He was made intendant of the monastery, which proceeded to grow and develop a good reputation for discipline and for hospitality. Pope Demetrius brought Hanna in to Cairo, advanced him to *hegoumenos* (archpriest), and put him on the staff of the patriarchal cathedral, until the pleas of his brother monks were heard, and he was able to return to his monastery. His continued success there caused the electors to choose him to be patriarch, the government having finally allowed the election after four years.

Hanna was elevated to the office of patriarch as Cyril V in 1875. He showed his interest in education by opening new schools and expanding the school curriculum. He improved monastery and church facilities and sponsored study for clergy and monks, especially through the publication of religious literature and the opening of monastic schools. He also developed programs for a better understanding of the Coptic language. Cyril was honored by governments in Egypt and Ethiopia and by the Ottoman Sultan, and he served on the Advisory Council of the national deputies. By 1894 Cyril had consecrated nineteen metropolitans and other bishops. It seems that he was very active, and was described by his biographer, who finished his work in 1894, as ascetic, charitable, and a good pastor.

Nevertheless, the long conflict between Cyril and the lay leadership had already begun before 1894—as his biographer put it tactfully: "there befell this father some reproaches in [1892-1893] . . . on account of disputes which occurred at that time."[71] But that part of the story belongs to our next chapter. In fact, things went well enough in the early days of Cyril V. He "found the Council in office at his accession, and their collaboration augured well by their joint approval of the foundation of the Coptic Theological Seminary,"[72] but when they got to money matters Cyril withdrew from the Council, which thus lost its power to act. Also, the patriarch arbitrarily closed the seminary for clergy and a girls' school.

Without the cooperation of the patriarch in a church so hierarchically structured, all the reformers could do was to organize voluntary societies like the Furtherance of Christianity in Egypt and the Coptic Charitable Society (in 1881)[73] to help with schools and work with the poor as best they could. The distinguished Butrus Ghali Pasha headed up the Society, the purpose of which was to revive reform ideas.[74] One of Egypt's leading twentieth-century intellectuals, Salama Musa, a Copt, learned to read in a primary school opened by the Society.[75]

Khedive Ismail created the "basis for the genesis of an Europeanized Egyptian elite in government, education and letters." This elite "became the leader of the reform and later nationalist movements of the early twentieth century." And in Ismail's reign public works improved the cities and the communications infrastructure, arts and letters were encouraged, and agricultural production rose significantly.[76]

The Copts generally benefited from Ismail's government. The move toward equality for Copts, begun by Said, was made real by Ismail.[77] Copts rose in government and in business, so that the "era of Ismail" could be seen as their "golden age."[78] Finally, it may be said of this reign: "Egypt's Renaissance began with Ismail."[79] Having given "the devil his due," we must remember that Ismail's personal extravagance and irresponsible continuation of the build-up of huge foreign debts caused his own downfall and the end of the Egyptian independence Muhammad Ali had worked so hard to achieve.

A tragic aspect of the final failure of the Ismail government was that the new educated and liberal Egyptian elite, which state and church had both helped prepare, was simply too inexperienced in politics and had too little power to play a creative role in the chaotic situation that led to the British occupation. So the six years before the Occupation were simply a struggle between the khedives, the new Egyptian army, the Ottoman Empire, and the "Great Powers" (above all, Britain and France, but also Italy and Austria) to decide who would determine what would happen to Egypt and its people.

The story of events from 1876, when European creditors forced the appointment of the Debt Commission or Caisse and the Dual Control, to the British Occupation in 1882 is too complex for us to try to give in any detail. We may summarize the three years before the Occupation, however, in the words of the *History of the Patriarchs* which were written soon after, and from a Coptic point of view:[80]

> There occurred [in 1879] the abdication of the mentioned Khedive [Ismail]. And his son, Tawfik Pasha governed. . . . And in the days of this Khedive an important event occurred which spread abroad in all the world . . . Towards the end of the year [1882] Ahmad Urabi Pasha, director of the Egyptian military service, . . . rebelled against this Khedive. And the two states, England and France, threatened him, and they commanded him to desist, and he did not desist. And they both sent their fleets to the harbour of Alexandria, and they threatened him with bombardment. And he began to fortify the forts and to raise armies. And the British fought against him, and they routed him at Tall al-Kabir [in September of 1882]. And they dispersed the gathering of his troops, and their armies marched to Cairo, and they entered it on the following day without the least resistance; and there did not occur from them the least harm to anyone, and this was marvelous

to us. And they took the Citadel, and they seized Urabi and his company, and they proclaimed the supremacy of the Khedive [Tawfik]. And after they had judged [Urabi and his company] and proved their treason, they exempted them from the death penalty, and they exiled them to the island of Ceylon in India. And this is the cause of the entry of the English into the Land of Egypt, and their interference in its administration together with the Khedive, but it did not cease to be subject to the Ottoman State, as before.

The Copts had no argument with Urabi, or the British, it would seem, although in May the Patriarch, along with other religious leaders, had begged the Khedive to reinstate Urabi as Minister of War, as he had threatened to kill them if they failed in this mission![81]

We now leave the century beginning with the French invasion and ending with the coming of the British occupation. In retrospect, it is hard to say which was most important for the future of the Coptic Orthodox Church, the modernizing of Egypt by the House of Muhammad Ali or The Awakening associated with the name of Cyril IV. Together they created new classes of Copts able to revive their church. But the new classes would also precipitate tensions within the Coptic Church, which were to last three quarters of a century and sometimes explode into open conflict between reforming laity and reacting clergy.

There can scarcely be any argument, however, about whether the Coptic Church was significantly stronger in 1882 than it was in 1798, by almost any measure. Here again we turn to the ending of the *History of the Patriarchs* for the point of view of a leading Copt writing at the end of the period he is describing: "In a word we say that the Egyptian State [1874-1894] was at the highest degree of justice and good order and arrangement. And it removed religious fanaticism, and almost established equality between its subjects, Christian and Islam, and it eliminated most of the injustice, and it realized much in the way of beneficial works for the benefit of all the inhabitants." The writer goes on to mention improvements in national and international communications, in irrigation, mechanization and industrialization, "and enactments of regulations and laws and severe control together with the generalization of personal and religious liberty, and the opening of schools and diffusion of sciences and arts." Cairo and Alexandria were greatly improved. Scholarship abounded "and engineering and scientific and political works have come into existence, in order to organize the country. The beginning of these organizations was in the days of Muhammad Ali Pasha, and they have not ceased to increase up to our present time [1894]. And, in short, the Land of Egypt was similar to the European kingdoms in organizations; and praise to God for His graces!"[82] The next century was to be even more exciting for the Coptic Christians, including achievements and setbacks, as we shall see in our concluding chapters.

[1]A useful history is found in P. J. Vatikiotis, *The History of Egypt*, 3rd ed. (Baltimore: Johns Hopkins Univ. Press, 1985), pp. 33-38.

[2]G. Young, *Egypt* (New York: Scribner's, 1927), p. 28.

[3]Vatikiotis, p. 38.

[4]Severianus, "Les coptes de l'Égypte musulmane," *Études Méditerranéennes*, 6 (winter, 1959), 74-75.

[5]Young, p. 30.

[6]*History of the Patriarchs of the Egyptian Church: Known as the History of the Holy Church by Sawirus ibn al-Mukaffa (HPEC)*, Vol. 3, trans. and annotated by A. Khater and O. H. E. KHS-Burmester (Cairo: Société d'archéologie copte, 1968 et seq.), p. 299.

[7]Vatikiotis, p. 45.

[8]*HPEC* 3, 298-302.

[9]I. Habib el-Masri, *The Story of the Copts* (Cairo: Middle East Council of Churches, 1978), pp. 498-499.

[10]*HPEC* 3, 302.

[11]H. Motski, "Jirjis al-Jawhari," *Coptic Encyclopedia*, 1991.

[12]For his life see A. S. Atiya, *A History of Eastern Christianity* (London: Methuen, 1968), pp. 101-103.

[13]The title of a widely read book of Henry Dodwell, *The Founder of Modern Egypt: A Study of Muhammad Ali* (Cambridge: Cambridge Univ. Press, 1931).

[14]Vatikiotis, pp. 49-50.

[15]P. M. Holt, "The Later Ottoman Empire in Egypt and the Fertile Crescent," in *The Central Islamic Lands from Pre-Islamic Times to the First World War*, Vol. 1 of *The Cambridge History of Islam*, ed. P. M. Holt, A. K. S. Lambton, and B. Lewis (Cambridge: Cambridge Univ. Press, 1970), p. 386.

[16]Vatikiotis, p. 60. These paragraphs on modernizing Egypt draw heavily from his chapter 4.

[17]A. L. al-Sayyid Marsot, *Egypt in the Reign of Muhammad Ali* (Cambridge: Cambridge Univ. Press, 1984), pp. 258-260; and Young, chap. 2, especially pp. 82-85.

[18]Vatikiotis, pp. 100-101.

[19]al-Sayyid Marsot, pp. 261-262; also, e.g., Young, pp. 47-48; T. Little, chap. 4 and especially p. 31: "the army became an integral part of the national movement and an instrument of liberation within a self-contained nation."

[20]Vatikiotis, pp. 67-69.

[21]Young, p. 48.

[22]Habib el-Masri, p. 508.

[23] *HPEC* 3, 304-308.

[24] The story and the quotation are found in *HPEC* 3, p. 303.

[25] *HPEC* 3, 307-308.

[26] O. F. A. Meinardus, *Christian Egypt: Faith and Life* (Cairo: American Univ. at Cairo Press, 1970), p. 17.

[27] Quoted in *Outline Histories for C. M. S. Missions* (London: Church Missionary Society, 1905), p. 17.

[28] See, e.g., *Missionary Register* (London: Church Missionary Society, 1829), pp. 233 and 411.

[29] *The Egypt and Sudan Missions* (London: Church Missionary Society, 1910), p. 12.

[30] *Church Missionary Record*, 2 (1831), 52 and 10 (1839), 182.

[31] *Church Missionary Record*, 14 (1843), 83, for December 26, 1842.

[32] *Missionary Register* (London: Church Missionary Society, 1829), p. 173.

[33] *Church Missionary Record*, 11 (1840), 104-105.

[34] *The Egypt and Sudan Missions*, p. 15; also, cf. S. Seikaly, "Coptic Communal Reform: 1860-1914," *Middle Eastern Studies*, 6 (October, 1970), 248; troubles of the theological students are set forth in "a Coptic layman" (Markus Simaika), "The Awakening of the Coptic Church," *The Contemporary Review*, 71 (1897), 735.

[35] O. V. Volkoff, ed., *Voyageurs russes en Égypte* (Cairo: Institut français d'archéologie orientale, 1972), p. 173.

[36] Habib el-Masri, pp. 509-510. She calls this "one of the famous incidents, often recounted."

[37] al-Sayyid Marsot, p. 264.

[38] Young, p. 42; also, cf. T. Little, p. 31.

[39] W. Jowett, *Christian Researches in the Mediterranean from 1815 to 1820 in Furtherance of the Objects of the Church Missionary Society* (London: Church Missionary Society, 1824), p. 91.

[40] *Church Missionary Record*, 10 (1839), 179-180 and 184.

[41] Letter from M. Martin, June 9, 1992.

[42] The paragraph is largely drawn from an unpublished paper, "Église et communauté coptes dans l'Islam égyptien," dated 3 February 1982, in the library of the Jesuit Institute in Cairo, put together by M. P. Martin who says it was a group effort.

[43] J. Heyworth-Dunne, "Education in Egypt and the Copts," *Bulletin de la Société d'Archéologie Copte*, 6 (1940), 92-101.

[44] Cyril's biography is found in *HPEC* 3, 308-310; it is quite brief and may indicate that there was more doubt about Cyril in the late nineteenth century than one might have thought.

[45]Habib el-Masri, p. 516.

[46]*The Egypt and Sudan Missions*, pp. 102 and 105.

[47]Markus Simaika (writing as "a Coptic layman"), p. 739n; also see Meinardus, p. 20.

[48]Quotation and the rest of the paragraph are from Habib el-Masri, p. 517.

[49]We are depending here on *HPEC* 3, 309-310.

[50]In Habib el-Masri, pp. 517-518, she also blames British and French diplomats for feeding the Khedive's suspicions. She states that he had Cyril poisoned.

[51]Meinardus, p. 20.

[52]Little, pp. 37-38.

[53]Little, pp. 37-38; cf. also Young, pp. 66-67.

[54]S. J. Staffa, *Conquest and Fusion: The Social Evolution of Cairo A.D. 642-1850* (Leiden: E. J. Brill, 1977), p. 242.

[55]E. Wakin, *A Lonely Minority: The Modern Story of Egypt's Copts* (New York: William Morrow, 1963), p. 10; cf. also Meinardus, p. 19.

[56]Vatikiotis, p. 73; cf. also Little, p. 41.

[57]His biography is found in *HPEC* 3, 310-312.

[58]S. Seikaly, pp. 247-275.

[59]Meinardus, p. 20.

[60]Salama Musa, *The Education of Salama Musa*, trans. L. O. Schuman (Leiden: E. J. Brill, 1961), pp. 14-15.

[61]*Letters from Egypt (1862-1869)* (1865; rpt. with additional letters by Gordon Wakefield; New York: Praeger, 1969), pp. 320, 323 (first quotation), 58 (second quotation), 108, 229, and 256-257—in that order.

[62]Habib el-Masri says as much, p. 523; also see E. E. Elder, *Vindicating a Vision* (Philadelphia: Presbyterian Board of Missions, 1958), pp. 59-61 and 72-73.

[63]Elder, pp. 201-202.

[64]*HPEC* 3, 312.

[65]Seikaly, pp. 247-275.

[66]Simaika, pp. 737-739.

[67]*HPEC* 3, 312 and 321.

[68]S. Seikaly, "Prime Minister and Assassin: Butrus Ghali and Wardani," *Middle Eastern Studies*, 13 (1977), 40-41.

[69]Meinardus, pp. 21-24; the quotation is from p. 22.

[70]His career until 1894 is taken up in *HPEC* 3, 312-322.

[71] *HPEC* 3, 321.

[72] Atiya, p. 109.

[73] Seikaly, "Coptic Communal Reform," pp. 247-275.

[74] Seikaly, "Prime Minister and Assassin," p. 45.

[75] Salama Musa, p. 22.

[76] The quotations are from Vatikiotis, pp. 73-74; a discussion of the improvements is found on pp. 78-80.

[77] Seikaly, "Coptic Communal Reform," p. 263.

[78] D. Behrens-Abouseif, "The Political Situation of the Copts, 1798-1923," in *Christians and Jews in the Ottoman Empire: The Function of a Plural Society*, ed. B. Braude and B. Lewis, Vol. 2 of *The Arabic Speaking Lands* (New York: Holmes and Meier, 1982), p. 192.

[79] Salama Musa, "Intellectual Currents in Egypt," *Middle Eastern Affairs*, 2 (1951), 267.

[80] *HPEC* 3, 323-324. The translation is awkward and literal but it is brief and written by an Egyptian.

[81] The Earl of Cromer (Evelyn Baring), *Modern Egypt*, 2 vols. (New York: Macmillan, 1908), 1, p. 277; cf. also M. Rowlatt, *Founders of Modern Egypt* (New York: Asia Publishing House, 1962), pp. 73 and 114.

[82] *HPEC* 3, 325-326. The rest of the manuscript outlines the situation of all the monasteries and dioceses of the Coptic Church as of 1894.

Chapter Ten

The Twentieth Century, I

✠ ——————————————————————————— ✠

1882 to 1959

EGYPT AS A NATION AND THE COPTIC CHURCH as a community have both had ups and downs throughout what we are calling "the twentieth century," the period from 1882, when the British occupation of Egypt was initiated, to the present. This chapter will deal with events of the first seven decades, during which the nation went from being run by the greatest of the nineteenth-century imperialist powers of the West to a measure of self-rule during the "Liberal Experiment" in constitutional democracy in the '20s and '30s to the return to authoritarian and military rule, this time, at last, by Egyptians, beginning in 1952.

Leading Coptic laymen were taking prominent roles in national life during the first half of the century, while leadership within the Coptic Church itself was going through decades of crisis. Seeds were being sown, however, that enabled the church in the 1950s to make a dramatic return to the Reform movement initiated and symbolized by Patriarch Cyril IV and to enter what has been called its "renaissance" in church life.

Many Copts began our century with high hopes. In 1894, a prominent Coptic intellectual and writer, finishing the quasi-official *History of the Patriarchs of the Egyptian Church*, had painted an optimistic picture of Egypt's progress begun by Muhammad Ali early in the nineteenth century and of the initial impact of the British occupation begun in 1882.[1] Such an optimistic outlook was based on the educational opportunities in the schools which the Reform had created for the Coptic laity and also on the wealth of many Coptic notables who had taken advantage of the opportunities created by the Muhammad Ali dynasty for private land-owning and for business activities. Education and wealth easily translate into power. Also, the Coptic

Christians expected better treatment by the Christian British than what they had received from the Muslim Ottoman Empire and its agents in Egypt.

The British disappointed the Copts, however, for they, like the French invaders of the previous century, decided that it would be wiser to associate their rule with the dominant Muslim majority than to seem to be identified with a despised minority. And, ironically, the very power and self-confidence of the Copts' lay leadership caused it for the three quarters of a century after 1882 to be often caught up in conflicts with the hierarchy of patriarchs and bishops over church reform and the proper management of church affairs. So much for the 1894 optimism among the Copts!

Let us consider now the state of the Coptic Church at the turn of the century. The patriarch, Pope Cyril V, had been in office since 1874 and continued in it until he died in 1927. This means that this devout but stubborn and narrowly educated man ruled the Coptic Church for a fifty-three year period during which modern Egypt was going through momentous changes and Copts like Butros Ghali were becoming leaders in national life and influencing the evolution of nationalist ideologies. Cyril's conservatism made it impossible for him to try to relate the Coptic Church positively or creatively to these important developments.

It could have been otherwise. It has been said that, a century before, several of those who drew up the Constitution of the United States also drew up the Constitution of the Episcopal Church in the United States. Thus that church had close connections with the national mood toward change and with the creation of a new kind of government and society. This is in sharp contrast with the Coptic Church hierarchy in the first half of the twentieth century. But, of course, the Copts were overwhelmingly outnumbered and outweighed by the Muslims in Egypt. Still, the ethos of the Coptic Church could have been influenced by its members who were joining in the efforts to create a national government and a national sense of purpose of their own, if their hierarchy had permitted it. Perhaps it was inevitable that a patriarch with Cyril's background would conscientiously resist any effort that seemed to erode the patriarch's almost mystically perceived right and obligation to manage all the affairs of the church. Steadfastness had brought the Copts through almost twelve centuries of difficulties, and Cyril viewed his actions as steadfast.

The laymen's reform efforts began with the Copts' majlis al-milli (religious council) which had been authorized by the ruling khedive and elected in 1874. It claimed important powers to reform and had been put in place just before Cyril's elevation to the patriarchate. The lay leaders felt they were better prepared to handle the church's finances, especially the endowments (waqfs) which were a major support of the church's charitable activities and of the monasteries. The lay leaders also felt they were better educated to handle the legal matters regarding the "personal status" laws, such as marriage and divorce, which the government entrusted to each religious community. Finally, the laymen wanted more control over the church press and church schools, and they wanted a more broadly educated clergy.

Cyril was able to block the efforts of the first majlis al-milli, since he was its chairman. He rejected the council outright, and it was soon dissolved. The lay leaders then redoubled their efforts through the Tawfik Society and the Coptic Relief Society to marshal church resources to meet the needs of the masses of Copts. In 1883, the majlis al-milli was reinstated and the struggle continued. When Cyril disapproved the 1892 election to the council, it appealed to the government. Cyril was exiled to his monastery, but after five months he was able to return in triumph to resume his struggle with the laymen over control of the waqfs, schools, benevolent societies, and the regulation of personal status matters.[2]

One is tempted to side with the laity who were trying to reform the church structure while the clergy were protecting their prerogatives. One sympathetic chronicler of recent Coptic history, an American journalist, stated simply, "The Coptic Church is probably the only Christian Church whose laity in the twentieth century has been more dedicated than the clergy."[3] Another writer, a French Dominican, equally sympathetic to the Copts, in a section entitled "the rebellion of the laity," began thus: "The renewal of the Coptic Church is, almost entirely, the work of laymen." He adds that "good intentions governed their action," and begins his explanation of why the struggle with the clergy was so "laborious": "First, because the two partners, no longer living in the same universe, no longer spoke the same language: the laymen benefited from a Western education and a humanistic culture which could scarcely be possessed by a hierarchy recruited exclusively from monks, outside of the powerful current of modernity which took possession of the country's elites."[4]

A Coptic scholar[5] distinguished the perspectives of laity and clergy by agreeing to the conservatism and relative ignorance of the clergy but focusing more on the leading laymen's experience in seeing how things can move ahead rather than focusing on their superior education. He found both clergy and laity to have been dedicated, but to different things. Also, he noted that the old "millet" system, under which the Ottoman Empire had made the religious head of each minority group responsible for his community, made a clergy-laity struggle inevitable once there were lay members strong enough to challenge the religious leadership of the Coptic community on matters of community life.

When Pope Cyril returned to Cairo in triumph in 1893, he must have realized that some concessions had to be made to the laymen who were so eager to see the church reformed. He opened new schools and reopened the schools and the theological college which he had closed. He published an encyclical calling for the parish priests to be diligent in their pastoral responsibilities. He started a library at the patriarchate and he secured more land for church use.[6] A prominent Coptic layman, writing anonymously in an English review in 1897, showed increased optimism about the Copts' coming together to reform and strengthen their church.[7]

For the statistics on the Copts' church life in the early 1900s we have contemporary reports from two Anglican clergymen in Egypt and from recent estimates by two Copts. Douglas Thornton in a 1906 report on Christian schools noted that there were over 600,000 church members and 100 Coptic Orthodox schools, of which twenty-seven were passing students for the primary certificate.[8] Also, there was "a small majority of Copts over Muslims in the primary and secondary schools of Egypt, while in the higher schools during last year the Copts numbered more than one third."[9]

Archdeacon Dowling, in one of the few books of the period giving a brief but thorough and reliable account of the Copts, reported that there were 850 priests, 460 churches, twelve monasteries, 450 monks, fifty-five nuns, sixty-five lay preachers and slightly under a million church members,[10] eight metropolitans and twelve bishops.[11] Dowling perceived that the difference over the doctrine of Christ, which was supposed to separate Copts from Catholics and Protestants, "has become a mere matter of terminology."[12] And Dowling pointed out "that Lane's familiar *Modern Egyptians* is practically valueless as regards the Egyptian Church and the Copts as a people, for his information was from a Moslem pervert [that is, convert]."[13]

A more recent article by a Coptic scholar reported[14] that in 1901 Copts made up more than forty-five percent of government employment and almost 100 percent of "sarrafs" (tax collectors). And Copts paid nineteen percent of the land tax.

Another Coptic scholar and specialist in the period reported[15] that in 1906 Coptic monasteries and churches had about 15,000 feddans (a feddan is about one acre) of valuable land, and that in 1907 Copts were about seven percent of the population, owned sixteen percent of cultivated land and buildings, with perhaps twenty-five percent of the nation's wealth, and in control of sixty percent of Egyptian commerce. Copts were found in the professions, in government service, in the crafts, and in the peasantry, and it could be possibly said that Copts were leading Egypt into the future.

It is clear from these four reports that the Copts in the early 1900s were by no means a community to be overlooked in an Egypt ready to take important steps into the modern world of national states, increasing technology and industrialization, aggressive Western culture and values, and the world market.

While the Copts were entering the twentieth century with some strengths but in some disarray, the British occupation was dominating Egypt's government and economy and Egypt's relations with the rest of the world. European intervention had become almost inevitable in light of Egypt's unmanageable foreign debts. The surprise was that the intervention was not French, for France had maintained influence and important interests in Egypt since Napoleon's invasion and the rise of Muhammad Ali and his dynasty, whereas the British had characteristically sided with the Ottoman Empire's interest in Egypt. The British had expected the French to join them in what they planned to be a brief occupation, as the French had participated in the bombardment of Alexandria in the first step in the occupation. But a change in government in France left the British alone in the adventure, and Britain had no intention of backing down. Britain's special interest was the Suez Canal—her vital link with India, which made Egypt so important to the British Empire that it did not completely free Egypt until 1956.

Evelyn Baring, soon to be made Lord Cromer, dominated the early part of the Occupation. He had participated in earlier economic negotiations with Egypt, and after a tour in India, he was recalled to take charge in Egypt. He was a master administrator, with no interest in the political dimensions of Egypt's situation. He insisted that Britain's invasion was approved by "the lawful rulers of Egypt" and the mass of Egyptians, and that the British then acted "with all the practical common sense, the scorn for theory, and the total absence of any fixed plan based on logical reasoning, which are the distinguishing features of his race."[16] These words were a crack at the French, but they also fit perfectly with his two simple and clear-cut goals for Egypt: financial solvency and governmental stability.

There would be no doubt about who was to reform and rule Egypt. Lord Granville declared officially: "It should be made clear to the Egyptian ministers and governors of provinces that the responsibility which for the time rests on England obliges H. M. Government to insist on the adoption of the policy which they recommend; and that it will be necessary that those ministers and governors who do not follow this course should cease to hold their offices."[17]

Cromer attained his goals, but of course there were other results of his administration. The Copts' high hopes were dashed. Cromer had no use for Islam, which he found anti-female, intolerant, and disastrous in its social impact, but he felt that it was necessary that Islamic customs be honored.[18] Ironically, it was this British Christian, who found Islam "politically and socially moribund,"[19] who really made Friday the Egyptian sabbath by declaring it the government's day off, made the Quran the only officially recognized religious book, and the Muslim sheikh the only religious teacher allowed in government schools. In the words of an American missionary, "the British Occupation has greatly strengthened the position of Mohammedanism in Egypt."[20] As late as 1911, a distinguished English specialist in Egyptian history could write, "To exalt the Mohammedan and to tread down the Christian, to license the majority and to curb the minority, is the policy which our Government has not avowed but practiced."[21]

Cromer found the Copts steadfast but not morally superior to the Muslims, whose practices influenced the Copts. He thought the Copts unfriendly, although they expected to be treated with favoritism. In the struggle between Pope Cyril and the lay leadership in the Coptic Church, Cromer supported the lay reformers,[22] finding the hierarchy's position incomprehensible. He thought Copts good at "measuring skills" but preferred to employ Syrians and Armenians in administration. He stated that the Syrian Christians constituted "the intellectual cream of the Near East" but that Europeanized Egyptians hated Christians even more than the masses did.[23]

Cromer's economic policies, typical of nineteenth-century imperialism, were to favor a wide variety of organizational and technological improvements in agricultural production for export, coupled with keeping import taxes low to discourage industrial production which would compete with British imports.[24] Wealthy Copts benefitted from improved agricultural production and suffered no more than any other businessmen or industrialists from Cromer's policies.

The influence of the Occupation on education was damaging. The British actually lowered the investment in education from what it was during the century before.[25] Perhaps the imperialism of the day looked upon education as a potential threat to its domination. As to the broader cultural impact of the Occupation, Westernizing forces became, perhaps inevitably, relatively more British and less French, though French influences remained strong. The non-believing radical Copt, Salama Musa, argued that "Egypt's renaissance began with Ismail (1863-1879)" and that the British Occupation actually held Egypt back.[26] (It is interesting that the "era of Ismail" has also been called the Copts' "golden age."[27])

Cromer's final months in Egypt were marred by the notorious "Dinshawai Incident" in 1906 in which villagers, inflamed by a hunting accident, contributed to the death of a British officer and suffered the most drastic reprisals. The leading Coptic layman, Butros Ghali, as minister of justice had to preside over the special court that decided the case—hardly a good way for a Christian to gain popularity among Egyptians.[28] Actually, Egypt had entered an economic recession in the months before Cromer was replaced by Eldon Gorst, so that Cromer was not able to leave Egypt as prosperous and subdued a country as he had wished.

Gorst distinguished himself by instituting liberalizing policies. These reflected the ideas of the Liberal Party which now governed England and adopted the theory that Britain's goals in Egypt should include some movement toward participation of Egyptians in the government of their country. Butros Ghali was named prime minister, apparently a great honor for the Coptic community. He had been tainted in the Dinshawai Incident, however, and in 1898, as foreign minister, he had signed for Egypt the unpopular Anglo-Egyptian Condominium which placed the Sudan (which Egyptians considered their backyard) under the joint rule of Britain and Egypt. Ghali was unpopular for other reasons as well,[29] and it has been said that he "was surely not the right Copt to become the prime minister."[30] It is no wonder that he was soon assassinated, in early 1910, by a Muslim member of the Nationalist movement. Worried Copts gathered at the Upper Egypt city of Asyut, where they were strong. They demanded a Sunday holiday, employment based on merit, religious instruction for Copts in schools, and a Coptic representation in governing bodies. A rival "General Egyptian Congress" met in the spring of 1911, but "no serious decisions were reached."[31] The Copts' demands went unheeded.[32]

While these great events were going on, a major effort was begun which was to have a bigger effect than they on Coptic Christians: Sunday Schools, which were called by a learned observer in 1961 "today one of the most solid institutions of the Coptic Church, begun modestly about 1910 in imitation of the Protestant Sunday Schools."[33] Imitation or not, the Sunday Schools, which imparted more than just specifically religious instruction, quickly became a major influence in church life and involved a wide variety of devout lay persons in the spiritual uplift of the Coptic community. No one was more important in the evolution of Coptic Orthodox Sunday Schools than the indefatigable Habib Guirguis.[34] At the age of seventeen he had entered the first class of the reconstituted Coptic theological school in 1893, with which he associated himself the rest of his long life.

> He had to ask the help of the teachers and students of the theological school and other volunteers in order to establish new classes in . . . major Egyptian cities. In 1918 he formed the central committee of Sunday Schools . . . responsible for preparing the curricula and the picture lessons . . ., and for extending the work by opening new branches even in small cities and villages. For years it was not easy to convince the Church leaders, the priests and the parents of the importance of the Sunday Schools. But . . . Habib Guirguis lived to see Sunday School in every church in Egypt. They became the centers of spiritual activity, with classes for every grade, youth meetings, meetings for the teachers and prayer groups. Bishops attended Sunday School conferences and

the successive Patriarchs blessed the work and prayed for its success.[35]

We return to the French Dominican writing in 1961 on Coptic renewal: "The entire Coptic renewal has its origins in the Sunday Schools. It is in transmitting the faith to the younger generations that the Copts have found it for themselves with new eyes and have deeply engaged themselves in its service."[36]

It was also in the early 1900s that nationalism began to emerge as an important force in Egypt, with special consequences for the Coptic community. Would nationalism favor the Copts, who seemed to have the best claim to being pure Egyptians? Or would nationalism threaten Copts by demanding that all Egyptians be of one ethnic group (Arab) or one religion (Islam)? As it turned out, a variety of nationalist movements arose in Egypt and have continued throughout the twentieth century.

There are ironies of Egyptian nationalism. During the ancient and classical periods of history, Egypt was the most clearly defined region by geography and culture; and yet, beginning that far back in history, Egypt has almost continuously found itself a province of some foreign empire or ruled by foreign elements, from the days of the Assyrian Empire in the seventh century B.C., up through the British Occupation. In 1900 Egypt had the distinction of being a province of one Empire (the Ottoman), subject to the rule of another (the British), and with a head of state (Abbas II) who did not speak Arabic. As late as the early 1920s it could be said of Egypt that,

> Most of the high-ranking [military] officers were British; the Muslim ones were still mainly of Turkish or Circassian descent. So indeed were most high-ranking officials of the Egyptian government. Nearly all public utilities, manufacturing firms, transportation companies, hotels, banks, and insurance companies were owned and managed by foreigners . . . [and there were] some 200,000 foreign residents, who were still exempted from local laws and taxes.[37]

Historically, nationalism as we know it began in the modern, Western world. Arabic-speaking nationalism began in the Middle East among Christians in Syria and Lebanon who had been educated in colleges run by Westerners. This development was almost inevitable, since neither Islam nor the Arab heritage has a place in its political philosophy for the territorial state which commands the primary loyalty of its inhabitants. Thus, for example, it is no accident that virtually every national boundary in the Arabian peninsula and the Fertile Crescent was drawn by European powers, in the interest of their empires.

Egyptian nationalism was born as opposition to British rule. It intensified in the early years of war against the Sudanese uprising led by the

"Mahdi," in which so many Egyptian soldiers were killed but after which the British assumed for themselves the governance of the defeated Sudan. Lest the nationalism be simply negative and lest "Egypt for Egyptians" be only a moving slogan or nationalism be only a theory to discuss, Egyptian nationalism sought to bolster its position and develop popular support. Thus, it variously allied itself, in some cases with the Ottoman Empire, in others with pan-Islam or pan-Arabism, and sometimes with "Egyptianism," an outlook "that took pride in Egypt's pre-Islamic civilization rather than Islam or Arabism."[38]

Egyptianism fit perfectly with the world-wide interest roused by archeological finds in Egypt, for it insisted that that which is to this day truly Egyptian is what developed in the ancient world. Thus it was also called "Pharaonism," a term preferred by Salama Musa, the Coptic intellectual, who claimed there was an actual biological basis for it.[39] Egyptianism was popular with Copts, for it implied that the Arab Conquest and the spread of Islam in Egypt were actually extraneous to what is truly Egyptian.

Mirrit Butros Ghali, a grandson of Butros Ghali and one of the leading Coptic laymen of the twentieth century, took in a 1978 essay[40] a somewhat different position. He stated that "most historians and publicists . . . [tend] to overlook the deep unity between the various elements of [Egypt's] cultural heritage." This unity is basically the essential religious consensus of Mediterranean civilization which is built on the revelation to Moses of the oneness of God, human justice and dignity, and social morality. Ghali does not believe that Arab culture and Islamic religion are foreign to the Egyptian heritage but rather laments that they have not been integrated with it in the historic sense of the Egyptian people, since "the Egyptian national consciousness" (the title of his essay) must include all of Egypt's history.

Muslim reformers like al-Afghani and also Muhammad Abduh (whom Cromer admired but disagreed with) were keys to initiating Egyptian nationalism but were soon overshadowed in influence by others. Some leading Copts were drawn to the pioneering nationalism of Mustafa Kamil, who died too young to develop his ideas and movement fully, for he was uncompromising in his insistence on getting the British out. A lay Coptic historian recently wrote of him that he "unfurled the banner of an intellectual movement round which all the elite rallied."[41] But Copts were put off by Kamil's turning for support to the Ottoman Empire.

Kamil was never really anti-Copt, but a certain movement towards violence and an increase in pan-Islamism began to worry the Copts from about 1903. There was no real political consensus among the Copts and not all were nationalists. Some suspected nationalism for its tendency to fanaticism and its frequent appeal to Ottoman power; and many Copts feared the loss of economic growth if the British withdrew from Egypt. Copts were not really badly off under the Occupation. Indeed, the Coptic community was "not secluded . . . ; its members were educated, and used their education to acquire immense wealth . . . ; its clergy [were] gradually awakening to the need for education. An inferior religious minority had become an integrated and equal part of Egyptian society."[42]

One historian of modern Egypt, in arguing that by World War I Copts were no longer nationalists, stated that Gorst "succeeded in breaking the homogeneity of the national [i.e., nationalist] movement by drawing the Copts away from it" and said of Butros Ghali that he "personified Coptic collaboration."[43] Be that as it may, many leading Copts were nationalist.

Salama Musa in a 1951 article[44] wrote that most Coptic writers belonged to the group that are more Western, more liberal on religion, race, and social reform and that they believed in separation of church and state and in equality for women. A sympathetic American writer has written of Copts a dozen years later that they have stood for Western values and that they "along with the other Christians [in Egypt] have been the main transmitters of Western and modern attitudes."[45]

It is not surprising that Copts came to prefer nationalists like Ahmad Lutfi as-Sayyid (much admired by Mirrit Ghali), who opposed the Ottoman relation and "developed the concept of secular nationalism in Egypt, of an Egypt for the Egyptians, and Egypt neither Turkish nor Arab."[46] This movement helped the Copts' relation to the nation and its nationalism, up until the 1930s, as we shall see. Actually, still in the 1930s a civics textbook could state: "the Arabs . . . blended into the original local population, the Copts, and out of this mixture was formed a single nation, the Egyptian nation."[47]

The problem for the Copts turned out to be that secular nationalism was, indeed, Western-inspired, as its critics insisted. Thus the eventual disillusionment of Egyptians with Western ideas, and also with the "liberal experiment" in government that broke down after World War II, put Copts in the precarious position they still occupy in Egypt.

Actually, it was World War I, however, that was the real turning point for Egyptian nationalism. At its beginning in 1914, the occupying British went to war with the Ottoman Empire, which had been in theory the ruler of Egypt; the Ottomans' khedive, Abbas, was deposed and exiled, and Egypt became a protectorate of Britain in name as well as in fact. The Egyptians were forced by the British to gear their economy to Britain's war needs and their foreign policy to Britain's imperial designs. Large numbers of imperial troops were quartered on Egypt. "Nationalists still in Egypt were put under house arrest, the Legislative Assembly was adjourned indefinitely, and political life went into suspension . . . Increasingly, . . . the British ran Egypt like a crown colony."[48]

Britain and its allies won the war, and some Egyptians, including the Copts who were in business and industry or were landowners, benefitted financially from it. Nevertheless, leading voices in Egypt, including many Copts, called for a totally new relationship with Britain, doubtless encouraged by Woodrow Wilson's call for "self-determination of peoples"—which the United States did not follow through on in the case of Egypt.[49] Egyptians wanted a "wafd" (delegation) at the peace conference to press the case for Egyptian self-rule.

The British at first totally ignored or rejected Egyptian efforts to be heard, and in reaction a Wafd party ("the largest and most important political organization in Egypt down to the Revolution of 1952"[50]) was organized, led by the nationalist Saad Zaghlul who had been vice president of the Legislative Assembly in early 1914, before it was abolished. "Wissa Wasef, George Khayyat, Makram Ebeid, are only a few of the Copt leaders who became prominent in the Wafd."[51]

When Zaghlul was exiled for his efforts, the 1919 Revolt broke out, and "Coptic priests mounted the *minbars* of mosques and Muslim *khatibs* stood in the pulpits of churches to preach the nearly forgotten lessons of national solidarity."[52] Qummus (archpriest) Sergius was at the great al-Azhar mosque in 1919 and when the British shut it down, he invited Muslim nationalists to meet at his church—a high point of Copt-Muslim relations (the same Sergius was saddened by the lack of Muslim-Christian cooperation after the 1952 Revolution[53]).

After a series of failed efforts to reach agreement between the British government and the determined Wafdists, independence for Egypt was finally proclaimed by General Allenby in 1922, and in the following year a Constitution was agreed upon, drawing heavily on Belgium's as a model. Four "Reserved Points" issued by Britain in 1922 claimed residual military and diplomatic powers in Egypt, by which, in fact, Britain remained a prominent factor in Egyptian affairs. Indeed, for decades more there was a three-way conflict between the Egyptian government, the monarchy (Muhammad Ali's successors became "sultan" in 1914 and "king" in 1922 when independence was acknowledged), and British imperial authorities. Furthermore, the effective functioning of the government was not only limited by the British and the machinations of Egypt's kings but also suffered from excessive partisanship and efforts of prime ministers to circumvent or even replace the Constitution. Even Saad Zaghlul, once in power, began to withdraw civil liberties that he had earlier demanded for the people.

Despite many setbacks, self-government for Egypt was making some progress. A formal treaty was drawn up with Britain in 1936, the same year in which King Fuad was succeeded by King Faruq; but already the Great Depression of the 1930s was causing serious suffering for the Egyptian people and their economy.

Meanwhile, the aged Pope Cyril V had died, in 1927, after decades of struggle with the lay leadership over the powers of the majlis al-milli to manage church affairs and over his own powers and responsibilities. Changes had been made in the council's constitution in 1908 and 1912, "but the laity struggled until their rights were restored by the constitution of 1927 [which settled the controversies with the monasteries over their waqfs.] . . . On hearing of the news of the passing of the new constitution, Cyril V died."[54]

The reader cannot help but notice that in our consideration of the first quarter of the 1900s our attention has concentrated on lay Copts. Even in the section on Sunday Schools we noted that the original activists in it were lay persons. This does not mean, however, that Copts did not honor and virtually revere their clergy and live out their church life overwhelmingly through participation in the sacraments presided over by their clergy. Our focus on Coptic lay persons does mean that the leaders were participating in the public dialogue, the big events, and the historic changes going on in Egypt during this crucial period in a way in which the clergy and hierarchy were not. Mrs. Iris Habib el-Masri, who is from a distinguished Coptic family and herself a historian and a veteran of the Egyptian Senate, does not seem to agree with this point. She has written that Copts, "as an integral part of their nation, . . . participated in full force in all the national movements . . . Clergymen and laymen got so passionately immersed in the patriotic expressions of love of their country that they put their fortunes, their lives and all they held dear in its service."[55] Except for the volatile Qummus Sergius, however, it is the laymen whose names appear in the literature in European languages on twentieth-century Egypt as the Coptic leaders in nationalist efforts.

There is some question as to whether an influential writer like Salama Musa, whom we have often mentioned as a Coptic writer, should even be included in a history of Coptic Orthodox Christianity. In a chapter entitled "At the Age of Seventy" of his *The Education of Salama Musa*[56] he said, "I believe in Christianity and in Islam and in the Jewish faith. I love Christ, and I admire Mohammed, and I seek enlightenment from Moses." He died in 1958 and might be called a non-believing radical Copt. But he was editor of the influential Coptic periodical *Misr,* and do not his background, his liberal ideas many would think of as Christian, and his professed love for Christ make Musa a Christian Copt? We shall come up against this kind of question again in the next chapter.

As we turn to the three patriarchs (John XIX, 1928-1942, Macarius III, 1944-1945, and Youssab II, 1946-1956) who came after Cyril V it may be useful to quote the summary statement of Mrs. Iris Habib el-Masri about them:

> One common feature these three Patriarchs shared was that they
> had been Bishops when they accepted to become patriarchs . . .
> This was a deviation from the long-inherited, established tradition

of the Church [of electing as patriarch a monk who was not already a bishop]. Needless to say, there were many among the Copts who strongly disapproved this deviation, the author's father [a leader in the majlis al-milli from 1930-1945] being one of them . . . The whole period of these three patriarchs was indeed turbulent to the Copts.[57]

In the words of Maurice Martin, the years 1927 to 1956 (the period of these three), "showed the fragility of the Copts' position."[58]

This turbulence was particularly true under the latter two patriarchs, as we shall see. The first of the three, John XIX, who had been Bishop of the Bohaira province, served first as "locum tenens" from 1927 and became patriarch the following year. He tried to make peace over the waqfs issue by appointing a committee of laymen and bishops. At first there was satisfaction, but in 1932 the committee was dropped.[59]

In 1928, the majlis al-milli decided to send five young men to England to prepare for teaching in the theological seminary to train priests.[60] Bishops and people were against the idea, lest the pure Coptic faith become infected. Pope John XIX announced that he would not ordain them, but he did promise to send some youths abroad. In reaction to this rebuff, a group of Coptic university students organized a new impetus in the Sunday School movement as volunteer cathechists, and they started a monthly magazine, *madaris al-ahad* (Sunday School). This activity led to vocations to the priesthood and to the monastic life, with a certain focus on the Suriani monastery in Wadi Natrun. Professor Murad Kamil of the University of Cairo was an important force in encouraging university graduates and professionals to consider vocations to be nuns or monks.

In the second quarter of the 1900s, social problems were beginning to become acute in Egypt, along with the economic problems intensified by the Great Depression of the 1930s. Egypt's population was rising sharply in the first half of the twentieth century. This put a burden on the food supply and on the ability of Egypt to keep its population productively employed. In fact, in spite of increased agricultural production, per capita real income was declining. Parallel to the threat of overpopulation was sharply increasing urbanization, which was creating problems of housing and schooling and providing adequate streets, water distribution, garbage collection, and utilities.

Mirrit Butros Ghali published (in Arabic) in 1938 in Egypt an important book entitled *The Policy of Tomorrow*,[61] in which he criticized the government and nationalist ideologies for concerning themselves exclusively with independence, even after the 1936 treaty, and ignoring needs for social and economic reform. He predicted disaster for Egypt, using "statistical and other data about conditions in Egypt . . . [in] a social-scientific, critical analysis of the country's problems." Ghali was an enthusiast for capitalism and favored agricultural development as a way to halt and reverse the "lowering in standards of living" that was a fact of Egyptian life in the 1930s.[62]

Under Pope John XIX the Coptic community was not mobilized to confront Egypt's serious problems. Upon his death, things got worse, not better, for the Copts. The bishop of Girga in Upper Egypt became acting patriarch from 1942-1944, until the office was filled by Macarius III,[63] who had been "the popular and powerful Bishop of Assiut."[64] He proposed various reforms, mostly about waqfs, and was determined to get along with the majlis al-milli. But his principal proposal was designed to concentrate power in the patriarchate, and the council rejected it. "Disputes between the clergy and the laity dominated the patriarchate of Macarius III. Every time a dispute would arise, however, the Patriarch left Cairo and went to the monastery." He died, no longer a reformist, the year after he was installed as patriarch.

In 1946, the bishop of Girga was instituted as patriarch as Youssab II. With his elevation, the clergy-laity controversy intensified. He renounced his pre-institution promises of letting the council manage the monastic endowments, and major disputes erupted between the patriarch and his constituency,[65] which were never resolved in his lifetime. Thus, in the last years before the 1952 Revolution, we see that the Coptic hierarchy was paralyzed with internal problems and in no position to consider broader problems of Egypt and its people.

While these rather unedifying struggles were going on between Coptic laity and clergy, the Sunday School movement continued to be an important revitalizing feature of Coptic church life, as was also a monastic revival. We have already seen that the two were rather closely linked. Our learned Dominican found that there had developed "a veritable movement toward the monastic life among the Sunday School leaders at the University of Cairo as well as the University of Alexandria. [He felt that] these monastic vocations are a test of the depth of the spiritual renewal which is beginning to win over the Coptic Church."[66] The extent to which the monastic revival has deepened current Coptic piety is not yet clear. We have also noted Protestant influences in the Sunday School movement. Father Jeremias of Saint Macarius' monastery and a long-time associate of Matta el-Mesqin (the best known of this century's Egyptian monastics, whose work we take up in the next chapter) confirms this when he comments on the twentieth century Coptic revival ("nahda"). He has stated[67] that various writings in English have had a significant influence on Copts—including the King James version of the Bible! *Pilgrim's Progress* and the English version of the *Imitation of Christ* have also been important elements of the religious revival. Stranger still as an influence on Coptic piety have been Bible studies like the *Pulpit*

Commentary and the works of Matthew Henry, long staples of English Evangelical and "fundamentalist" biblical interpretation.

Turning back to Egypt's governments, we find that the challenges to them in the decades before the 1952 Revolution were not only the power struggles among king, the British, and parliament. The social and economic problems of Egypt in the second quarter of the 1900s would have taxed the resources of any government anywhere—no matter how united—as Ghali had pointed out.

The 1936 treaty with Britain was encouraging, and the Copts were proud that their own Makram Ebeid, who had become general secretary of the Wafd in 1927, promoted it. (In 1923, Copts had comprised almost forty-four percent of the Wafd executive committee,[68] so having a Copt in such a high position was no surprise.) But social and economic problems remained and threatened the experiment in liberal government. In 1937, King Faruq was encouraging "the new extreme right (fascist) organization, Misr al-Fatat (Young Egypt), with its Green Shirts youth organization" which was to "become a party of extreme Egyptian nationalism, mixed with religious fanaticism, and a xenophobic platform."[69] Of greater long-term importance than Young Egypt were the Muslim Brothers. Founded in 1928, and "advocating an orthodox Islamic view of society and politics, the Brethren did not eschew forceful modern techniques of organization for political action. They presented themselves as an alternative to the rule of the so-called secular politicians."[70] These militant organizations not only threatened Egypt's "liberal experiment" in general but also, because of their Islamic emphasis, the Copts in particular. Both organizations hated the Wafd party, which was already suffering divisions and increasingly losing its ability to control the parliament and make progress against the social and economic ills of the late 1930s.

World War II brought back British domination, and Egypt was thrust, willy-nilly, into supporting Britain. Masses of Allied troops were stationed in Egypt, and German General Rommel brought his desert army into the country until his defeat at El Alamein. On February 4, 1942, when King Faruq tried to steer his own course, the British brought up tanks to force him to appoint a cabinet that would cooperate with Britain. Thus the Wafd came back into power, but now under the curse of being the servant of British interests. Before long, Makram Ebeid, now the powerful finance minister, broke with his prime minister and exposed the corruption in the Wafd party and brought it even more enemies. The British lost interest in supporting the Wafd after the assurance of defeating the Axis powers, and the party fell from power in 1944.[71]

Egyptians were not dragooned during the second World War as they had been in the first, and many Egyptians actually benefitted from World

War II. Allied forces employed many Egyptians and made large purchases of Egyptian food and goods. Egypt's manufacturers, who had had some protection since 1930, had almost no foreign competition during the war and at its end were poised to develop markets in nearby countries. Copts who owned land or were in business or manufacturing were beneficiaries of this economic boon for Egyptian investors.

A historian of modern Egypt entitled a chapter on Egyptian politics 1930-1950, "The Failure of Liberalism and the Reaction against Europe."[72] This apt title reminds us that the West was being doubly rejected. Its political, economic, and military domination of Egypt and the Middle East were to be fought against on every front, including the establishment of the State of Israel. And Western political, social, and cultural ideas were under fire—including the West's preference for secular government, a matter of great concern for Copts, who realized that a union of state and religion in Egypt would create very serious problems for them.

Another historian of Egypt has said of the postwar period, "Embittered young Egyptians were losing faith in parliamentary democracy and the prewar political parties and were turning to militant, anti-democratic movements," referring to the Muslim Brothers and Young Egypt, now renamed "Islamic Socialist Party."[73] To this tendency towards "radical conservative movements," P. J. Vatikiotis adds "a radical leftist tendency among Western-educated intelligentsia," including the novelist Najib Mahfuz (destined to win the Nobel Prize for Literature in 1988) and the Copt literary and cultural historian, Louis Awad.[75] Thus was the ideology of liberal parliamentary government discredited.

The process of overthrowing parliamentary government in Egypt took seven years,[76] helped along by the frustrating war in the late 1940s over the establishing of the State of Israel. Much more important, however, was Egypt's apparently never-ending struggle with Britain over its military forces on Egyptian soil and over the independence of the Sudan. Indeed, it was the British troops' violent defense of their position in the Suez area that precipitated the breakdown in law and order and parliamentary government in 1952. The Wafd party had regained control of government in the elections of 1950, but it was no match for the disorders of two years later that led to the Revolution which ended the "liberal experiment."

The coming of 1952 confronted the Coptic Christians with the dangers of the increasing take-over of nationalist leadership by radical Islamic groups and the collapse of the Wafd movement that had been so important to them. Many Coptic leaders had become rich during the various economic developments of the seventy years since 1882, so the political instability and the spread of radical economic ideas must have caused them a great deal of worry.

The root problems of the 1952 Revolution for the Copts were that "no officer of the Revolution was a Copt" and that Nasser's brand of nationalism risked leaving the Copts out in its "return to Islam."[77] The Copts had not had an important military tradition, and, although there were Copts who were officers in the army, none of the "Free Officers" who made the Revolution was a Copt. Also, the 1952 Revolution was really a military coup which lacked the popular base or the ideology that had linked Copts and Muslims so prominently in 1919. Indeed, there was no popular base for government in Egypt.[78]

In some ways 1952 marked a return to despotism or "dictatorship without brake."[79] One historian of modern Egypt has implied that "the [Nasser] era in mid-century ushered in a more extreme period of oppression than Sidqi's" (Sidqi being an autocratic right-wing prime minister forced on Egypt by the king in the 1930s), which "accentuated the belief that constitutional institutions were incapable of taking hold in so hostile a political soil as Egypt seemed to be."[80] Be that as it may, Copts found themselves on the outside looking in in a way that had not been true for them at any time earlier in the century.

In addition to this loss of political influence, the Coptic community faced serious economic challenges. The Free Officers may have lacked political ideology, but they did act quickly to bring about agrarian reform, which was probably long overdue. Initially, in the 1952 decrees, individual ownership of land was limited to 200 feddans[81] (a feddan is about an acre), but this maximum was progressively lowered in the years following. A number of Copts had acquired large land holdings, as this had long been the best way for them, as a sometimes threatened minority, to gain protection and some form of power: wealth invested in land. Thus, land reform fell heavily on Copts. When nationalization of industries was added to land reform,[82] leading Copts lost another way to develop economic power as leverage for influence and position in Egyptian society and government.

It has been argued that "land reform and nationalization of companies benefited Muslims exclusively" but also that there were compensatory benefits of land reform to previously landless Coptic peasants.[83] It is unlikely, however, that an Egyptian government without Copts and "returning to Islam" would have given Coptic fellahin an even break in the distribution. Still, it may well be that "by 1952 the landowning elite had become a useless burden to the peasants" and thus "the revolution was, if anything, overdue."[84] In the words of a scholar on the scene, "the agrarian reform on the one hand and the suppression of political parties on the other had the same effect: the abolition of the influence of the notable Coptic laymen in the affairs of the state and therefore in those of the [church] community, which thenceforth has two directions but one head—the church hierarchy."[85]

The decline of Coptic notables is part of the sad story of the early 1950s for the Copts. The other part is the trouble about the patriarch, Pope Youssab II. He had quickly gone back on his word to the majlis al-milli to let them supervise the monastic waqfs, and disputes sharpened between the patriarch on the one hand and the majlis al-milli and the community on the other. The patriarch allowed his valet, who had no qualifications for church administration, to become his agent. "Corruption within the hierarchy had reached an unbelievable height."[86] A virtual revolution was developing. The Holy Synod, which included clergy, asserted itself in 1954 to try to gain control of the patriarchate.

A new organization, *umma qibtiya* (Coptic Nation), had been founded by Coptic law students. It called for a Christian nation founded on the Gospels as its constitution, using Coptic as its official language.[87] This extremist group demanded Youssab's resignation; and members actually kidnapped him in July in a vain effort to force the issue, but the police were able to free him. 1955 was a particularly difficult year for Copts. The government, now headed by Gamal Nasser, was called in; it intervened by calling in a new majlis al-milli, but transferring the "personal status" responsibilities to itself rather than to the council. Majlis al-milli and Holy Synod effected Youssab's deposition, and in September a member of the umma qibtiya tried to assassinate him.[88] Things had gone too far. Nasser banned Youssab from the patriarchate,[89] and a trio of bishops was appointed to administer its affairs. Finally, Youssab died in 1956, and it became possible to name an acting patriarch, the bishop of Beni Suef, who served for two and a half years, until April 29, 1959.

During those extremely difficult years for the Copts, things had not stood still for the government of Egypt.[90] At the beginning of the 1952 Revolution, still in July, King Faruq was forced to abdicate in favor of a regency; and the junta constituted itself as a Revolution Command Council, with Nasser as chairman. A strike in early August was violently put down and punished. In early September, a move was made to try to get the National Assembly, which was dominated by landowners, to institute land reform, which was simply proclaimed when the Assembly refused. The civilian prime minister resigned, and the government was headed by the popular General Najib, one of the few Egyptian heroes of the '48-'49 war in Palestine over the creation of Israel, although Najib was not one of the "Free Officers." Many political arrests were made, and the Constitution of 1923 was abrogated before the end of 1952.

Early in 1953, political parties were abolished, and a "Liberation Rally," headed by Nasser, was instituted to try to mobilize popular support. Governmental administration was widely taken over by military men. By midyear the regency was unseated and Egypt became a republic. In early

1954, Nasser, who had always been the leader of the Free Officers, pushed Najib aside and, in the power struggles, emerged as unchallenged leader. The Muslim Brothers were proscribed, and after their assassination attempt on Nasser, they were strongly put down and six of their leaders were executed. In early 1956, "a new constitution was promulgated" which 1) created a strong presidency, 2) called Egypt an Arab nation, 3) included socialist principles, and 4) created "a National Union to replace the Liberation Rally, which was to screen and select nominees for election to the National Assembly." Nasser was installed as president in late June.[91]

A historian of modern Egypt summarized Nasser's rule thus:

The main feature . . . was the highly personalized 'system' he devised. The brief period of collective decisions and responsibility under the Free Officer regime lasted barely two years . . . From a *primus inter pares*, he had become a native sultan. The issue of his legitimacy was resolved, in a manner of speaking, by his charisma and his acceptance by an enthusiastic public . . . During his rule he produced five parliaments with an average life of two years. He promulgated six constitutions. His cabinets had an average life span of thirteen months . . . He had the right to interfere in all areas of national, political, social, economic, and cultural life of the country.[92]

He interfered in the religious life as well, as we saw in the banishment of Pope Youssab II. Although many problems remained unresolved, because of Nasser's unusual ability to identify himself with the aspirations of the Egyptian people, the nation was to weep openly when he died.

1956 saw many challenges for Nasser in foreign affairs as he gained prominence in the Arab world. He also annoyed the Secretary of State of the United States by his efforts to destabilize conservative monarchies in the Middle East and by his activities in the non-aligned nations movement (dramatized at the Bandung Conference in 1955). Secretary Dulles blocked assistance for building a high dam at Aswan—a key element for Nasser's plan for industrial and agricultural development. When Nasser reacted to Dulles' action by nationalizing the Suez Canal, Israel, Britain, and France ganged up on Egypt in the Suez War of 1956. Egypt was saved by joint diplomatic efforts of the Soviet Union and the United States, and by the beginning of the new year, Britain's last instrument of control over Egypt was ended when the British troops guarding the canal departed.

During this dramatic year of 1956, nationalizations of businesses and industries were initiated, in accordance with Nasser's efforts to meet Egypt's desire for economic justice and to finance solutions for Egypt's many needs, including feeding its rapidly growing population. We have already noted that nationalization turned out to serve the country little better than what it had had before, and in the process the Coptic class of "notables" was hurt.

In 1958, the United Arab Republic was formed by merging Egypt and Syria, necessitating a new constitution. The UAR marriage lasted only until Syria withdrew in 1961. The 1964 constitution necessitated by Syria's departure reaffirmed Egypt's being an Arab nation with a "democratic socialist" system of government.[93] How were the Copts going to fit into that picture? During the first part of the century, leadership from the Patriarchate had been controversial when it had not been actually damaging. What now? We shall see in the next, concluding chapter.

[1]*History of the Patriarchs of the Egyptian Church: known as the History of the Holy Church by Sawirus ibn al-Mukaffa (HPEC)* Vol. 3, trans. and annotated A. Khater and O. H. E. KHS-Burmester (Cairo: Société d'archéologie copte, 1970), pp. 323-326; also see the conclusion of our chapter 9; according to O. F. A. Meinardus, *Christian Egypt: Faith and Life* (Cairo: American University in Cairo Press, 1970), p. 211, the writer was Filuthaus Ibrahim.

[2]A thorough treatment of this history is found in S. M. Seikaly, "The Copts under British Rule, 1882-1914" (Diss. University of London, 1967); a summary of many of his findings appeared in his article, "Coptic Communal Reform: 1860-1914" in *Middle Eastern Studies*, 6 (1970), 247-275; a useful sketch of the purpose and evolution of the majlis al-milli and its struggles with Cyril V is found in Meinardus, pp. 21-25.

[3]E. Wakin, *A Lonely Minority: the Modern Story of Egypt's Copts* (New York: William Morrow, 1963), p. 130.

[4]H.-M. Legrand, "Le renouveau copte," *Istina*, 8 (1961-62), 134-135.

[5]Seikaly, "The Copts under British Rule," pages 68 et seq., and 17.

[6]Seikaly, "Coptic Communal Reform," p. 263.

[7]"The Awakening of the Coptic Church," *The Contemporary Review*, 71 (1897), 747. The author was Markus Simaika.

[8]Douglas Thornton, "The Educational Problem in Egypt in Relation to Religious Teaching," *Church Missionary Intelligencer*, 57 (1906), 651-658.

[9]Thornton, p. 656.

[10]T. E. Dowling, *The Egyptian Church* (London: Cope and Fenwick, n.d., but about 1909), p. 12.

[11]Dowling, p. 14.

[12]Dowling, pp. 5 and 6.

[13]Dowling, p. 4; the book is E. W. Lane, *The Manners and Customs of the Modern Egyptians* (London: Murray, 1836); in her useful book, *Coptic Egypt* (Edinburgh: Scottish Academic Press, 1988), Barbara Watterson feature's Lane's descriptions throughout pp. 161-167.

[14]M. M. Assad, "The Coptic Church and Social Change in Egypt," *International Review of Missions*, 61 (1972), 120.

[15]Seikaly, "Coptic Communal Reform," pp. 247-275; the 15,000 feddans figure was taken from G. Baer, *A History of Land Ownership in Modern Egypt, 1800-1950* (London, 1962), p. 179.

[16]Cromer, *Modern Egypt*, 2 vols. (London: 1908), 1, 123 and 125.

[17]D. S. Margoliouth et al., "Egypt," *Encyclopedia Britannica*, 1957 ed.

[18]Cromer, 1, 143.

[19]Cromer 2, 184.

[20]Thornton, pp. 656-657.

[21]A. J. Butler, Introd., *Copts and Moslems under British Control: A Collection of Facts and a Résumé of Authoritative Opinions on the Coptic Question 1911*, by K. Mikhail (Port Washington, New York: Kennikat Press, 1971).

[22]Cromer 2, 211-212.

[23]Cromer 2, 203-220 (the quotation is from p. 220) and 231.

[24]P. J. Vatikiotis, *The History of Egypt*, 3rd ed. (Baltimore: Johns Hopkins Univ. Press, 1985), p. 211.

[25]A. Goldschmidt, Jr., *Modern Egypt: The Formation of a Nation-State* (Boulder, Colo.: Westview Press, 1988), pp. 38 and 48.

[26]"Intellectual Currents in Egypt," *Middle Eastern Affairs*, 2 (1951), 267-268.

[27]D. Behrens-Abouseif, "The Political Situation of the Copts, 1798-1923," in *The Arabic-Speaking Lands*, Vol. 2 of *Christians and Jews in the Ottoman Empire: the Functioning of a Plural Society,* ed. B. Braude and B. Lewis (New York: Holmes and Meier, 1982), p. 192.

[28]Vatikiotis, pp. 204-205.

[29]Vatikiotis, p. 207.

[30]Behrens-Abouseif, p. 197.

[31]Vatikiotis, p. 208.

[32]This is clear from the efforts of K. Mikhail to influence English public opinion in *Copts and Moslems under British Control* (London, 1911); Meinardus, pp. 39-40, includes a useful summary of the proposals.

[33]Legrand, p. 138.

[34]We are here dependent on R. Yanney, "Light in the Darkness: Life of Archdeacon Habib Guirguis (1876-1951)," *Coptic Church Review,* 5 (1984), 47-52.

[35]Yanney, p. 49.

[36]Legrand, p. 139.

[37]Goldschmidt, pp. 59-60.

[38]I. Gershoni and J. P. Jankowski, *Egypt, Islam, and the Arabs: the Search for Egyptian Nationhood, 1900-1930* (New York: Oxford Univ. Press, 1986), p. 153. Egyptianism, or "Egyptianity," is dealt with especially in "Conclusion: the Triumph of Egyptianism" (in the 1920s); see also Vatikiotis, pp. 310-311 and 477-481; B. L. Carter, *The Copts in Egyptian Politics, 1918-1952* (Bechenham, Kent: Crook Helm, 1986), pp. 95-96 and 107; M. Perlmann's summary of *The Education of Salama Musa* in *Middle Eastern Affairs,* 2 (1951), 279-285. Fouad Ajami, *The Arab Predicament: Arab Political Thought and Practice since 1967, Updated Edition* (Cambridge: Cambridge Univ. Press, 1992), chap. 2.

[39]According to Gershoni and Jankowski, p. 165.

[40]M. B. Ghali, "The Egyptian National Consciousness," *Middle East Journal,* 32 (1978), 59-77.

[41]I. Habib el-Masri, *The Story of the Copts* (Cairo: Middle East Council of Churches, 1978), p. 527.

[42]Seikaly, "The Copts under British Rule," pp. 133-140 and 341-348; the quotation is from p. 348.

[43]T. Little, *Modern Egypt* (New York: Praeger, 1967), pp. 65 and 66.

[44]"Intellectual Currents in Egypt," p. 272.

[45]Wakin, pp. 4 and 30.

[46]Perlmann, summary of *The Education of Salama Musa,* p. 280.

[47]Gershoni and Jankowski, p. 155.

[48]Goldschmidt, p. 53.

[49]Goldschmidt, p. 58.

[50]P. M. Holt *Egypt and the Fertile Crescent 1516-1922: A Political History* (Ithaca, New York: Cornell Univ. Press, 1966), p. 295.

[51]Vatikiotis, p. 260.

[52]Goldschmidt, p. 57.

[53]J. Jomier in "Les Coptes," chap. 3 of M. C. Aulas et al., *L'Égypte aujourd'hui: Permanence et changement, 1805-1976* (Paris: CNRS, 1977), pp. 69-84.

[54]Meinardus, p. 25.

[55]Habib el-Masri, pp. 527-528.

[56]Trans. L. O. Schuman (Leiden: E. J. Brill, 1961); the quotation is from p. 227.

[57]Habib el-Masri, p. 529; and p. 534 for her father.

[58]in M. Martin, "L'église et communauté copte dans l'Islam égyptien," unpublished paper dated 3 February 1982, made available by the author in December of 1989 at the Jesuit Library in Cairo.

[59]Meinardus, pp. 26-27.

[60]This paragraph depends on the "Chronique" from Egypt in *Proche-Orient Chrétien*, 4 (1954), 244-245.

[61]For an English translation, see M. B. Ghali, *The Policy of Tomorrow* (Washington, D.C.: American Council of Learned Societies, 1953).

[62]Vatikiotis, pp. 312-313.

[63]Meinardus, p. 41.

[64]Habib el-Masri, p. 529.

[65]Meinardus, p. 26.

[66]Legrand, p. 141.

[67]In an interview in early December of 1989 at Saint Macarius' monastery.

[68]Carter, p. 195.

[69]Vatikiotis, pp. 292 and 318.

[70]Vatikiotis, p. 317.

[71]Vatikiotis, p. 354.

[72]Vatikiotis, pp. 317-342. Afaf Lutfi al-Sayyid Marsot entitled her important book on the period *Egypt's Liberal Experiment, 1922-1936* (Berkeley: Univ. of California Press, 1977).

[73]Goldschmidt, p. 75.

[74]Vatikiotis, pp. 341-342.

[75]Vatikiotis, chapter 16, especially pp. 355-371, where there is a helpful sketch of these years leading up to the 1952 Revolution.

[76]M. Martin, p. 8.

[77]Amira Sonbol, "Society, Politics, and Sectarian Strife," in I. M. Oweiss, *The Political Economy of Contemporary Egypt* (Washington: Georgetown Univ. Center of Contemporary Arab Studies, 1990), p. 266.

[78]M. B. Ghali, "The Egyptian National Consciousness," p. 63.

[79]A. L. al-Sayyid Marsot, p. 5.

[80]English translation in *Middle East Journal*, 7 (1953), 74 et seq.

[81]Wakin, pp. 38, 39.

[82]S. F. Karas, "Egypt's Beleaguered Christians," *Worldview*, 26 (1983), 13; for a contrary view, see J. D. Pennington, "The Copts in Modern Egypt," *Middle Eastern Studies*, 18 (1982), 164.

[83]Goldschmidt, p. 93.

[84]Martin, p. 7.

[85]Meinardus, p. 26.

[86]L. Barbulesco, ed., *Les Chrétiens égyptiens aujourd'hui: Éléments de discours* (Cairo: Centre d'étude et de documentation économique, juridique, et social, 1985), p. 29.

[87]Wakin, pp. 93-94; and cf. Pennington, p. 163.

[88]Meinardus, p. 27.

[89]For this history, see Vatikiotis, pp. 376-384, or Goldschmidt, pp. 90-99.

[90]Vatikiotis, pp. 384-385.

[91]Vatikiotis, pp. 421-422.

[92]Vatikiotis, pp. 400-401.

Chapter Eleven

Twentieth Century, II

✠ ——————————————————————— ✠

1959 -

D IVIDING THE TWENTIETH CENTURY in Egyptian political and diplomatic history is quite easy, for the 1952 Revolution of the "Free Officers" was clearly the dominant factor for the last half of the century. 1952 is, unfortunately, not so good a dividing point for the internal development of Coptic Church history, for that year found the Copts in the middle of a low point for the church. So, we chose 1959 as our dividing point. The second half of the twentieth century has been crucially important for the Coptic Church, in spite of the general environment the church and its membership have found themselves in since 1952. As we saw in the preceding chapter, most of the changes wrought by the 1952 Revolution significantly eroded the economic and political power of Copts, and many Coptic families were soon beginning to wonder what future there was for Copts in Egypt. Then the 1970s brought serious troubles for the Copts from Islamic organizations like student groups, the Islamic Group, and the Muslim Brothers, and the Coptic leadership found itself caught in conflicts with the government of Egypt which were to stretch on into the middle 1980s.

Yet, during all the difficult time from 1952 to this writing, a renaissance has been going on in Coptic Church life, including strong leadership from a hierarchy which had become, for the first time, well educated[1] as well as devout. The great turning point for the Coptic Church of the twentieth century was the 1959 election and consecration of Coptic Pope Cyril VI (after a two and a half year interregnum which followed the tragic patriarchate of Youssab II). The ongoing revival in the Coptic Church since 1959 is the principal focus of this chapter.

The future Cyril VI was born in 1902, educated in Alexandria, and employed as a young adult by a travel agency. He entered the Baramus monastery in Wadi Natrun at the age of twenty-five, inspired by his reading in the *Lives of the Desert Fathers*. His monastic vocation was opposed by his parents and by the patriarchal assistant, Bishop Youannis, on the basis of the young man's good education and wealthy upbringing, which were thought to make the monastic life too hard for him,[2] but he persevered. We have already noted how the beginnings of monastic reform were bringing a variety of results, of which this was a major one.

After two years at the Helwan School for Monks, he was back at Wadi Natrun where he moved to a cave near his monastery—his first anchorite experience. In 1936, he began another period of solitude, this time near and then in Old Cairo until he became Qummus Mina, as head of Saint Samuel monastery, from which he was elected patriarch. The government of Egypt, in a 1957 presidential decree, had approved the regulations for the election but it had not allowed the election to take place for two and a half years. The regulations were announced in April of 1959 as in accord with church law by "Dr. Kamal Ramzi Stino, Central Minister of Supply, a Copt who served as the church's representative in the cabinet of the United Arab Republic."[3]

The election was not easy, but in the elimination ballot Qummus Mina was one of the three that got the highest number of votes. Then, a five-year old deacon drew by lot the name of Mina, who was declared elected. Four days later, President Nasser designated the newly-elected as Pope of Alexandria in a presidential decree.[4] Mina was consecrated to the office within the month as Cyril VI, whose "religious value made possible broad unanimity within the [Coptic] community and the flourishing once again of the dignity of the [patriarchal] function"[5] after some difficult times.

One of the first things Pope Cyril undertook was to solve the serious problems the Coptic Church was having with its daughter church in Ethiopia,[6] which had always received its hierarchy from Egypt. For one thing, the Emperor and the Ethiopians had been wanting their own hierarchy at least since Ethiopia regained its independence (from Italy) in 1942. Also, the Ethiopians had been upset over the deposition of Youssab II, for it was he who had consecrated their chief bishop (abuna) and allowed him to consecrate five Ethiopian bishops. A 1958 agreement between the two churches stipulated that the Ethiopian Church would participate in the election of the new Coptic patriarch and that Ethiopian aspirations about the powers of their abuna would be reexamined after the election. Pope Cyril followed through conscientiously, so that by mid-1959 a joint declaration of the two churches was issued, in which the abuna was enthroned "as the first Patriarch-Catholicus of the Church of Ethiopia," although the Alexandrian pope remained "the supreme spiritual head of the Church of Ethiopia."[7]

Pope Cyril's monastic policies did not have universal support.

Realizing that the future of the church depends upon the integrity and spirituality of the monks, and believing in strict monastic discipline, Cyril VI ordered all the monks to return to their respective monasteries to fulfill their monastic vows. While most monks followed the patriarchal order, some of the anchorites of the Western Desert disobeyed [in 1960-61] the law and thus were penalized by being suspended from the Church.[8]

Among those unwilling to comply was the conservative but deeply spiritual Matta el-Mesqin,[9] who was soon to recover his place, however, as a leader of the monastic revival in the Coptic Church.

Cyril proposed to work closely with the majlis al-milli, but by 1960 the waqfs had been placed under a special committee, leaving the council only educational and building duties,[10] and in 1962 Nasser simply abolished it, on the theory that the patriarch could handle those matters better. Patriarch and president got along quite well.[11] When Nasser laid the foundation-stone of the new Saint Mark's Cathedral in Abbasiya in 1965, he emphasized the brotherhood of Christians and Muslims and the lack of distinctions between them; Pope Cyril "pledged his full allegiance to the government" in his reply, and "the official proclamations of the patriarch became more numerous in which he condemned the American involvement in Vietnam, imperialism and colonialism in Africa, racism in Israel, and proposed the introduction of studies in socialism for the Coptic clergy."[12] These positions fit well with Nasser's. By the time of the 1967 war with Israel Cyril had been proclaiming "the basic identity of goals of the Christian Gospel with the aspirations of the Arab Socialist Society."[13]

The Coptic Church showed another side of its opposition to colonialism in Africa by its efforts to link up with Christian communities in Uganda, Kenya, and Tanzania as well as South Africa. Pope Cyril stated in 1962 that "the Coptic Church carries the banner of Orthodox Christian doctrine, and wherever Orthodox Christianity exists, full liberty and permanent peace prevail. For the Coptic Church throughout its long history has not given a chance to imperialism to dominate through religious teachings." By 1964, it was thought "that there were several African Christian communities, that wished to cut relations with Western Churches and establish independent African Churches," and waqfs funds were set aside for non-imperialist missionary efforts.[14]

In a 1964 article,[15] an Egyptian Jesuit wrote, "The Coptic Orthodox Church . . . has today about five million members who are among the hardest working and most patriotic citizens [of Egypt]." He described them as religious people, but "in this second half of the twentieth century [the Church] presents herself as at once weakened and renewed," largely because of internal fights in which "the richest and best educated laymen, and some-times the more zealous, wish to direct the Church." The state had taken over the Copts' schools, but through the improved educational level of the monks and the Sunday Schools, institutions like the Coptic Archeological Society and the Coptic Institute, Copts were able to maintain a certain focus on lit-eracy and learning. Their newspaper, *al-Watani*, was said to have 50,000 readers. Furthermore, the Copts had been very active in placing Bibles in the hands of their members through the Egyptian Bible Society and their own Bible societies, including heroic efforts to reach isolated Coptic families through the Rural Diakonia movement and focusing on Bible study in the education of the clergy.

1962 was a key year for Egypt and for Copts. Nasser created the Arab Socialist Union, which was "intended to create a new Arab society in Egypt as well as outline the basic characteristics of the desirable Muslim, national-ist, socialist Arab society everywhere. It was also the prelude to another reor-ganization of the country's political and constitutional life."[16] Also in 1962, Egypt began its five-year intervention in Yemen which was to be inconclu-sive, but which drained Egypt dangerously of blood and resources and soured some of Egypt's natural allies.

Still in 1962, Pope Cyril began consecrating "general bishops" to share in the church's leadership. Bishop Shenouda, who was to succeed Cyril as patriarch, was given special responsibilities in Christian education at all lev-els. Bishop Samuel was to have special responsibility in ecumenism and in the social service work in the church. Bishop Gregorios was consecrated for higher education and to head the Coptic Institute. Since they were not "mar-ried" to any diocese, these general bishops were free to exercise leadership throughout the church—and were eligible for the patriarchate. They were to play an important part in the continuing renaissance in the Coptic Church, and Shenouda was to increase their number once he became patriarch.

The Six Days War with Israel in June of 1967 was a turning point in Egyptian history. Although Nasser was able to deflect from himself much of the popular dismay over Egypt's humiliating and costly defeat, it was a terri-ble blow to Egypt. The war finally made it clear that Egypt could not afford the investment it would take to make itself Israel's military equal, and, cou-pled with the costs of the war in Yemen, the Six Days War left Egypt's econ-omy in a very precarious position. It seemed that grim failure was now fac-ing the ambitious efforts to build up Egypt's economy to make possible solu-tions for the many problems and challenges to Egypt created by the contin-uing acceleration of population growth, rapid urbanization, unemployment, and underemployment.

The widespread response to the 1967 defeat was a sharp turning to religion and to the religious communities. This took place among Muslims as well as among the Coptic Christians. Paradoxically, no event was more important to both than a series of apparitions in 1968 of the Virgin Mary. A Muslim historian called them "the most interesting post-defeat phenomenon" which, she goes on to say, took place at

> a small church in a remote suburb of Cairo. The Virgin holds a special place in the hearts of all Egyptians, Christian or Muslim . . .Thousands of Egyptians lined up outside the church every night . . .A wave of religious fervour swept the country. Coptic monasteries . . . had waiting lists, and such long ones that they would only admit university students. Koran study groups mushroomed among all classes of society, who turned to religion for consolation.[17]

Indeed, it would seem that a Muslim was the first to see the phenomenon, and the Egyptian government encouraged visitors to try to see it.[18] The sharp inward turning of Christians and Muslims toward their religious communities was a potential danger to the Copts, a religious minority in an Islamic state. The inevitable push for islamization was to heighten religious strife in Egypt[19] as the end of the century approached.

Nasser died in 1970 and was succeeded by his vice president, Anwar Sadat, another of the Free Officers who had made the 1952 Revolution. "The hero had died, leaving behind him a country partly under foreign domination, and facing overwhelming problems. If the hero had had feet of clay, at least he had been larger than life, a true colossus who had dominated the Middle East for nearly two decades and caused it to follow the beat of his drum."[20] None of Egypt's social or economic problems had vanished, however, and, as if this were not enough, Egypt had found itself since 1967 embarrassingly dependent on the Soviet Union and Saudi Arabia for economic and military support. Both of these countries, in their own ways, were to inhibit Egypt's freedom of action.

Sadat was considered rather colorless, and people wondered if he would be able to survive as president. He did survive, of course, and in his "rectification revolution" he quickly moved his supporters into key positions and began a series of significant shifts away from various of Nasser's policies. In the realm of ideology he countered leftist influences by encouraging Muslim organizations, especially among the politically important university students. He exchanged Egypt's relation with the Soviet Union for one with the United States. The socialized economy, which had been so large a part of Nasser's program for Egypt, was modified with a new policy of openness (infitah) to private investment and foreign businesses.

Even more dramatic than these moves, which had only a minimum of success in solving Egypt's problems, were Sadat's efforts to confront the challenge of Israel. The first was war. In October of 1973, Sadat was able to coordinate with Syria a surprise attack on Israel on the Jewish Day of Atonement (Yom Kippur) which made significant short-term gains, even though the Israelis quickly recovered and launched a counterattack that threatened Egypt more than ever before. Although the Yom Kippur War was a military defeat for Egypt, it was an important symbolic victory, psychologically and politically. The economic and social problems of Egypt, however, had scarcely been touched; and when almost in desperation Sadat had ordered in 1977 the end of the expensive subsidies for food, riots erupted which endangered the very survival of the regime.

Sadat made his decision, then, to make peace with Israel in order to end the continual drain of Egypt's resources from the seemingly interminable and fruitless state of war with that most powerful state in the Middle East. Making this separate peace with Israel cost Egypt the friendship and support of other Arab countries, but was by no means unpopular at home. The Egyptians hoped that, at last, this would be the breakthrough that would begin to improve their standard of living. Unfortunately, they were to be disappointed once again. Sadat had "reversed [Nasser's] policies toward the superpowers, socialism, and, and the conflict with Israel . . . [for which he was] lauded in the West,"[21] but he was by no means idolized in Egypt, partly because of increasing corruption growing out of his and his family's love of ostentation. He seemed to be more practical-minded than Nasser about what Egypt could hope to do to solve its problems, but what was working for him?

In March of 1971, Pope Cyril VI died. The Coptic Church was then unified in a way that it had sadly lacked during the time of his three immediate predecessors. He was a saint and a solitary at heart, "a genuine [miracle worker], a deeply pious and religious person of extraordinary spiritual gifts who, among other things, has stopped the ill practice of simony (sale of religious office), at least at the episcopal level," but who may have lacked some administrative skills that a patriarch could use with great profit.[22]

In Cyril's day, a movement had begun to flourish which was to rival the Sunday Schools and the monastic revival in importance to the life and mission of the Coptic Orthodox Church. This was the Rural Diakonia Program pioneered by Abuna Bulus Bulus in Damanhur in 1957 and broadened in impact, from 1959, by the head of the Department of Social Studies of the Coptic Institute, the future Bishop Samuel.[23] It was designed to serve Coptic families in villages that had no church. The program included "the distribution of Bibles and [other] religious literature" and visits of priests to bring the church's sacraments to the people. To these spiritual ministrations was added invaluable instruction in social and economic matters such as family care, improved agriculture, health, and home economics. The program trained workers, supervised them, and brought them together for evaluation and further training.

Cyril had created a notable leadership through the general bishops he consecrated, and one of them was to be his successor, Shenouda III, who was to extend the practice substantially. He had been the bishop for Coptic Church Educational Institutions and rector and professor of Old Testament of the Coptic Orthodox theological seminary. He was enthroned as patriarch in late 1971, at the age of 47.[24] Before his monastic career, he had graduated from Cairo University in history and had served as an officer in the Egyptian army during the 1948 war with Israel. He was active in the Sunday School movement from 1950 to 1953, a movement he was later to supervise as a general bishop. He was seen as a "charismatic and uncompromising figure," which may have boded ill for his relations with the volatile Sadat. After "fruitful years in youth work, he went to the desert as a monk . . . For six years he lived in a cave in seclusion from his monastery [Bishoi in the Wadi Natrun] that he might give himself to prayer, study, and contemplation."[25] He was influenced by a famous ascetic and hermit, Abuna Abd al-Massih, who had also inspired Pope Cyril VI.[26]

As patriarch, Shenouda "soon gained prominence as theologian, New Testament exegete, journalist [he has edited his own weekly, *al-Kiraza*] and preacher, . . . called by Patriarch Maximos Hakim of the Syrian Orthodox Church . . . 'the most gifted preacher of the Word in the Middle East today.'" The attendance at his Bible studies at the Patriarchal Cathedral in Cairo ranged "from 5,000 to 7,000."[27]

One way Pope Shenouda could give leadership to his church and the Copts of Egypt was to establish himself as an ecumenical force. The Coptic Church had had an interesting relationship with the ecumenical movement since World War II. The future Bishop Samuel had represented the Copts in the World Council of Churches' 1954 meeting in Evanston, Illinois, and the Copts have maintained[28] this relationship ever since, despite opposition of some conservatives like Abuna Matta el-Mesqin, who criticized the Council for discouraging patriotism and for being pro-Jew.[29]

A foretaste of what was to come showed up when the Ecumenical Patriarch of Constantinople visited Cairo and was told by a professor at the Institute of Coptic Studies, "There is no difference between you and us . . . the [differences] are only verbal. There is no reason for us to remain separated . . . We do not follow Eutyches (the heretic in whose teachings the humanity of Jesus seemed to disappear) and you do not follow Nestorius (the heretic in whose teachings the oneness of Christ seemed to disappear)." The Ecumenical Patriarch responded, "I sense and have the assurance of entering into contact with a sister Orthodox Church."[30] By 1971 Bishop Shenouda himself had become involved in ecumenical activities. At Vienna at the Pro Oriente Conference, a joint statement was drawn up by him and other theologians of the Oriental, i.e., non-Chalcedonian, Orthodox Churches on the one hand, and the Eastern (Chalcedonian) Orthodox Churches which are in communion with the patriarch of Constantinople on the other. (These two Orthodox communions had been separated since 451 and have maintained rival hierarchies in the East, e.g., the Eastern Orthodox have a patriarch of Alexandria of their own.) The Vienna statement[31] was addressed to the heads of the Orthodox churches as a call for unity.

Note was taken of the prominence of non-theological differences that developed during the centuries of separation—differences agreed to be ultimately peripheral, which should not be allowed to hinder unity. Emphasis was put on the common faith of the Orthodox churches expressed in the ecumenical Nicene Creed, the Doctrine of the Trinity, the seven sacraments, the honor due the Virgin Mary, together with traditional religious practices of Eastern Christians like fasting, venerating icons and relics, and invoking the prayers of saints. Most important was the ability of the theologians to express in common their faith in the oneness of Jesus Christ and in his perfect divinity and perfect humanity. The Council of Chalcedon of 451 was not mentioned nor was its controversial doctrine of two "natures" of Christ "after the union" of the divine and human in Jesus. Surprisingly, there was little problem in reaching an agreed statement about a doctrine that had seemed to separate churches for so long. The importance of this concord on the doctrine of Christ was crucial not only for the Copts' relations to the Eastern Orthodox churches but also for their relations to the Western Churches, Catholic and Protestant, for they also had accepted the Council of Chalcedon which was rejected by the Copts and the other Oriental Orthodox churches.

Pope Shenouda, who was elevated to the patriarchate in 1971, visited Rome in 1973 where he and Roman Pope Paul VI issued a joint statement on Christology[32]. In a discourse at his cathedral in 1974,[33] he expressed many of his convictions about church unity. "We are a conservative and traditional church and nevertheless we have held out our hands towards unity in all domains because unity is the commandment of Christ; it is his will." He cited the Vienna "Common Formula": "We all believe that our Lord, God and Saviour Jesus Christ is the Incarnate Word, the Incarnate God. We believe that He was perfect in His Divinity and Perfect in His Humanity, and that His Divinity never departed His Humanity not even a single instant nor a twinkle of an eye."

In subsequent years, Pope Shenouda also cultivated relations with the Anglican Communion. In 1979, he visited England to consecrate Coptic Churches and visit the Archbishop of Canterbury.[34] In 1987, the Archbishop of Canterbury visited Pope Shenouda at his monastery (Bishoi) in Egypt, and they issued a joint statement based on the Nicene Creed and an agreed statement on the doctrine of Christ almost word for word like those we have referred to above.[35] Later in 1987, Pope Shenouda organized a meeting at his monastery with the Greek Orthodox Patriarch of Alexandria, the two rival Patriarchs of Antioch (Chalcedonian and non-Chalcedonian), and the Armenian Catholicon. They confessed the same faith in Christ, "fundamentally and essentially."[36]

That the great difference on Christology between Anglicans (typical of Western orthodoxy on the doctrine of Christ) and the Oriental Orthodox Churches was really only a verbal one had actually been perceived, first by a lay missionary of the Episcopal Church (an Anglican church) in 1841: "They attach to the one nature precisely the same idea that we attach to the one person, the difference is only the word,"[37] and then by Archdeacon Dowling in the early part of this century when he observed that the difference in belief about Christ "has become now a mere matter of terminology."[38]

In 1988, there were meetings between Coptic Orthodox and Coptic Catholics and Coptic Evangelicals, participated in by leaders at the highest levels.[39] The Copts seemed to recognize now what these small minority churches in Egypt had taught them by example, e.g., in Christian education and social services. Relationships seemed to be friendlier than ever. The question remained whether Coptic Orthodox and Roman Catholic could ever become really reconciled, in light of conflicting claims between the two Popes, of the condemnations of the others' heroes on both sides (like Leo the Great of Rome and Dioscorus of Alexandria), and of the cultural differences that had taken root over centuries of separation—especially those that emerged after the Reformation in Europe.

While all this ecumenism was going on in the 1970s and 1980s, the Copts were finding themselves in increasingly dangerous circumstances in Egypt. The "process of militant religious resurgence was accelerated by Nasser's failing socialist policies, followed by Sadat's pro-Western economic liberalization policy and his alliance with the rich, oil-producing Arab states after 1971."[40] Pope Shenouda was the capstone of the effort of the renewal movement to be a power to serve Copts, so that they would not be so dependent on government.[41] He was thought by many Egyptians to have "rather aggressive activist views regarding the promotion and defence of the rights of the Coptic community." Many felt that there was too much Coptic militancy, especially among Coptic youth, and that the Copts were building too many churches. By 1980, many Muslims were alarmed by "the significant upsurge in the political consciousness and activity of the Coptic community—its determined effort to resurrect the Coptic language (at the expense of Arabic), its efforts to proselytize and to develop new churches, schools and socio-political organizations."[42] On the other hand, Copts feared that pushing legislation was "undermining the secular fundamentals that bind a nation-state together."[43]

Some Muslims saw the Coptic Church as "now like a political party under the leadership of the patriarch, breaking the national unity."[44] Copts were perceived as opposing constitutional moves toward making the Islamic "sharia" the main source—or as simply *the* source of Egyptian law.[45] Muslims argue that the sharia is no threat to Copts but rather arises from fears stimulated by Western interests.[46] Copts were also complaining that official censuses were deliberately undercounting them in order to justify their under-representation in government and in other walks of life.[47]

Islamic societies of university students, encouraged by Sadat to counteract leftist influences, began organized attacks on Coptic students, who also engaged in activities perceived as Coptic militancy. Conservative Copts, alarmed at what was happening, may have wished that a more diplomatic candidate, say, like Bishop Samuel, had been chosen in 1971.

Conflicts arose most dramatically and decisively over church-building. For many years there had been Muslim lawyers who argued that any church-building should be illegal in an Islamic country.[48] Nasser had promised that twenty-five churches a year could be built; but only sixty-eight were authorized throughout the 1960s, so Copts put up buildings called "philanthropic," not without conflicts between Christians and Muslims.[49] Still in the 1990s congregations had to petition for a presidential decree to allow even minor repairs.

By 1980, things were so bad, as a result of bombings of churches, that Pope Shenouda canceled Easter celebrations—a drastic step, as many Muslim friends, including high officials, joined Christians in many of the Easter festivities. Not long after, militant Copts in the United States embarrassed Sadat by demonstrating against him during his visit to that country. Sadat blamed Pope Shenouda, and accused him "of conspiring to erect a separate Christian state in Upper Egypt."[50]

In 1981, Sadat was desperate. His political support was weak and his economic plans were not really improving life in Egypt for most Egyptians. His efforts to use Muslims against leftists had opened Pandora's box, and a bloody Christian/Muslim riot in a section of Cairo in June of 1981 brought communal rivalry to the crisis stage. Sadat's main problem was generally with Muslim militants, but, in order to appear even-handed, he sent Pope Shenouda to his monastery to stay under what was effectively house arrest, and tried to replace him. Other bishops and Coptic clergy were arrested, and various militant Muslim organizations, including the Muslim Brothers, were banned.

This was happening in September of 1981. Weeks later, Sadat was dead, assassinated by militant Muslims; and the popular Coptic Bishop Samuel had died at his side. Vice-president Hosni Mubarak was installed as president immediately. An air force officer who had been too young to participate in the 1952 Revolution of the Free Officers, he had been trusted by Sadat and now moved strongly against those directly responsible for the assassination. Otherwise his policy was more reconciliation than retribution, and he tried to move things slowly back to normal. His policy was "gradualism and moderation at all costs whether or not a more dynamic course of action is called for."[51] The Coptic hierarchy was able to block an effort to replace the Patriarch in 1983. Pope Shenouda was not encouraged to return to his patriarchate in Cairo, however, until January of 1985.

In an election called for 1984 the Wafd party, in which Copts had served prominently in earlier times, made common cause with the Muslim Brothers. Thus, the Copts felt they no longer had a place in the Wafd, choosing rather to take their chances with the official party. In 1985, when in an interesting test case a motion to adopt the sharia directly into Egyptian law came before the Assembly, it was severely defeated. It appeared that Egypt would continue to have a secular government.

Still, highly educated Copts—the ones who were not migrating to Canada or the United States or Australia—were turning more and more to life within the bosom of the church, often as monks and nuns. Two visitors to Coptic monasteries had written in 1978 in a Russian Orthodox journal[52] of the "vast expansion of monasticism and recovery of the tradition of the desert fathers" and how "monastic revival was initially associated with the educated middle class of Cairo. The monasteries of the Wadi Natrun are full of doctors and engineers from the capital." In thirty years the number of monks there grew eight-fold.[53] Otto Meinardus, in reviewing his work on Coptic monasteries, found forty monks associated with Saint Anthony's, forty with Saint Paul's, eighty-three with Baramus, 120 with Bishoi, sixty each with Suriani and al-Muharraq.[54] And the monastic vocation still has a powerful appeal for many Copts.

The bishops have been drawn more and more from among the better educated monks, who add higher education to the traditional asceticism and years of solitude which have always characterized leading Coptic monks. The best known Coptic monk is still Matta al-Mesqin, although he has come down strongly behind the more conservative elements and has expressed strong reservations about Coptic participation in ecumenical activities. His monastery, Saint Macarius', is expansive and beautifully rebuilt. Famous for its hospitality and spiritual atmosphere, it is a favorite of hosts of Egyptian and foreign pilgrims; and it is making the desert bloom through a variety of innovative projects, a number of which have stimulated considerable government interest. At the Bishoi monastery in the Wadi Natrun, Pope Shenouda has created a visitors' residence in which both international and Egyptian church leaders can stay and participate in top-level discussions about common Christian concerns and plans. The center is already serving these uses, as we have seen.

A Coptic scholar wrote in 1982, "The Coptic Church is like a histori-cal museum; the old and the new are to be found side by side, for the antiq-uity of the culture leads to their being simply juxtaposed with no thought of the dialectical relationship between the two."[55] Whether or how long this remains true is problematic. The experience of Western Christianity has tended to be quite different; for centuries it has generally been in some kind of dialogue with new ideas and new environments. In fact, many Copts crit-icize Western Christianity for being so strongly influenced by its environ-ment that Western Christians lose contact with the original, historic faith. Be that as it may, it is hard to see how a trend to more secular education for cler-gy as well as lay leaders is not destined to create for Copts a "dialectical rela-tionship" between the old and the new in Coptic Christianity, in spite of its intense emphasis on the traditional. Another Coptic writer stresses "a deep split in the leadership of the church" between traditionalists and moderniz-ers, the latter "being highly educated Copts who went into church service to revitalize the decaying church's structure."[56] Thus, as they approach the end of the twentieth century, Copts are old and new, modernizers and tradition-alists. It remains to be seen whether they will interact and move toward a progressive synthesis or whether conservatism will limit the modern world's impact on the Coptic Church to technological improvements.

As we turn to the relationship of the Coptic Orthodox Church to the cultural and political environment in which Copts and the majority of their fellow Egyptians find themselves, we begin with statistics. Already we are in trouble. Are there three to four million Copts or seven to ten million? One serious statistical study made in 1967 concluded that Copts have comprised seven to eight percent for the last two centuries, so that the lower figure, which is closer to the government's, is the better one.[57] The medians of totals and percentages found in several articles,[58] however, would suggest six mil-lion Copts and about ten percent to twelve percent of the population of Egypt, but most of the articles are by Copts, who have an interest in higher percentages. The *1985 Handbook: Member Churches*[59] of the World Council of Churches proposed 3.9 million members in 1200 parishes with 1500 priests, gathered into forty dioceses and led by sixty bishops.

Copts look like other Egyptians, but they are often distinguishable by their names[60] and, especially if they are villagers, by a cross tattooed[61] on the inside of their right wrist. There are still Copts who convert to Islam, often to escape an unpleasant marriage or to get a better job, and doubtless there are Copts who would like to blend into the landscape so as not to draw atten-tion to themselves. Still, Copts are generally quite unashamed of their com-munity. This may be particularly true of young Copts. "For the majority of educated young Copts today, religion is the dominant ideology, and the church the main social outlet."[62] This writer had the point driven home to him when one Monday night in 1989 he attended, along with no fewer than five hundred young adults, their regular weekly gathering at the Coptic metropolitan cathedral in Beni Suef.

There is a negative side of this religious loyalty. Maurice Martin has written eloquently in 1982 of the self-isolation of Copts, especially the youth, who are feeling more and more excluded from national life. Like the devout Muslim youth who "have turned to traditional forms of self-identity,"[63] young Copts are opposing Western modernity, which they feel has eroded traditional values in Egypt, especially moral and family values. Religion is seen as a universal cure, especially the more traditional and the more ascetical forms of religion. "At present," it was observed in 1982, "the Coptic Church seems to offer the model of people turning to serve it, a people integrated into, and consecrated to, their religious community."[64]

On the other hand, Pope Shenouda, in a newspaper interview explaining the purposes of a long overseas tour he was about to undertake in 1989, seemed to signal a drop in religious extremism in Egypt: "Our children living overseas must know that what they hear about religious extremism is exaggerated . . . The reality is different. Extremism is not dominant. It is true of a minority and does not find an important echo, as some pretend. Intellectuals as well as the state oppose it . . . I want everyone to know that extremism is in retreat in Egypt."[65] It is also argued that most "educated Egyptians remain loyal to the ideals of secular nationalism,"[66] and that "it would seem unlikely that in the present circumstances religion would exercise much influence on judicial decision making."[67] And yet the issue does not seem to be dead by any means. A dramatic academic debate in Cairo over legal decision making drew a tremendous crowd of strict Islamicists, and the few legal scholars who questioned shifting Egyptian law to meet Islamicist demands were scarcely given a hearing.[68] Perhaps there is a paradox that despite little public defense of secular government and law there is little chance that the Mubarak regime will replace it.

A sociological study[69] of a rural village in Upper Egypt drew some conclusions about the Coptic community there which illustrate Coptic efforts to secure their place in Egypt. It is to be noted that the observations were made in the late 1970s. The town is in the Minya province, which has a significant proportion of Copts. About one-fourth of the 25,000 townspeople are Christians, who have their own representatives on the village council. Only the tattooed cross distinguishes them in outward appearance. Copts have a kind of persecution complex (the late '70s were dangerous times in el-Minya) and suspect that a Nasser is needed to control hostile Muslims.

The Copts were said to "have sublimated their minority feelings of frustration and persecution into an intense, individualistic drive for self-realization."[70] Thus, Copts owned fifty-eight percent of the town's private enterprises (especially in the more technically advanced and profitable business-es), three-fifths of the factories, and all the pharmacies, photographic stu-dios, and electrical and plumbing outlets. Nine of the eleven medical doc-tors were Copts. A Christian grocer commented: "We Christians here can-not spend our nights in social activities; . . . we have to work hard and edu-cate our children to protect ourselves against the Muslim majority." The study notes how sharply this attitude frustrates cooperation in the village to resolve common problems.[71] It must be said, however, that Coptic business success has certainly appeared to be the best guarantee of Coptic survival for the thirteen and a half centuries of Arab/Muslim domination of Egypt.

At the other end of the Coptic social spectrum would be the garbage collectors of Cairo. Many poor Copts who had been left without a way to live in agricultural Egypt migrated to Cairo without jobs or prospects but found a niche for themselves working with garbage—work without a taboo for Christians. They were able to earn money from their clients, who had to pay to get their garbage carted off. Equally important to them was finding them-selves the possessors of a vast source of re-usable materials. The atmosphere where they live and work is most unpleasant, and the inevitable social prob-lems of urbanization have not been escaped. Christian organizations seeking to minister to the families often feel quite inadequate to the enormous chal-lenge. And yet once again, in this way also, Copts have been able to show their determination to survive. A 1980 study heard it said of Christians, apparently in contrast with others, that they "cooperate and help each other and they have compassion."[72]

One of the challenges to Egypt since the 1952 Revolution is the result of the heroic push toward free education at almost all levels: how to have adequate schools for such a huge quantity of students. All schools were nationalized and made free in an effort to equalize the chance of young peo-ple to gain access to education. Parents have understandably tried to take full advantage of opportunities for their children, but this has caused serious overcrowding at all levels and a dangerous watering down of instruction at most schools. Nowhere is this more true than at the university level. A fur-ther complication arose when government employment was offered in 1962 to all who completed degree programs.[73] Not only has this created a giant government expense and inefficiency but it has not offered sufficient incen-tive for students to aim at programs of study most likely to have good jobs waiting for their graduates.[74] There is a glut in the prestigious programs in the arts, in law and commerce, in the humanities and in the theoretical sciences but a serious lack of qualified workers in the middle range of technical man-power. Higher education as the road to personal success has been more important for Coptic youth than for the majority, so it may be that they will continue preferring courses of study leading to steady jobs.

The Coptic intellectual Louis Awad has been particularly critical of the damage being done to Egyptian universities by the serious overcrowding.[75] Awad represents the highest level Copts have been able to achieve in the intellectual pursuits most valued in the West, but this has created problems for him. He has been bitterly attacked recently for using "Western" criteria in criticizing the common Muslim evaluation of the place of an important Muslim writer in the evolution of Egyptian nationalism.[76]

On the other hand, when a mature and devout layman of the Coptic diaspora and a visiting monk from Egypt were asked recently about the relation of intellectuals like Awad to the Coptic Church, the pair responded, "there are no intellectuals in the Coptic Church." This response sounds astonishing and calls for some explanation. It does seem to be the case that the Coptic Orthodox Church as a religious community has not been invaded by the secular and humanistic presuppositions of the Renaissance, which have given the West such marvelous tools of literary, linguistic, and historical criticism. Secular and humanistic thinking as applied to scientific and technical questions does not dismay Copts. On the contrary, Copts have welcomed technical advances in engineering, for example, and even in studies like law. But Copts have no history of applying this kind of modern critical technique to matters of religion. If, then, intellectuals are those for whom secular and humanistic criticism is their stock in trade, a comment like "there are no intellectuals in the Coptic Church" becomes less startling.

Still, Copts are vulnerable to the charge of being anti-intellectual. For example, an active Coptologist, who has been a driving force for vigorous Coptic language and textual studies at the Coptic Archeological Society, has not hesitated to call Copts to account. In a recent article she spoke of the "pervasive anti-intellectual stance of the Coptic ethos . . . [and] the Coptic devaluation of learning" over the centuries, explaining that learning has not been traditional in Coptic monasteries and "never became a holy act in Coptic culture."[77] Her complaints are designed not really to humiliate but to stimulate Copts to achieve excellence in the kind of Coptological studies she and other Western scholars admire. And it is doubtful whether, in fact, anti-intellectualism is a useful term to describe Coptic Christians. Their overriding concerns are, first, to preserve unchanged the traditional beliefs and practices of their church which they consider to be unequaled in fidelity to the way Jesus and his apostles constituted them; second, to survive as an intact community which has suffered much but which has maintained a dignified presence in a country which is theirs with a great history which is theirs; and, third, to create and support institutions which are designed to help Copts to share actively in the life of their church in a wide variety of ways and to succeed in the world, regardless of how hostile it may be or appear to be.

A parallel to the Copts' apparent indifference to the Western intellectuality is their non-achievement in Arabic studies. A sympathetic English missionary almost a century ago recognized the fact that for Copts "Arabic is a foreign tongue that has displaced their own historic language . . . [Therefore] very few of the Christians of Egypt have become proficient scholars of what is not their classical language."[78] Salama Musa explained in an article a half-century later that Copts had little chance to study Arabic at the university level and would not have been motivated to do so anyway, as they would not have been accepted as teachers.[79] Also, standard literary Arabic is closely tied to a religion and to a culture that have not respected the Copts or offered them a chance to show their literary ability.

It is now a quarter of a century since emigration became for Copts a real alternative to the historic discriminations suffered so long in their own country. Many young Egyptians were then emigrating[80] in search of better prospects, but Copts had the added incentive. One list speaks of there being four churches in England, ten in Canada, forty-one in the United States, and fourteen in Australia.[81] Many Copts went to Australia and Canada between 1962 and 1967,[82] but then a flood seemed to start to the United States.

These overseas communities of Copts received a historic four-month pastoral visit from Pope Shenouda in 1989.[83] The Coptic Pope was greeted in Toronto by fifty-four Coptic priests serving in Canada and the United States, and opportunity was taken to discuss pastoral and educational challenges in ministering to the many communities of émigrés in America. In Jersey City, a Coptic school of theology was opened to prepare clergy and others for church leadership, and a Coptic monastery was inaugurated in the desert of southern California. Before going on to Australia, Pope Shenouda met with the president of the United States, opened a session of the U. S. Congress with a prayer, and was present to greet the arrival of President Mubarak in Washington.

One can only speculate about the future of the Coptic Church in the diaspora. Copts adjust well and find adequate employment in the countries to which they are scattered (two of the psychiatrists in a mid-sized city in North Carolina are Copts from Egypt), and many maintain their ties to their traditional church. Whether complex and lengthy rituals featuring two ancient Middle Eastern languages (one sacred to Copts but long since unspoken) will long maintain the loyalty of a people making a life for themselves in a very different and friendly environment, only time will tell.

In Egypt itself, the Coptic Orthodox Church seems to be well prepared to play the role it will be called upon to play. As to common worship:[84] on Sundays, and often also on Saturdays, the Divine Liturgy[85] is celebrated; and on weekdays the Evening and the Morning "Raising of Incense" and the Hours[86] are observed. Churches are full of enthusiastic worshippers, including many young adults with their small children. Monasteries are well supplied with monks and draw more pilgrims than ever to enjoy their quiet beauty and the wisdom and hospitality of the monks. Indeed, the crowds of visitors may sometimes even threaten to disrupt the monastic life.[87] Coptic church art is robust, combining traditional symbols and techniques with striking colors and contemporary style, especially in frescos found in many twentieth-century churches. The Patriarchate in Cairo includes an atelier, under the direction of the distinguished Isaac Fanous, both to create sacred art and to teach young artists.

Sunday Schools are attended by hordes of lively children taught often by dedicated and attractive university students. One, named Mervat, helps her mother at work as a housekeeper, excels in classes at the university, is regular at Sunday and weekday worship at her church, and teaches a Sunday School class of sixty-five.

Social service programs reach out more and more to isolated communities of Copts in increasingly broad programs. For example, the Daughters of Mary in Beni Suef pray constantly, operate a clinic, a day care center for hundreds of children, an orphanage for girls, a state-supported inoculation clinic, a school for retarded children, an old folks home, a conference center in a nearby town; and in Cairo they serve the Copts who are garbage workers (who may otherwise have no schools or medical services).

Children are baptized. Couples are married. Families are close, e.g., "married children usually attempt to live as near to their parents as they possibly can."[88] The dead are buried with great dignity. Members' morals are drawn from the traditional teachings of their church. For the Copts of Egypt, as for most Christians in predominantly Muslim lands, their Christianity "provides the skeletal form" and "moral authority" in "shaping the character of [their] social life."[89] Many Christian groups in the world would envy the lively church life of Egypt's Copts.

That Pope Shenouda and his church have not simply shut themselves off from the world around them may be illustrated by two visits to Pope Shenouda in late 1988. In November, Palestine Liberation Organization chief Yasser Arafat brought a delegation to the Patriarch to receive congratulations for his efforts to create a Palestinian state and to achieve a just peace. In December, Nobel Prize for Literature winner Najib Mahfuz was received by the pope who discussed with him the "concrete way in which the national unity is expressed in the works of this great Egyptian author."[90] These meetings suggest that the Coptic community has not simply been marginalized in late twentieth-century Egypt.

The traditional Christianity of Egypt is closing the twentieth century with vigor and with a loyalty to Egypt exceeded only by its loyalty to Christianity. And in 1992 their own Butros Butros Ghali became Secretary-

General of the United Nations! A history records rather than predicts, but the evidence in the 1990s suggests that the Coptic Orthodox will be as confident in 2001 about their future as they were in 1901.

[1]Maurice P. Martin, Christian van Nispen, Fadel Sidarous, "Les nouveaux courants dans la communauté copte orthodoxe," *Proche-Orient Chrétien*, 40 (1990), 249.

[2]Raphael Ava Mena, "Days in the Life of a Contemporary Saint," *Coptic Church Review*, 7 (1986), 22; for the rest of this account of Cyril VI before his consecration, I am depending on O. F. A. Meinardus, *Christian Egypt: Faith and Life* (Cairo: American University in Cairo Press, 1970), pp. 43-44.

[3]A thorough account of the regulations and process is found in Meinardus, pp. 128-139; the quotation is from page 139.

[4]Meinardus, pp. 140-141.

[5]H.-M. Legrand, "Le renouveau copte," *Istina*, 8 (1961-62), 137.

[6]For a complete account, see M. B. Ghali, "Ethiopian Church Autocephaly," *Coptic Encyclopedia,* 1991, and cf. Meinardus, pp. 392-398.

[7]Meinardus, pp. 398 and 395.

[8]Meinardus, pp. 44-45.

[9]Meinardus, p. 46; and cf. Legrand, pp. 142-144.

[10]Meinardus, p. 27.

[11]J. D. Pennington, "The Copts in Modern Egypt," *Middle Eastern Studies*, 18 (1982), 166.

[12]Meinardus, p. 49.

[13]Meinardus, p. 50.

[14]Meinardus, p. 469, quoting *Middle East News Agency* for 20 July 1962, 6 January 1964, and 19 February 1964.

[15]H. H. Ayrout, "Regards sur le christianisme en Égypte hier et aujourd'hui," *Proche-Orient Chrétien*, 15 (1965), 3-42.

[16]P. J. Vatikiotis, *The History of Egypt*, 3rd ed. (Baltimore: Johns Hopkins Univ. Press, 1985), p. 400.

[17]A. L. al-Sayyid Marsot, *A Short History of Modern Egypt* (Cambridge: Cambridge Univ. Press, 1985), p. 126.

[18]*New Middle East,* 51, 19-22.

[19]Amira Sonbol, "Society, Politics, and Sectarian Strife," in I. M. Oweiss, *The Political Economy of Contemporary Egypt* (Washington, D. C.: Georgetown Univ. Center for Contemporary Arab Studies, 1990), pp. 266-267.

[20]Al-Sayyid Marsot, p. 128.

[21]A. Goldschmidt, *Modern Egypt: The Formation of a Nation State* (Boulder, Colo.:Westview Press, 1988), p. 137.

[22]Meinardus, p. 45.

[23]Meinardus, pp. 445-446, and M. Assad, "The Coptic Church and Social Change in Egypt," *International Review of Missions,* 61 (1972), 127.

[24]This fact and the rest of this paragraph are drawn from Pennington, p. 167.

[25]"Blessed Be Egypt My People," editorial in *Missiology,* 5 (1977), 406.

[26]Meinardus, p. 435.

[27]"Blessed Be Egypt My People," p. 406.

[28]See, e.g., B. Dupuy, "Où en est la dialogue entre l'orthodoxie et les églises dites monophysites," *Istina,* 31 (1986), 357-370.

[29]O. F. A. Meinardus, "Recent Developments in Egyptian Monasticism," *Oriens Christianus,* 49 (1965), 79-89.

[30]"Chronique" section of *Proche-Orient Chrétien,* 10 (1960).

[31]An English translation was provided me by the Coptic Archbishop of Jerusalem in August of 1982.

[32]*Acta Apostolicae Sedis,* 63 (30 April 1973), 299-301.

[33]English translation in *Coptic Church Review,* 6 (1985), 4-8.

[34]See Fr. Malaty's paper delivered to the Anglican/Oriental Orthodox Forum, October, 1985, in *Coptic Church Review,* 6 (1985), 103-105.

[35]A photocopy of the four-page "Common Declaration," signed by both prelates on each page, was provided me by the Anglican Consultative Council in London.

[36]*Encyclopedia Britannica: 1989 Book of the Year Supplement,* p. 297.

[37]Horace Southgate in the official missionary review of the Episcopal Church in the United States of America, *The Spirit of Missions,* 6 (1841), 369.

[38]T. E. Dowling, *The Egyptian Church* (London: Cope and Fenwick, c. 1909), pp. 5 and 6.

[39]Vatikiotis, p. 418.

[40]*Proche-Orient Chrétien,* 39 (1989), 331-332 and 334-336; and see M. P. Martin et al., "Les nouveaux courants dans la communauté copte orthodoxe," pp. 250-252.

[41]Abd al-Monein Said Aly and M. W. Wenner, "Modern Islamic Reform Movements: The Muslim Brotherhood in Contemporary Egypt," *The Middle East Journal*, 36 (1982), 358.

[42]Sonbol, pp. 263-276.

[43]Vatikiotis, p. 418.

[44]Sonbol, p. 265.

[45]For "sharia" laws, see F. M. Najjar, "The Application of Sharia Laws in Egypt," *Middle East Policy*, 1 (1992), 62-73.

[46]S. M. Solihin, *Copts and Muslims in Egypt: A Study on Harmony and Hostility* (Markfield, Leicester: The Islamic Foundation, 1991), pp. 79-82.

[47]H. Ansari, "Sectarian Strife in Egypt and the Political Expediency of Religion," *The Middle East Journal*, 38 (1984), 397 and 403.

[48]For example, al-Damanhuri in *On the Churches of Cairo* trans. and ed. Moshe Perlmann (Berkeley: Univ. of California Press, 1975) and Muhammad al-Ghazzali in *Our Beginning in Wisdom* trans. Isma'il R. el Faruqi (New York: Octagon Books, 1975).

[49]G. Kepel, *The Prophet and Pharaoh: Muslim Extremism in Egypt* (London: Al Saqi Books, 1985) covers the rioting, e.g., pp. 207-210; and cf. also H. Ansari, pp. 408-412.

[50]Vatikiotis, p. 420.

[51]D. A. Roy and W. T. Irelan, "Law and Economics in the Evolution of Contemporary Egypt," *Middle Eastern Studies*, 25 (1989), 179.

[52]J. and A. Millbank, "A Visit to the Coptic Church," *Sobornost*, 2 (1980), 57-64.

[53]For monastic revival, see D. O. R., "Revivescence du monachisme oriental" in "notes et documents," *Irenikon*, 33 (1960), 385-388; and see M. P. Martin et al., "Les nouveaux courants dans la communauté copte orthodoxe," pp. 249-250.

[54]O. F. A. Meinardus, *Monks and Monasteries of the Egyptian Deserts*, rev. ed. (Cairo: American Univ. in Cairo Press, 1989), pp. 31, 46, 70, 120, 143, and 167.

[55]G. Bebawi, "The Bishop in the Coptic Church Today," in *Bishops: But What Kind?*, ed. P. C. Moore (London: SPCK, 1982), p. 68.

[56]N. R. Farah, *Religious Strife in Egypt: Crisis and Ideological Conflict in the 70s* (Montreux, Switzerland: Gordon and Breach, 1986), p. 49.

[57]J. Ducruet, "Statistique chrétienne d'Égypte," *Travaux et Jours*, 24 (1967), 65-68; and see M. P. Martin et al., "Nouveaux courants," p. 254.

[58]Ducruet, pp. 65-68; Bishop Gregorios, "Christianity, the Coptic Religion, and Ethnic Minorities in Egypt," *Geojournal*, 6 (1982), 57; F. N. Ibrahim, "A Social and Geographical Analysis of the Egyptian Copts," *Geojournal*, 6 (1982), pp. 63-67; B. Watterson, *Coptic Egypt* (Edinburgh: Scottish Academic Press, 1988), p. 174; R. H. Dekmejian, *Patterns of Political Leadership: Egypt, Israel, Lebanon* (Albany: SUNY Press, 1975), p. 170; Goldschmidt, p. 159; R. B. Betts, *Christians in the Arab East* (London: SPCK, 1981);

S. F. Karas, "Egypt's Beleaguered Christians," *Worldview,* 26 (1983), 13; M. Samaan and S. Sukhary, "The Copts and Muslims in Egypt," in *Muslim-Christian Conflicts: Economic, Political, and Social Origins,* ed. S. Joseph and B. L. K. Pillsbury (Boulder, Colo.: Westview Press, 1978), pp. 128-155; and Pope Shenouda's 1977 figure of seven million in A. Tamura, "Ethnic Consciousness and its Transformation in the Course of Nation Building: The Muslim and the Copt in Egypt, 1906-1919," *Muslim World,* 75 (1985), 104.

[59]See "Egypt" in Ans J. van Bent, ed., *Handbook: Member Churches* (Geneva: World Council of Churches, 1985).

[60]For a convenient listing, see Meinardus, *Christian Egypt,* pp. 10-14.

[61]Meinardus, pp. 4-6.

[62]Pennington, p. 167.

[63]Sonbol, p. 266.

[64]M. Martin, "L'église et la communauté copte dans l'Islam égyptien," TS, Jesuit Institute Library, L'École Ste. Famille, Cairo, pp. 8-11.

[65]*Proche-Orient Chrétien,* 39 (1989), 324.

[66]Goldschmidt, p. 167.

[67]Roy and Irelan, p. 177.

[68]N. E. Gallagher, "Islam v. Secularism in Cairo: An Account of the Dar al-Hilman Debate," *Middle Eastern Studies,* 25 (1989), 208-215.

[69]R. H. Adams, *Development and Social Change in Rural Egypt* (Syracuse, N. Y.: Syracuse Univ. Press, 1986).

[70]Adams, p. 185.

[71]Adams, p. 187.

[72]U. Wikan, *Life among the Poor in Cairo,* trans. Ann Henning (London: Tavistock Publications, 1980), p. 47.

[73]Goldschmidt, p. 118; and see Fouad Ajami, *The Arab Predicament: Arab Political Thought and Practice since 1967. Updated Edition* (Cambridge: Cambridge Univ. Press, 1992), p. 103.

[74]Mahmud A. Faksh, "The Chimera of Education for Development in Egypt: The Socio-economic Role of University Graduates," *Middle Eastern Studies,* 13 (1977), 229-240.

[75]Vatikiotis, p. 460; and on p. 454 he points out the lack of technical education. For another critique of the universities, see G. Kepel, pp. 135-136.

[76]R. Matthee, "Jamal al-Din al-Afghani and the Egyptian National Debate," *International Journal of Middle East Studies,* 21 (1989), 151-169.

[77]L. S. B. MacCoul, "The Strange Death of Coptic Culture," *Coptic Church Review,* 10 (1989), 35-43; and cf. her earlier article, "Coptic Orthodoxy Today: Ethnicism, Dead End, or Mere Survival," *Coptic Church Review,* 4 (1983).

[78]D. M. Thornton, "The Educational Problem in Egypt in Relation to Religious Teaching," *Church Missionary Intelligencer*, 57 (1906), 654-655.

[79]"Intellectual Currents in Egypt," *Middle Eastern Affairs*, 2 (1951).

[80]Ajami, pp. 150-152.

[81]Pope Shenouda III et al., "Migration," *Coptic Encyclopedia*, 1991.

[82]A. E. Hillal Dessouki, "The Shift in Egypt's Migration Policy," *Middle Eastern Studies*, 18 (1982), 53-68; and see M. P. Martin et al., "Les nouveaux courants," pp. 255-257.

[83]The visit is described in *Proche-Orient Chrétien*, 39 (1989), 323-326.

[84]For anything about Coptic worship and sacraments, see O. H. E. KHS-Burmester, *The Egyptian or Coptic Church: A Detailed Description of Her Liturgical Services and the Rites and Ceremonies Observed in the Administration of Her Sacraments* (Cairo: Société d'archéologie copte, 1967).

[85]For a useful English rendering of the typical liturgy see *The Divine Liturgy of Saint Basil the Great: and the Evening and the Morning Raising of Incense Prayers* (Troy, Mich.: St. Mark Coptic Orthodox Church, 1982); for most of the rite the Arabic or the Coptic text is in a parallel column—or both Arabic and Coptic.

[86]For the hours, see the useful volume which has English and Arabic in parallel columns, *The Agpeya: Being the Coptic Orthodox Book of Hours according to the Present-day Usage in the Church of Alexandria* (Los Angeles: Sts. Athanasius and Cyril of Alexandria Publications, 1982); for Coptic and Arabic and English texts, see O. H. E. KHS-Burmester, ed. and trans., *The Horologion of the Egyptian Church: Coptic and Arabic Text from a Medieval Manuscript* (Cairo: Centro Francescano di Studi Orientali Cristiani, 1973).

[87]M. P. Martin et al., "Les nouveaux courants," p. 253.

[88]A. B. Rugh, *Family in Contemporary Egypt* (Syracuse, New York: Syracuse Univ. Press, 1984), pp. 209-210.

[89]Rugh, p. 6.

[90]*Proche-Orient Chrétien*, 39 (1989), 326-327.

Conclusion

✠ ———————————————————————————————— ✠

NY HISTORY WRITTEN IN THE 1990s must end if and when it reaches the 1980s, but a conclusion about that history may also be drawn. The conclusion we seek is an answer to the question implicit in the original title ("Continuities in Traditional Egyptian Christianity") of the project that led to this book: Was there one Egyptian Christianity, or were there, in fact, three—or perhaps two? The question is in no way frivolous, for Egypt has had three languages and three cultures during the period since 1 A.D. It would not be far-fetched, then, to assume that three distinct cultures would mean three churches, or even three Christianities.

First, there was the Greek-speaking Hellenistic culture, which dominated the great city of Alexandria and the other Hellenistic cities of Egypt. It was in these cities that Egyptian Christianity had its origins and early growth.

Parallel to the Hellenistic culture of those cities was the Egyptian—or Coptic-speaking culture of Upper Egypt and the mass of Egyptians everywhere in their country. Symbolic of the duality of these cultures was the Alexandrian custom of referring to any trip south of that northernmost city as "going to Egypt."

Then, after the Arab conquest of Egypt in 640, both the Hellenistic and the Coptic cultures of Egypt gave way gradually to the Arabic-speaking and predominantly Islamic culture which has quite dominated Egypt for at least the last thousand years.

Greek

The earliest Christianity of Egypt was Hellenistic; indeed, Egypt became the center of Hellenistic theology from the beginning of the third century because of the great influence of Clement and Origen. Subsequently, in the fourth and fifth centuries, the Egyptian theologian-patriarchs, Athanasius and Cyril, as the leaders of Hellenistic Christianity, dominated ecumenical efforts up until 451 toward resolution of the controversies over the two fundamental Christian doctrines: the Trinity and the Incarnation.

Coptic

Already before 451, Coptic-speaking Christianity had become important in Egypt through the monastic movement, which had begun in the third century and come to flower in the fourth. There had been Christian preaching in Coptic by late third century, and, by the end of the next century, Abbot Shenoute had shown that a high standard of writing could be achieved in sermons in the Coptic language.

After 451, when communion among the great churches was being broken as a result of the Council of Chalcedon, the Byzantine Empire tried for almost two centuries to force Egyptian Christians to accept as patriarchs the pro-Chalcedonians the Empire intruded. They were, however, simply the heads of an imperial (Melchite) church which accepted the council. The mass of Egyptians continued to associate themselves with the patriarchs and hierarchy which rejected Chalcedon. This church became progressively Coptic-speaking, and its leadership survived the Arab conquest and Arab domination intact, together with the masses that remained loyal to their traditional Christian faith.

Arabic

When the Muslim Arabs overran Egypt in the 640s, they may have assumed that the Egyptians would remain Christian and Coptic-speaking. The rewards of conversion to Islam were too strong, however, so it was not many centuries before most Egyptians were Muslim. Similarly, the Arabic language of the rulers spread itself widely, if gradually, beginning with the Coptic administrators employed to serve the rulers. It was not too long before the triumph of Arabic was complete and Coptic became a language used only in Christian worship. It became necessary for church writers in Egypt to create a Christian literature in Arabic in order to reach church members. Even today, the renewal of interest of Copts in the traditional language has scarcely lessened their dependence on Arabic in their services of worship.

A Response

This book is designed to allow careful readers to make their own informed decision about whether the Coptic Orthodox Church is the same church as the ancient Egyptian church of Athanasius and Cyril I—or the same church after the Arab conquest as it was before.

For both doctrinal and ecclesiastical reasons Western Christians and the Eastern Christians in communion with Constantinople have tended to consider the true successor of the early church in Egypt to be the Greek-speaking Melchite church, rather than the "heretical" church of the mass of Egyptian Christians, which has opposed the Council of Chalcedon. This is comparable to the traditional Roman Catholic theory that the Church of England or the Church of Sweden ceased to be continuous with their original churches when communion with Rome was broken in the sixteenth century.

For this writer, it is both wrong-headed and insensitive to deny the continuity of the Coptic Orthodox Church with Egypt's earliest Christianity—and the nineteen centuries of Christian Egypt since its beginnings. It is wrong-headed, for it overlooks the institutional continuity as well as the loyalty of the mass of church membership which the anti-Chalcedonian church maintained through the two centuries of competition with the Melchites after 451 and then through the succession of Islamic governments initiated by the Arabs after 640.

In addition, continuity has been maintained by the remarkable traditionalism of Egyptian Christians. Western Christians tend to be critical of the Copts for never changing anything in their religious practices or in the way they hold or proclaim the traditional beliefs. This profound resistance to change has not only helped the Copts preserve their continuity with the early days of their church but should help demonstrate this continuity to doubters.

It would also be insensitive to deny the continuity, in view of the many and seemingly endless disabilities most Egyptian Christians have been willing to undergo since 451 in order to hold on to the Christian beliefs and practices which they inherited from their forebears—for the express purpose of perpetuating that continuity.

A conclusion may end on a more specifically positive note: a church which has survived so long, often in difficult circumstances, and has expressed herself in three different cultures and languages (one Indo-European, one Hamitic, one Semitic) should be as encouraged about her future as she is proud of her long past.

Bibliography

Abd al-Malik, Butrus. "The Christian Church in Egypt in the Tenth Century," *Tome commémoratif du millénaire de la bibliothèque patriarcale d'Alexandrie*. Alexandria, Egypt: Publications de l'Institut d'Étude Orientale de la Bibliothèque Patriarcale d'Alexandrie, 1953.

Abd al-Masih, Yassa. "The Faith and Practices of the Coptic Church." *Tome commémoratif du millénaire de la bibliothèque patriarcale d'Alexandrie*. Alexandria, Egypt: Publications de l'Institut d'Étude Orientale de la Bibliothèque Patriarcale d'Alexandrie, 1953.

Abudacnus. *The History of the Copts Commonly Called Jacobites under the Dominion of the Turk and Abyssinian Emperors with Some Geographical Notes or Descriptions of the Several Places in Which They Live in Those Dominions*. Trans. from original in Latin, E. S. Sadleir. 2nd ed. London: R. Baldwin, 1693.

Abu Salih. *The Churches and Monasteries of Egypt: And Some Neighboring Countries*. Ed. and trans. B. T. A. Evetts with added notes by A. J. Butler. Oxford: Clarendon Press, 1895.

Adams, Francis William Lauderdale. *The New Egypt*. London: T. Fisher Unwin, 1893.

Adams, Richard H. *Development and Social Change in Rural Egypt*. Syracuse, N. Y.: Syracuse Univ. Press, 1986.

Adams, William Y. *Nubia: Corridor to Africa*. Princeton: Princeton Univ. Press, 1977.

Adeney, W. F. *The Greek and Eastern Churches*. New York: Scribner, 1939.

189

The Agpeya: Being the Coptic Orthodox Book of Hours according to the Present-day Usage in the Church of Alexandria. Los Angeles: Sts. Athanasius and Cyril of Alexandria Orthodox Publications, 1982.

Alcock, Anthony, ed. and trans. *Isaac the Presbyter's The Life of Samuel of Kalamun.* Warminster, Engl.: Aris and Phillips, 1985.

Alexandrina: Héllénisme, judaïsme et christianisme à Alexandrie: Mélanges offerts au P. Claude Mondésert. Paris: Éditions du Cerf, 1987.

Alla, Waheed Hassab. *Le Baptême des enfants dans la tradition de l'église copte d'Alexandrie.* Fribourg, Switz.: Éditions Universitaires, 1985.

Amélineau, Émile Clément, ed. and trans. "Encomium of Pisentios, Bishop of Keft." In his *Étude sur christianisme en Égypte au septième siècle.* Paris, 1887.

- - - - - - -. *La Géographie de l'Égypte à l'époque copte.* Paris, 1893.

- - - - - - -. *L'Histoire de l'Égypte chrétienne.* Paris, 1895.

- - - - - - -. *Monuments pour servir à l'histoire de l'Égypte chrétienne au IVe et Ve siècles.* Volume 4 of *Mémoires publièes par les membres de la mission archéologique française au Caire.* Paris: Ernest Léroux, 1888.

- - - - - - -. *Oeuvres de Schenoudi: Texte copte et traduction française.* Paris, 1907.

Anawati, Georges C. "The Christian Communities in Egypt in the Middle Ages." In *Conversion and Continuity: Indigenous Christian Communities in Islamic Lands Eighth to Eighteenth Centuries.* Ed. Michael Gervers and Ramzi Gibran. Toronto: Pontifical Institute of Medieval Studies, 1990, pp. 237-251.

Ansari, Hamiel. *Egypt: The Stalled Society.* Albany, N. Y.: SUNY Press, 1986.

- - - - - - -. "The Islamic Militants in Egyptian Politics." *International Journal of Middle East Studies,* 16 (1984), 123-144.

- - - - - - -. "Sectarian Conflict in Egypt and the Political Expediency of Religion." *Middle East Journal,* 38 (1984), 397-418.

Arberry, A. J., ed. *Religion in the Middle East.* 2 vols. Cambridge: Cambridge Univ. Press, 1969.

Arnold, Duane Wade-Hampton. *The Early Episcopal Career of Athanasius of Alexandria.* Notre Dame: Notre Dame Univ. Press, 1991.

Assad, Maurice. "The Church and Family Life Education." *Bulletin of the Institute of Coptic Studies,* 1975, 49-62.

- - - - - - -. "The Coptic Church and Social Change in Egypt." *International Review of Missions,* 61 (1972), 117-129.

Athanasius, Bishop of Beni-Suef and Bahnasa. *The Copts through the Ages.* 5th ed. Cairo: State Information Service, n.d.

- - - - - - -. *The Doctrines of the Orthodox Church of Alexandria.* n.p., n.d.

Atiya, Aziz Surial. "Abu Shakir ibn al-Rahib." *Coptic Encylopedia,* 1991.

- - - - - - -. "al-As'ad Abu al-Faraj Hibat Allah ibn al-'Assal." *Coptic Encyclopedia.* 1991.

- - - - - - -. "Awlad al-'Assal." *Coptic Encyclopedia.* 1991.

- - - - - - -. "Copto-Arabic Literature." *Coptic Encyclopedia.* 1991.

- - - - - - -. *The Copts and Christian Civilization: The Forty-Second Annual Frederick William Reynolds Lecture.* Salt Lake City: Univ. of Utah Press, 1979.

- - - - - - -. *Crusade, Commerce, and Culture.* Bloomington, Ind.: Indiana Univ. Press, 1962.

- - - - - - -. *The Crusade in the Later Middle Ages.* London: Methuen, 1938.

- - - - - - -. *A History of Eastern Christianity.* London: Methuen, 1968.

- - - - - - -. "ibn Kabar." *Coptic Encyclopedia.* 1991.

- - - - - - -. "Makir, ibn al-'Amid al-." *Coptic Encyclopedia.* 1991.

Ayad, Boulos Ayad. "The Relationship between the Ancient Egyptian Culture and the Coptic Culture." *Bulletin of the Institute of Coptic Studies,* 1975, 81-84.

Ayalon, David. *L'Esclavage du mamelouk.* Jerusalem: Israel Oriental Society, 1951.

Ayrout, Henri Habib. *The Egyptian Peasant.* 1938; rpt. Boston: Beacon Press, 1963.

- - - - - - -. "Regards sur le christianisme en Égypte hier et aujourd'hui." *Proche-Orient Chrétien,* 15 (1965), 3-42.

Aziza, Hussein. "The Role of Women in Social Reform in Egypt." *Middle East Journal,* 7 (1953), 440-450.

al-Azmeh, Aziz. *Ibn Khaldun: An Essay in Reinterpretation.* London: Frank Cass, 1982.

Badawi, Alexandre. *Guide de l'Égypte chrétienne.* Cairo: Société d'archéologie copte, 1953.

Baer, Gabriel. *A History of Land Ownership in Modern Egypt, 1800-1950.* London: Oxford Univ. Press, 1962.

Bagnall, R. S. Rev. of *The Arab Conquest of Egypt and the Last Thirty Years of the Roman Dominion,* by Alfred J. Butler. *Classical Journal,* 75 (1979-1980), 347-348.

Barbulesco, Luc, ed. *Les Chrétiens égyptiens aujourd'hui: Éléments de discours.* Cairo: Centre d'études et de documentation économique, juridique, et social, 1985.

Bardy, Gustave. "Les premiers temps du christianisme de langue copte en Égypte," In *Mémorial Lagrange*. Paris: J. Gabalda, 1940, pp. 203-216.

Barnard, Leslie W. "St. Mark and Alexandria." *Harvard Theological Review*, 57 (1964), 145-150.

Batal, James. "Notes on the New Egypt." *Muslim World*, 44 (1954), 227-235.

Bauer, Walter. *Orthodoxy and Heresy in Earliest Christianity*. Trans. and ed. R. A. Kraft et al. Philadelphia: Fortress Press, 1977.

Bauwens-Preaux, Renée, ed. *Voyage en Égypte de Joos van Ghistelle, 1482-83*. Cairo: Institut français d'archéologie orientale, 1976.

Bebawi, George. "The Bishop in the Coptic Church Today." In *Bishops But What Kind? Reflections on Episcopacy*. Ed. Peter Clement Moore. London: SPCK, 1982.

- - - - - - -. "Saint Athanasios: The Dynamics of Salvation." *Sobornost*, 8 (1986), 24-41.

Behrens-Abouseif, Doris. *Die Kopten in der Ägyptischen Gesellschaft: von der Mitte des 19. Jahrhunderts bis 1923*. Freiburg: Klaus Schwarz, 1972.

- - - - - - -. "The Political Situation of the Copts, 1798-1923." In *The Arabic-Speaking Lands*. Vol. 2 of *Christians and Jews in the Ottoman Empire: The Functioning of a Plural Society*. Ed. Benjamin Braude and Bernard Lewis. New York: Holmes and Meier, 1982.

Bell, David N., ed. and trans. *The Life of Shenoute: By Besa*. Kalamazoo, Mich.: Cistercian Publications, 1983.

Bell, Harold Idris. *Cults and Creed in Greco-Roman Egypt*. New York: Philosophical Library, 1956.

- - - - - - -. *Egypt from Alexander the Great to the Arab Conquest: A Study in the Diffusion and Decay of Hellenism*. Oxford: Clarendon Press, 1948.

- - - - - - -. *Jews and Christians in Egypt: The Jewish Troubles in Alexandria, and the Athanasian Controversy, Illustrated by Texts from Greek Papyri in the British Museum*. London: British Museum, 1924.

Betts, Robert B. *Christians in the Arab East*. London: SPCK, 1979.

Bilanuik, P. B. T. "Florence, Copts at the Council of (1439-1442)." *Coptic Encyclopedia*, 1991.

Bishai, Wilson B. "The Transition from Coptic to Arabic." *Muslim World*, 53 (1963), 145-150.

Bleeker, C. J. "The Egyptian Background of Gnosticism." In *Le Origini dello Gnosticismo*. Ed. Ugo Bianchi. Leiden: E. J. Brill, 1967, pp. 229-236.

"Blessed Be Egypt, My People." Editorial. *Missiology*, 5 (1977), 403-405.

Bosworth, C. E. "Christian and Jewish Religious Dignitaries in Mamluk Egypt and Syria: Qalqashandi's Information on their Hierarchy, Titulature, and Appointment." *International Journal of Middle East Studies*, 3 (1972), 59-74.

- - - - - - -, ed. *The Islamic World from Classical to Islamic Times: Essays in Honor of Bernard Lewis*. Princeton: Darwin Press, 1989.

- - - - - - -. "The 'Protected Peoples' (Christians and Jews) in Medieval Egypt and Syria." *Bulletin of John Rylands Library*, 62 (1979-80), 11-36.

Bowie, Leland. "The Copts, the Wafd, and Religious Issues in Egyptian Politics." *Muslim World*, 67 (1977), 106-126.

Bowman, A. K. *Egypt after the Pharaohs: 332 B.C. - A.D. 642 from Alexander to the Arab Conquest*. London: British Museum, 1986.

Brett, M., ed. *Northern Africa: Islam and Modernization*. London: Frank Cass, 1973.

Brooks, E. W. "The Patriarch Paul of Antioch and the Alexandrian Schism of 575." *Byzantinische Zeitschrift*, 30 (1929), 468-476.

Brown, Peter. *Society and the Holy in Late Antiquity*. Berkeley: Univ. of California Press, 1982.

Brunner-Traut, Emma. *Die Kopten: Leben und Lehre der Frühen Christen in Ägypten*. Köln: Diederichs, 1982.

Bulliett, R. W. *Conversion to Islam in the Medieval Period*. Cambridge: Harvard Univ. Press, 1975.

Burmester, Oswald H. E. KHS-. "The Canons of Christodoulos, LXVI Patriarch of Alexandria." *Le Muséon*, 45 (1942), 71-84.

- - - - - - -. "The Canons of Cyril III ibn Laklak, Part II." *Bulletin de la Société d'Archéologie Copte*, 14 (1959), 116-150.

- - - - - - -. *The Egyptian or Coptic Church: A Detailed Description of Her Liturgical Services and the Rites and Ceremonies Observed in the Administration of Her Sacraments*. Cairo: Publications de la société d'archéologie copte, 1967.

- - - - - - -, ed. and trans. *The Horologion of the Egyptian Church: Coptic and Arabic Text from a Medieval Manuscript*. Cairo: Centro Francescano di Studi Orientali Christiani, 1973.

Butcher, Edith L. *The Story of the Church of Egypt*. 2 vols. London: Smith, Elder, and Co., 1897.

Butler, Alfred J. *The Arab Conquest of Egypt and the Last 30 Years of the Roman Dominion*. 1902; rpt. Ed. P. M. Fraser. New York: Oxford Univ. Press, 1978.

Carter, Barbara Lynn. *The Copts in Egyptian Politics*. London: Croom Helm, 1986.

Chadwick, Henry. *Early Christian Thought and the Classical Tradition: Studies in Justin, Clement, and Origen.* New York: Oxford Univ. Press, 1966.

— — — — — — —. *The Early Church.* Baltimore: Penguin Books, 1967.

— — — — — — —. *Origen Contra Celsum.* Cambridge: Cambridge Univ. Press, 1965.

— — — — — — —. "Pachomius and the Idea of Sanctity." In *The Byzantine Saint.* Ed. Sergei Hackel. San Bernardino, Calif.: Borgo Press, 1983, pp. 11-24.

— — — — — — —. "Philo and the Beginnings of Christian Thought." In *The Cambridge History of Later Greek and Early Medieval Philosophy.* Ed. H. H. Armstrong. Cambridge: Cambridge Univ. Press, 1967.

— — — — — — —. "Philoponus the Christian Theologian." In *Philoponus and the Rejection of Aristotelian Science.* Ed. Richard Sorabji. London: Duckworth, 1987.

Chalaby, Abbas. *Les Coptes d'Égypte.* Rouen : Samco-Offset-Rouen, 1973.

Charles, R. H., trans. and ed. *The Chronicle of John, Bishop of Nikiou: Translated from Zotenberg's Ethiopic Text.* London: Williams and Norgate, 1916.

Chauleur, Sylvestre. *Histoire des coptes d'Égypte.* Paris: La Colombe, 1960.

Chitham, E. J. *The Coptic Community in Egypt: Spatial and Social Change.* Durham, Engl.: Univ. of Durham, 1986.

Chitty, Derwas, J. *The Desert a City: An Introduction to the Study of Egyptian and Palestinian Monasticism under the Christian Empire.* Oxford: Basil Blackwell and Mott, 1966.

— — — — — — —, trans. *The Letters of Saint Antony the Great.* Oxford: SLG Press, 1975.

Church Missionary Record 1-29. London: Church Missionary Society Press, 1930-1958.

Clarke, Somers. *Christian Antiquities in the Nile Valley.* Oxford: Clarendon Press, 1912.

Clarke, W. K. Lowther. *The Lausiac History of Palladius.* London: SPCK, 1918.

The Coptic Liturgy. Cairo: Coptic Orthodox Patriarchate, 1963.

Cramer, Maria. *Das Christlich-koptische Ägypten: Einst und Heute, Eine Orientierung.* Wiesbaden: O. Harrassowitz, 1959.

Creed, J. M. "Christian and Coptic Egypt." In *Legacy of Egypt.* Ed. S. R. K. Glanville. 1st ed. Oxford: Clarendon Press, 1942.

Cromer, Lord (Evelyn Baring). *Modern Egypt.* 2 vols. New York: Macmillan, 1908.

Crouzel, Henri. *Origen.* Trans. A. S. Worrell. San Francisco: Harper and Row, 1989.

Crum, W. E. "Eusebius and Coptic Church Histories." *Proceedings of the Society of Biblical Archeology*, 24 (1902), 68-84.

- - - - - - -. "Sévère d'Antioche en Égypte." *Revue de l'Orient Chrétien*, ser. 3, 3 (1922-23), 92-104.

The Cry of Egypt's Copts: Documents on Christian Life in Egypt Today. New York: Phoenicia Press, 1951.

al-Damanhuri, Ahmad ibn Abd al-Mur. *Shaykh Damanhuri On the Churches of Cairo (1739).* Ed. and trans. Moshe Perlmann. Berkeley: Univ. of California Press, 1975.

Day, Peter D. *Eastern Christian Liturgies: The Armenian, Coptic, Ethiopian and Syrian Rites.* Shannon, Ireland: Irish Universities Press, 1972.

Dehérain, H. *L'Égypte turque: Pachas et mamelukes du XVIème au XVIIIème siècle: L'Expédition du Général Bonaparte.* Vol. 3 of *Histoire d'Égypte.* Ed. G. Hanotaux. Paris: Librairie Plon, 1931.

Dekmeijian, R. Hrair. *Patterns of Political Leadership: Egypt, Israel, Lebanon.* Albany, N. Y.: SUNY Press, 1975.

den Heijer, Johannes. "*L'Histoire des patriarches d'Alexandrie*: Recension primitive et vulgate." *Bulletin de la Société d'Archéologie Copte*, 27 (1985), 1-29.

- - - - - - -. *Mawhub Ibn Mansur Ibn Mufarrig et l'historiographie copto-arabe: Etude sur la composition de l'Histoire des Patriarches d'Alexandrie* (= *Corpus Scriptorum Christianorum Orientalium*, Vol. 513: Subsidia, tomus 81). Louvain, 1989.

- - - - - - -. "Quelques Remarques sur la deuxième partie de *L'Histoire des patriarches d'Alexandrie.*" *Bulletin de la Société d'Archéologie Copte*, 25 (1983), 107-124.

Dennett, D. C. *Conversion and the Poll Tax in Early Islam.* Cambridge: Harvard Univ. Press, 1950.

Dessouki, Ali E. Hillal. "The Shift in Egypt's Migration Policy." *Middle Eastern Studies*, 18 (1982), 53-68.

Détré, Jean-Marie. "Contributions à l'étude des relations du patriarche copte Jean XVII avec Rome de 1735 à 1738," *Studia Orientalia Christiana Collecteana*, No. 5 (1960), 123-169.

Dick, I. "Difficultés suscités à l'église copte pour sa participation au Conseil Oecumenique des Églises." *Proche-Orient Chrétien*, 13 (1963), 55-63.

Diehl, Charles. *L'Égypte chrétienne et byzantine.* Vol. 3 of *Histoire de la nation égyptienne.* Ed. G. Hanotaux. Paris: Librairie Plon, 1937.

The Divine Liturgy of St. Basil the Great: And the Evening and the Morning Raising of Incense Prayers. Troy, Mich.: St. Mark Coptic Orthodox Church, 1982.

Dodwell, Henry. *The Founder of Modern Egypt: A Study of Muhammad Ali.* Cambridge: Cambridge Univ. Press, 1931.

D. O. R. "Reviviscence du monachisme oriental." *Irenikon,* 33 (1960), 385-388.

Doresse, Jean. *Des Hieroglyphes à la croix: Ce que le passé pharaonique a légué au christianisme.* Istanbul: Nederlands Historisch-Archeologisch Instituut, 1960.

Dowling, Theodore Edward. *The Egyptian Church.* London: Cope and Fenwick, c. 1909.

Downey, Glanville. "Coptic Culture in the Byzantine World: Nationalism and Religious Independence." *Greek, Roman, and Byzantine Studies,* 1 (1958), 119-135.

Drescher, James, ed. and trans. *Apa Mena: A Selection of Coptic Texts Relating to St. Menas.* Cairo: Publications de la société d'archéologie copte, 1946.

du Bourget, Pierre. *Les Coptes.* Paris: Presses universitaires de France, 1988.

Duchesne, Louis Marie Olivier. *L'Église au sixième siècle.* Paris: Fontemoing et cie., E. de Boccard, Successeurs, 1925.

Ducruet, Jean and Maurice Martin. "Statistique Chrétienne d'Égypte." *Travaux et Jours,* 24 (1967), 65-68.

Dupuy, Bernard. "Où en est le dialogue entre l'orthodoxe et les églises dites monophysites?" *Istina,* 31 (1986), 357-370.

Ebied, R. Y. and L. R. Wickham.. "A Collection of Unpublished Syriac Letters of Timotheus Aelurus." *Journal of Theological Studies,* NS 21 (1970), 321-369.

The Egypt and Sudan Mission. London: Church Missionary Society, 1910.

Elder, Earle E. *Vindicating a Vision.* Philadelphia: Presbyterian Board of Missions, 1958.

Evagrius Scholasticus. *The Ecclesiastical History of Evagrius with Scholis.* Ed. J. Bidez and L. Parmentier. 1898; rpt. New York, 1979.

Evelyn-White, Hugh Gerard. *The Monasteries of Wadi Natrun.* 1933; rpt. New York: Arno Press, 1973.

Evetts, B. T. A. "Un Prélat reformateur, le patriarche Cyril IV (1854-1861)." *Revue de l'Orient Chrétien,* 17 (1912), 3-15.

Faksh, Mahmud A. "The Chimera of Education for Development in Egypt: The Socio-Economic Role of University Graduates." *Middle Eastern Studies,* 13 (1977), 229-240.

Farag, F. Rofail. *Sociological and Moral Studies in the Field of Coptic Monasticism.* Leiden: E. J. Brill, 1964.

- - - - - - -. "The Technique of Research of a Tenth Century Christian Arab Writer: Severus ibn Muqaffa." *Le Muséon*, 86 (1973), 37-66.

Farah, Nadia Ramsis. *Religious Strife in Egypt: Crisis and Ideological Conflict in the Seventies.* Montreux, Switz.: Gordon and Breach, 1986.

Fenoyl, Maurice de. "Les sacrements de l'initiation chrétienne dans l'église copte." *Proche-Orient Chrétien*, 7 (1957), 7-25.

- - - - - - -. *Le Sanctorale Copte.* Beirut: Imprimerie Catholique, 1960.

Ferré, André. "Abu al-Fadl Isa ibn Nasturus." *Coptic Encyclopedia.* 1991.

- - - - - - -. "Fatimids and the Copts." *Coptic Encyclopedia.* 1991

Fortescue, Adrian. *The Lesser Eastern Churches.* London: Catholic Truth Society, 1913.

Fowler, Montague. *Christian Egypt: Past, Present, and Future.* London: Church Newspaper Company, 1901.

Frederick, Vincent. "Abu al-Fakhr al-Masihi." *Coptic Encyclopedia.* 1991.

- - - - - - -. "Abu al-Khayr al-Rashid ibn al-Tayyid." *Coptic Encyclopedia.* 1991

- - - - - - -. "Butrus Sawirus al-Jamil." *Coptic Encyclopedia.* 1991.

- - - - - - -. "Yuhanna of Sammanud." *Coptic Encyclopedia.* 1991.

Frend, W. H. C.. "Athanasius as an Egyptian Christian Leader in the Fourth Century." *New College* (Edinburgh) *Bulletin*, 8, 1 (1974).

- - - - - - -. "The Church of the Roman Empire, 313-600." In *The Layman in Christian History.* Ed. M. I. Finley. London: Routledge and Kegan Paul, 1974, pp. 263-287.

- - - - - - -. "The Mission to Nubia: An Episode in the Struggle for Power in Sixth Century Byzantium." *Travaux du centre d'Archéologie Méditerranéenne de l'Académie Polonaise des Sciences,* Vol. 16, *Études de Travaux,* 8 (1975), 10-16.

- - - - - - -. "Nationalism as a Factor in Anti-Chalcedonian Feeling in Egypt." In *Religion and National Identity: Papers Read at the Nineteenth Summer and the Twentieth Winter Meetings of the Ecclesiastical History Society.* Oxford: Blackwell, 1982.

- - - - - - -. "Religion and Social Change in the Late Roman Empire." *The Cambridge Journal*, 2, 8 (1949), 491-495.

- - - - - - -. *The Rise of Christianity.* Philadelphia: Fortress Press, 1984.

- - - - - - -. *The Rise of the Monophysite Movement: Chapters in the History of the Church in the Fifth and Sixth Centuries.* Cambridge: Cambridge Univ. Press, 1972.

- - - - - - -. "Severus of Antioch and the Origin of the Monophysite Hierarchy." In *The Heritage of the Early Church: Essays in Honor of the Very Reverend G. V. Florovsky.* Rome, 1973.

- - - - - - -. "The Winning of the Countryside." *The Journal of Ecclesiastical History*, 18(1967), 1-14.

Friedeberg, Ilse. "Bishop Samuel." *Sobornost*, 4 (1982), 60-62.

Gairdner, W. H. Temple. *D. M. Thornton: A Study in Missionary Ideals and Methods.* London: Hodder and Stoughton, 1908.

Gallagher, Nancy E. "Islam v. Secularism in Cairo: An Account of the Dar al-Hilman Debate." *Middle Eastern Studies*, 25 (1989), 208-215.

Gellens, Samuel I. "Egypt, Islamization of." *Coptic Encyclopedia.* 1991.

Gershoni, Israel and J. P. Jankowski. *Egypt, Islam, and the Arabs: The Search for Egyptian Nationhood, 1900-1930.* New York: Oxford Univ. Press, 1986.

Gervers, Michael and Ramzi Jibran Bikhazi, eds. *Conversion and Continuity: Indigenous Christian Communities in Islamic Lands, Eighth to Eighteenth Centuries.* Toronto: Pontifical Institute of Medieval Studies, 1990.

Ghali, Mirrit Butros. "Essay: The Egyptian National Consciousness." *Middle East Journal*, 32 (1978), 59-77.

- - - - - - -. "Ethiopian Church Autocephaly." *Coptic Encyclopedia.* 1991.

- - - - - - - -. *The Policy of Tomorrow.* Washington: American Council of Learned Societies, 1953.

al-Ghazzali, Muhammad. *Our Beginning in Wisdom.* Ed. and trans. Isma'il R. el-Faruqi. 1953; rpt. New York: Octagon Books, 1975.

Giamberardini, P. Gabriele. "La Doctrine christologique des coptes." *Proche-Orient Chrétien*, 13 (1963), 211-220.

- - - - - - -. L'Incarnation inconditionnée du Christ dans la théologie copte." *Proche-Orient Chrétien*, 16 (1966), 113-119.

Gill, Joseph. *The Council of Florence.* Cambridge: Cambridge Univ. Press, 1959.

Glubb, John. *Soldiers of Fortune: The Story of the Mamluks.* New York: Stein and Day, 1973.

Goldschmidt, Arthur. *Modern Egypt: The Formation of a Nation State.* Boulder, Col.: Westview Press, 1988.

Goodspeed, Edgar J. *A History of Early Christian Literature.* Rev. and enlarged. Robert M. Grant. Chicago: University of Chicago Press, 1966.

Gordon, Joel. "The False Hopes of 1950: The Wafd's Last Hurrah and The Demise of Egypt's Old Orders." *International Journal of Middle East Studies*, 21 (1989), 193-214.

Gordon, Lucie Duff. *Letters from Egypt (1862-1869).* Ed. and with additional letters Gordon Wakefield. New York: Praeger, 1969.

Graf, Georg. *Geschichte der Christlichen Arabischen Literatur.* Vol. 2. Vatican City: Bibliotheca Apostolica Vaticana, 1947.

Grant, Robert M. "Theological Education at Alexandria." In *The Roots of Egyptian Christianity.* Ed. Birger A. Pearson and James E. Goehring. Philadelphia: Fortress Press, 1986, pp. 178-189.

Green, Henry A. "The Socio-Economic Background of Christianity in Egypt." In *The Roots of Egyptian Christianity.* Ed. Birger A. Pearson and James E. Goehring. Philadelphia: Fortress Press, 1986, pp. 100-113.

Gregg, Robert C. and D. E. Groh. *Early Arianism: A View of Salvation.* Philadelphia: Fortress Press, 1981.

Gregorios. "Baptism and Chrismation according to the Rite of the Coptic Orthodox Church." *Bulletin de la Société d'Archéologie Copte,* 21 (1971-73), 19-32.

- - - - - - -. "Christianity, the Coptic Religion and Ethnic Minorities in Egypt." *Geojournal,* 6 (1982), 57-62.

Gregorios, Paulos, William H. Lazareth, and Nikos A. Nissiotis. *Does Chalcedon Divide or Unite?: Towards Convergence in Orthodox Christology.* Geneva: World Council of Churches, 1981.

Griffith, Sydney H. "Eutychius of Alexandria on the Emperor Theophilus and Iconoclasm in Byzantium: A Tenth Century Moment in Christian Apologetics in Arabic." *Byzantion,* 52 (1982), 154-190.

Grillmeier, Alois. *Christ in Christian Tradition: From the Apostolic Age to Chalcedon (451).* Trans. J. S. Bowden. London: Mowbray, 1965.

Guillaumont, Antoine. "Copte (littérature spirituelle)." *Dictionnaire de spiritualité ascétique.* 1953.

- - - - - - -. "Kellia." *Coptic Encyclopedia.* 1991.

Hammerschmidt, E. "Some Remarks on the History of, and our Present State of Investigation into, the Coptic Liturgy." *Bulletin de la Société d'Archéologie Copte,* 19 (1967-68), 89-114.

Hanna, Malek. "Les livres liturgiques de l'église copte. In Vol. 3, *Orient chrétien,* of *Mélanges Eugène Tisserant.* pp. 1-35.

Hardy, Edward Rochie. *Christian Egypt, Church and People: Christianity and Nationalism in the Patriarchate of Alexandria.* New York; Oxford Univ. Press, 1952.

- - - - - - -. *The Large Estates of Byzantine Egypt.* New York: Columbia Univ. Press, 1931.

- - - - - - -. "The Patriarchate of Alexandria: A Study in a National Christianity." *Church History,* 15 (1946), 81-100.

Heikal, Mohammed. *The Autumn of Fury: The Assassination of Sadat.* New York: Random House, 1983.

Hewett, Gordon. *The Problem of Success: A History of the Church Missionary Society, 1910-1942.* 2 vols. London: Church Missionary Society, 1971.

Heyworth-Dunne, J. "Education in Egypt and the Copts." *Bulletin de la Société d'Archéologie Copte,* 6 (1940), 91-108.

- - - - - - -. *An Introduction to the History of Education in Modern Egypt.* London: Frank Cass, 1939.

Hill, Henry, ed. *Light from the East: A Symposium of the Oriental Orthodox and Assyrian Churches.* Toronto: Anglican Book Centre, 1988.

History of the Patriarchs of the Coptic Church of Alexandria. Ed. and trans. B. T. A. Evetts. In *Patrologia Orientalis.* Vol 1, pp. 105-211 and 383-518; Vol. 5, pp. 3-215; Vol. 10, pp. 358-540. Paris: Firmin-Didot, 1907-1915.

History of the Patriarchs of the Egyptian Church: Known as the History of the Holy Church by Sawirus ibn al-Mukaffa. Vol. 2, pt. 1. Trans. Yassa Abd al-Masih and O. H. E. Burmester. Cairo: Société d'archéologie copte, 1943. Vol. 2, pt. 2.. Trans. Aziz S. Atiya, Yassa Abd al-Masih, and O. H. E. Burmester. Cairo: Société d'archéologie copte, 1948. Vol. 2, pt. 3. Trans. Aziz S. Atiya, Yassa Abd al-Masih, and O. H. E. Burmester. Cairo: Société d'archéologie copte, 1959. Vol. 3, pts. 1-3. Trans. Antoine Khater and O. H. E. Burmester. Cairo: Société d'archéologie copte, 1968 and 1970. Vol. 4, pts. 1-2. Trans. Antoine Khater and O. H. E. Burmester. Cairo: Société d'archéologie copte, 1974.

Hitti, Philip. *The Arabs: A Short History.* 5th Paperback Printing. Princeton: Princeton Univ. Press, 1966.

Holt, Peter Malcolm. *The Age of the Crusades: The Near East from the Eleventh Century to 1517.* New York: Longman, 1986.

- - - - - - -. *Egypt and the Fertile Crescent, 1516-1922.* Ithaca, N. Y.: Cornell Univ. Press, 1966.

- - - - - -, ed. *Political and Social Change in Modern Egypt: Historical Studies from the Ottoman Conquest to the United Arab Republic.* New York: Oxford Univ. Press, 1968.

Hunter, F. Robert. *Egypt under the Khedives, 1805-1879.* Pittsburgh: Pittsburgh Univ. Press, 1984.

Husayn, Afandi. *Ottoman Egypt in the Age of the French Revolution: By Huseyn Efendi.* Trans. Stanford J. Shaw. Cambridge: Harvard Univ. Press, 1964.

ibn Khaldun. *The Muqaddimah: Introduction to History.* 3 vols. Trans. F. Rosenthal. New York: Pantheon Books, 1958.

Ibrahim, Fouad N. "Social and Economic Geographical Analysis of the Egyptian Copts." *Geojournal,* 6 (1982), 63-67.

Irwin, Robert. *The Middle East in the Middle Ages: The Early Mamluk Sultanate, 1250-1382.* Carbondale, Ill.: Southern Illinois Univ. Press, 1986.

Jaeger, Werner. *Early Christianity and Greek Paideia.* Cambridge: Harvard Univ. Press, 1961.

Jeremias (Monk of St. Macarius' Monastery). Personal Interview. 7 December 1989.

Johnson, David W. "Coptic Relations to Gnosticism and Manichaeism." *Le Muséon,* 100 (1987), 199-209.

- - - - - - -. "Further Remarks on the Arabic *History of the Patriarchs of Alexandria.*" *Oriens Christianus,* 61 (1977), 103-116.

Jomier, Jacques. "Les Coptes." In *L'Égypte d'aujourd'hui: Permanence et changements, 1805-1976.* Ed. M. C. Aulas et al. Paris: CNRS, 1977, pp. 69-84.

Jouguet, Pierre. "De l'égypte grecque a l'égypte copte." *Bulletin de l'Association des Amis des Églises et de l'Art Copte,* 1 (1935), 1-26.

Jowett, William. *Christian Researches in the Mediterranean: From 1815-1820 in Furtherance of the Objects of the Church Missionary Society.* 3rd ed. London: Church Missionary Society, 1824.

Judge, E. A. "The Earliest Use of Monachos for 'Monk' and the Origins of Monasticism." *Jahrbuch für Antike und Christentum,* 20 (1977), 72-89.

Judge, E. A. and S. R. Pickering. "Papyrus Documentation of Church and Community in Egypt in the Mid-Fourth Century." *Jahrbuch für Antike und Christentum,* 20 (1977), 47-71.

Kamil, Jill. *Coptic Egypt: History and Guide.* Cairo: American Univ. in Cairo Press, 1967.

Kamil, Murad. *Coptic Egypt.* Cairo: Le Scribe égyptien, 1968.

Karas, Shawky F. *The Copts Since the Arab Invasion.* Jersey City: American, Canadian, and Australian Coptic Associations, 1985.

- - - - - - -. "Egypt's Beleaguered Christians." *Worldview,* 26 (1983), 13-14.

Kasser, Rodolphe. "Les Origines du christianisme égyptien." *Revue de Théologie et de Philosophie,* 95 (1962), 11-28

Kelly, John Norman Davidson. *Early Christian Creeds.* 3rd ed. New York: D. McKay, 1972.

Kemp, E. W. "Bishops and Presbyters in Alexandria." *Journal of Ecclesiastical History,* 6 (1955), 125-142.

Kepel, Gilles. *Muslim Extremism in Egypt: The Prophet and the Pharaoh.* Trans. Jon Rothschild. Berkeley: Univ. of California Press, 1986.

Khella, Karan Nazir. *Naïssance et développement de l'église copte.* Paris: Cahier d'études chrétiennes orientales, 1967.

Kidd, Beresford James. *The Churches of Eastern Christendom from 451 to the Present Time.* London: The Faith Press, 1927.

King, Archdale A. *The Rites of Eastern Christendom.* Rome: Catholic Book Agency, 1947. Vol. 1.

Klijn, A. F. J. "Jewish Christianity in Egypt." In *The Roots of Egyptian Christianity.* Ed. Birger A. Pearson and James E. Goehring. Philadelphia: Fortress Press, 1986, pp. 161-175.

Kolta, K. S. *Das Christentum am Nil und die Heutige Koptische Kirche.* Munich: J. Pheiffer, 1982.

Kuhn, E. H. "A Fifth Century Egyptian Abbot." *Journal of Theological Studies,* NS 5 (1954), 36-48, 174-187.

Labib, Subhi. "Athanasius III." *Coptic Encyclopedia.* 1991.

- - - - - - -. "Badr al-Jamali." *Coptic Encyclopedia.* 1991.

- - - - - - -. "Benjamin II." *Coptic Encyclopedia.* 1991.

- - - - - - -. "Bulus al-Habis." *Coptic Encyclopedia.* 1991.

- - - - - - -. "The Copts in Egyptian Society and Politics, 1882-1919." In *Islam, Nationalism, and Radicalism in Egypt and the Sudan.* Ed. Gabriel R. Warburg and Uri M. Kupferschmit. New York: Praeger, 1983, pp. 301-320.

- - - - - - -. "Crusades." *Coptic Encyclopedia.* 1991.

- - - - - - -. "Cyril II." *Coptic Encyclopedia.* 1991.

- - - - - - -. "Gabriel II." *Coptic Encyclopedia.* 1991.

- - - - - - -. "John VII." *Coptic Encyclopedia.* 1991.

- - - - - - -. "Mark III." *Coptic Encyclopedia.* 1991.

- - - - - - -. "Peter V." *Coptic Encyclopedia.* 1991.

Lane, Edward W. *The Manners and Customs of the Modern Egyptians.* 1836; rpt. London: East-West Publications, 1978.

Lane-Poole, Stanley. *A History of Egypt in the Middle Ages.* 2nd ed. London: Methuen, 1913.

Lapidus, T. M. "The Conversion of Egypt to Islam." *Israel Oriental Studies,* 2 (1972). 248-262.

Lefort, Louis Théophile. "Catéchèse christologique de Chénoute." *Zeitschrift für Ägyptische Sprache und Altertumskunde,* 80 (1955), 40-45.

- - - - - - -. *Les Vies coptes de Saint Pachôme et de ses premiers successeurs.* Louvain: Muséon, 1943.

Legrain, G. *Une Famille copte de Haute-Égypte.* Brussels: La Fondation égyptologique Reine Elisabeth, 1945.

Legrand, Hervé-Marie. "Le Renouveau copte." *Istina,* 8 (1961-62), 133-150.

Leipoldt, Johannes. *Schenute von Atripe und die Enstehung des National-Ägyptischen Christentums. (Texte und Untersuchungen 25, 13).* Leipzig: Hinrichs, 1903.

- - - - - - -. "Zur Ideologie des Frühen Koptischen Kirche." *Bulletin de la Société d'Archéologie Copte,* 17 (1963-64), 101-110.

Lewis, Bernard. *The Arabs in History.* 4th ed. New York: Harper and Row, 1967.

- - - - - - -. "Egypt and Syria." In *The Central Islamic Lands from Pre-historic Times to the First World War.* Vol. 1 of *The Cambridge History of Islam.* Ed. P. M. Holt, A. K. S. Lambton, and B. Lewis. Cambridge: Cambridge Univ. Press, 1970, pp. 175-230.

Lewis, Naphtali. *Life in Egypt under Roman Rule.* Oxford: Clarendon Press, 1983.

Little, D. P. "Coptic Conversion to Islam under the Bahri Mamluks 692-755/1293-1354." *Bulletin of the School of Oriental and African Studies,* 39 (1976), 552-569.

- - - - - - -. "Religion under the Mamluks." *Muslim World,* 73 (1983), 165-181.

Little, Tom. *Modern Egypt.* London: Ernest Benn, 1958.

MacCoull, Leslie S. B. "Child Donations and Saints in Coptic Egypt." *East European Quarterly,* 13 (1979), 409-415.

- - - - - - -. "Coptic Orthodoxy Today: Ethnicism, Deadend, and Mere Survival." *Coptic Church Review,* 4 (1983), 25-29.

- - - - - - -. "The Strange Death of Coptic Culture." *Coptic Church Review,* 10 (1989), 35-43.

- - - - - - -. "Three Cultures under Arab Rule: The Fate of Coptic." *Bulletin de la Société d'Archéologie Copte,* 27 (1985), 61-70.

al-Makrizi, Taqi al-Din. *A Short History of the Copts and of their Church.* Trans. S. C. Malan. London: D. Nutt, 1873.

- - - - - - -. "Account of the Monasteries and Churches of the Christians of Egypt; Forming the Concluding Sections of the *Khitat* of al-Makrizi (died A.H. 845=A.D. 1441)." In Abu Salih. *The Churches and Monasteries of Egypt: And Some Neighboring Countries.* Ed. and trans. B. T. A. Evetts with added notes by A. J. Butler. Oxford: Clarendon Press, 1895, pp. 305-346.

Malaty, Tadros Y. "The Coptic Orthodox Church-Anglican Church Relations." *Coptic Church Review*, 6 (1985), 103-105.

- - - - - - -. *St. Mary in the Orthodox Concept.* Alexandria, Egypt: St. George Coptic Church, n. d.

Markos, Bishop Antonius. "Developments in Coptic Orthodox Missiology." *Missiology*, 17 (1989), 203-215.

Martin, Annik. "Aux Origines de l'église copte: L'Implantation et le développement du christianisme en Égypte." *Revue des Études Anciennes*, 83 (1981), 35-56.

- - - - - - -. "Les Premiers siècles du christianisme à Alexandrie: Essai de topographie religieuse (IIIe - IVe siècles.) *Revue des Études Augustiniennes*, 30 (1984), 211-225.

Martin, Maurice-Pierre. "Les Coptes catholiques 1880-1920." *Proche-Orient Chrétien*, 40 (1990), 33-35.

- - - - - - -. "Les Coptes en Égypte: Une minorité assiégée." *Choisir*, No. 310 (October, 1985).

- - - - - - -. "L'Église et la communauté copte dans l'Islam égyptien." TS. Jesuit Institute Library, L'École Ste. Famille, Cairo.

- - - - - - -. "Une Lecture de l'*Histoire des patriarches d'Alexandrie*." *Proche-Orient Chrétien*, 35 (1985), 15-36.

Martin, Maurice-Pierre, Christian van Nispen, and Fadel Sidarouss. "Les Nouveaux courants dans la communauté copte orthodoxe." *Proche-Orient Chrétien*, 40 (1990), 245-257.

Maspero, Jean. *Histoire des patriarches d'Alexandrie: Depuis la mort de l'Empereur Anastase jusqu'à la réconciliation des églises jacobites (518-616).* Paris: Librairie Ancienne Edouard Champion, 1923.

el-Masri, Iris Habib. "A Historical Survey of the Convents for Women in Egypt up to the Present Day." *Bulletin de la Société d'Archéologie Copte*, 14 (1958), 63-111.

- - - - - - -. *The Story of the Copts.* Cairo: Middle East Council of Churches, 1978.

Matthee, Rudi. "Jamal al-Din al-Afghani and the Egyptian National Debate." *International Journal of Middle East Studies*, 21 (1989), 151-169.

McCarthy, Justin A. "Nineteenth Century Egyptian Population." *Middle Eastern Studies*, 12, 3 (October, 1976), 1-40.

McMullan, Ramsey. "Nationalism in Roman Egypt." *Aegyptus*, 44 (1964), 179-199.

McNeill, William H. *The Rise of the West: A History of the Human Community.* Chicago: Univ. of Chicago Press, 1963.

Meinardus, Otto F. A. "The Attitudes of the Orthodox Copts towards the Islamic State from the Seventh to the Twelfth Century." *Östkirchliche Studien*, 13 (1964), 153-170.

- - - - - - -. *Christian Egypt: Ancient and Modern.* Cairo: Cahiers d'histoire égyptienne, 1965.

- - - - - - -. *Christian Egypt: Faith and Life.* Cairo: The American Univ. in Cairo Press, 1970.

- - - - - - -. "Damru." *Coptic Encyclopedia.* 1991.

- - - - - - -. *Monks and Monasteries of the Egyptian Desert*, Rev. ed. Cairo: The American Univ. in Cairo Press, 1989.

- - - - - - -. "Recent Developments in Egyptian Monasticism." *Oriens Christianus*, 49 (1965), 79-89.

- - - - - - -. "Zur Monastischen Erneuerung in der Koptischen Kirche." *Oriens Christianus*, 61 (1977), 59-70.

Mellini, Peter. *Sir Elden Gorst: The Overshadowed Proconsul.* Stanford, Calif.: Hoover Institution Press, 1977.

Mena, Raphael Ava. "Days in the Life of a Contemporary Saint." *Coptic Church Review*, 7 (1986), 22-28.

Meyendorff, John. *Christ in Eastern Christian Thought.* New York: St. Vladimir's Seminary Press, 1975.

Mikhail, Kyriakos. *Copts and Muslims under British Control: A Collection of Facts and a Résumé of Authoritative Opinion on the Coptic Question.* 1911; rpt. Port Washington, N. Y.: Kennikat Press, 1971.

Millbank, John and Allison. "A Visit to the Coptic Church." *Sobornost*, 2 (1980), 57-64.

Milne, Joseph Grafton. *A History of Egypt under Roman Rule.* 3rd ed. London: Methuen, 1924.

Moloney, Raymond. "Egypt, Ethiopia: Africa's Senior Churches in Dialogue with Rome." *African Ecclesiastical Review*, 30 (1988), 91-96.

Monks, George R. "The Church in Alexandria and the City's Economic Life in the Sixth Century." *Speculum*, 38 (1953), 349-362.

Morrison, S. A. *The Way of Partnership.* London: Church Missionary Society, 1936.

Motski, H. "Jirjis al-Jawhari." *Coptic Encyclopedia.* 1991.

Muir, William. *The Mameluke or Slave Dynasty of Egypt: A History of Egypt from the Fall of the Ayyubite Dynasties to the Conquest of the Osmanlis A.D. 1260-1517.* 1896; rpt. Amsterdam: Oriental Press, 1968.

Musa, Salama. *The Education of Salama Musa.* Trans. L. O. Schuman. Leiden: E. J. Brill, 1961.

-------. "Intellectual Currents in Egypt." *Middle Eastern Affairs,* 2 (1951), 267-272.

Najjar, Fauzi M. "The Application of Sharia Laws in Egypt." *Middle East Policy,* 1 (1992), 62-73.

Nationalism, and Radicalism in Egypt and the Sudan. Ed. Gabriel R. Warburg and Uri M. Kupferschmidt. New York: Praeger, 1983.

Neale, John Mason. *A History of the Holy Eastern Church: The Patriarchate of Alexandria.* 2 vols. London: Joseph Masters, 1847.

Nock, Arthur Darby. "Later Egyptian Piety." In *Coptic Egypt.* New York: Brooklyn Museum, 1944.

Non-official Ecumenical Consultation between Theologians of the Oriental Orthodox Churches and the Roman Catholic Church. Vienna-Lainz, September 7-12, 1971. Vienna: Herder, 1972.

Norris, Richard A., ed. *The Christological Controversy.* Philadelphia: Fortress Press, 1980.

Northrup, Linda S. "Muslim-Christian Relations during the Reign of the Muslim Sultan al-Mansur Qalawun (A.D. 1278-1290)." In *Conversion and Continuity: Indigenous Christian Communities in Islamic Lands Eighth to Eighteenth Centuries.* Ed. M. Gervers and R. Gibran. Toronto: Pontifical Institute of Medieval Studies, pp. 253-261.

O'Leary, De Lacy. *The Saints of Egypt.* London: SPCK, 1937.

-------. "Severus of Antioch in Egypt." *Aegyptus,* 32 (1952), 425-436.

-------. *A Short History of the Fatimid Khalifate.* London: Kegan Paul, Trench, Trubner, & Co., 1923.

Olster, David. "Chalcedonian and Monophysite: The Union of 616." *Bulletin de la Société d'Archéologie Copte,* 27 (1985), 93-109.

O'Neill, J. C. "The Origins of Monasticism." In *The Making of Orthodoxy: Essays in Honour of Henry Chadwick.* Cambridge: Cambridge Univ. Press, 1989.

Orlandi, Tito. "Coptic Literature." In *The Roots of Egyptian Christianity.* Ed. Birger A. Pearson and James E. Goehring. Philadelphia: Fortress Press, 1986, pp. 51-81.

Pearson, Birger A. *Gnosticism, Judaism, and Jewish Christianity.* Minneapolis: Fortress Press, 1990.

- - - - - - -. "Earliest Christianity in Egypt." In *The Roots of Egyptian Christianity*. Ed. Birger A. Pearson and James E. Goehring. Philadelphia: Fortress Press, 1986, pp. 132-160

Pearson. Birger A. and James E. Goehring, eds. *The Roots of Egyptian Christianity*. Philadelphia: Fortress Press, 1986.

Pennington, J. D. "The Copts in Modern Egypt." *Middle Eastern Studies*, 18 (1982), 158-179.

Perlmann, Moshe. "Notes on Anti-Christian Propaganda in the Mamluk Empire." *Bulletin of the School of Oriental and African Studies*, 10 (1940-42), 843-861.

- - - - - - -. "Shurunbulali Militant." In *Studies in Islamic History and Civilization in Honour of Professor David Ayalon*. Ed. M. Sharon. Jerusalem: Cana, 1986.

- - - - - - -. Rev. of *The Education of Salama Musa*, by Salama Musa. *Middle East Affairs*, 2 (1951), 279-285.

Petry, Carl. *The Civilian Elite of Cairo in the Late Middle Ages*. Princeton: Princeton Univ. Press, 1981.

- - - - - - -. "Copts in Late Medieval Egypt." *Coptic Encyclopedia*. 1991.

Poladian, Terenig. "The Doctrinal Position of the Monophysite Churches." *Bulletin de la Société d'Archéologie Copte*, 17 (1963-64), 157-175.

Poliak, A. N. *Feudalism in Egypt, Syria, Palestine, and the Lebanon, 1250-1900*. London: Royal Asiatic Society, 1939.

Remondon, R. "L'Égypte et la suprême résistance au christianisme (Ve - VIIe siècles)." *Bulletin de L'Institut Français d'Archéologie Orientale*, 51 (1952), 63-78.

Richmond, J. C. B. *Egypt 1798-1952: Her Advance Toward a Modern Identity*. London: Methuen and Company, 1977.

Ritter, Adolf Martin. "De Polycarpe à Clément: Aux Origines d'Alexandrie chrétienne." *Alexandrina: Héllénisme, judaïsme et christianisme à Alexandrie: Mélanges offerts au P. Claude Mondésert*. Paris: Éditions du Cerf, 1987, pp. 151-172.

Roberts, Colin Henderson. "Early Christianity in Egypt: Three Notes." *Journal of Egyptian Archeology*, 40 (1954), 92-96.

- - - - - - -. *Manuscript, Society and Belief in Early Christian Egypt*. Oxford: Oxford Univ. Press, 1979.

- - - - - - -. Rev. of *Orthodoxy and Heresy in Earliest Christianity*. 2nd (German) ed., by Walter Bauer. *Journal of Theological Studies*, NS 16 (1965), 183-185.

Robinson, James M. Gen. ed. *The Nag Hammadi Library in English.* Trans. and ed. members of the Coptic Gnostic Library Project of the Institute for Antiquity and Christianity, Claremont, Calif., 3rd ed. San Francisco: Harper and Row, 1988.

Roncaglia, Martiniano Pellegrino. *Histoire de l'église copte.* 4 vols. Beirut: Dar al-Kalima, 1966-1973.

Rousseau, Philip. *Pachomius: The Making of a Community in Fourth Century Egypt.* Berkeley: Univ. of California Press, 1985.

Rowlatt, Mary. *Founders of Modern Egypt.* New York: Asia Publishing House, 1962.

Roy, D. A. and W. T. Irelan. "Law and Economics in the Evolution of Contemporary Egypt." *Middle Eastern Studies,* 25 (1989), 163-185.

Rubenson, Samuel. *The Letters of St. Antony: Origenist Theology, Monastic Tradition, and the Making of a Saint.* Lund: Lund Univ. Press, 1990.

Rugh, Andrea B. *Family in Contemporary Egypt.* Syracuse, N. Y.: Syracuse Univ. Press, 1984.

Sadeque, Syedah Fatima. *Baybars of Egypt.* Dacca: Oxford Univ. Press, 1956.

Sagiv, David. "Judge Ashmawi and Militant Islam in Egypt." *Middle Eastern Studies,* 28 (1992), 531-546.

Said Aly, Abd-al and M. W. Wenner. "Modern Islamic Reform Movements: The Muslim Brotherhood in Contemporary Egypt." *Middle East Journal,* 36 (1982), 336-361.

St. Mark and the Coptic Church. Cairo: Coptic Orthodox Patriarchate, 1968.

Samaan, Makram and Soheir Sukkary. "The Copts and Muslims of Egypt." In *Muslim-Christian Conflicts: Economic, Political, and Social Origins.* Ed. S. Joseph and B. L. K. Pillsbury. Boulder, Colorado: Westview, 1978, pp. 129-155.

Samir, Khalil. "Abd al-Masih al-Israeli al Raqqi." *Coptic Encyclopedia.* 1991.

-------. "Abu al-Fath ibn Sahlan ibn Muqashir." *Coptic Encyclopedia.* 1991.

-------. "Abu Ishak ibn Fadlallah." *Coptic Encyclopedia.* 1991.

-------, ed. *Actes du deuxième congrès international d'études arabes chrétiennes.* Rome: Pontificalis Institutum Studiorum Orientalium, 1986.

-------. Intro., text, and trans. "Al-Safi ibn al-Assal: Brefs chapitres sur la trinité et l'incarnation." *Patrologia Orientalis* 42, fasc. 4, no. 192. Turhont, Belgium: Prepols, 1985.

- - - - - - -. "Fakhr al-Dawlah." *Coptic Encyclopedia*. 1991.

- - - - - - -. "Gabriel V." *Coptic Encyclopedia*. 1991.

- - - - - - -. "al-Safi ibn al-'Assal." *Coptic Encyclopedia*. 1991.

Sarkissian, Karekine. "Les Églises orientales et l'unité chrétienne." *Proche-Orient Chrétien*, 16 (1966), 109-112.

Saunders, J. J. *A History of Medieval Islam*. London: Routledge and Kegan Paul, 1965.

Savary, Claude Étienne. *Letters on Egypt*. London: G. G. J. and J. Robinson, 1786.

al-Sayyid Marsot, Afaf Lutfi. *Egypt in the Reign of Muhammad Ali*. Cambridge: Cambridge Univ. Press, 1984.

- - - - - - -. *Egypt's Liberal Experiment: 1922-1936*. Berkeley: Univ. of California Press, 1977.

- - - - - - -. *A Short History of Modern Egypt*. Cambridge: Cambridge Univ. Press, 1985.

Scott-Moncrieff, Philip David. *Paganism and Christianity in Egypt*. Cambridge: Cambridge Univ. Press, 1913.

Seikaly, Samir. "Coptic Communal Reform: 1860-1914." *Middle Eastern Studies*, 6 (1970), 247-275.

- - - - - - -. "The Copts under British Rule, 1882-1914." Diss. University of London 1967.

- - - - - - -. "Prime Minister and Assassin: Butros Ghali and Wardani." *Middle Eastern Studies*, 13 (1977), 112-123.

Severianus. "Les Coptes de l'Égypte musulmane." Trans. J. Baragnan. *Études Méditerranéennes*, 6 (1959), 70-87.

Shaw, Stanford J. *The Financial and Administrative Organization and Development in Egypt, 1517-1798*. Princeton: Princeton Univ. Press, 1962.

- - - - - - -. *History of the Ottoman Empire and Modern Turkey*. Vol. 1 of *Empire of the Gazis: The Rise and Decline of the Ottoman Empire, 1280-1808*. Cambridge: Cambridge Univ. Press, 1976.

Shenouda III, Pope. "Christian Unity." *Coptic Church Review*, 6 (1985), 4-8.

Shenouda III, Pope, et al. "Migration." *Coptic Encyclopedia*, 1991.

Shore, A. F. "Christian and Coptic Egypt." In *Legacy of Egypt*. Ed. J. R. Harris. 2nd ed. Oxford: Clarendon Press, 1971, pp. 390-433.

Sidarous, Sesostris. *Des Patriarcats: Les Patriarches dans l'empire ottoman et spécialement en Égypte*. Paris: Arthur Rousseau, 1907.

Sidarouss, Fadel. "Église copte et monde moderne." *Proche-Orient Chrétien*, 30 (1980), 211-265.

Simaika, Markus. "The Awakening of the Coptic Church." *The Contemporary Review*, 71 (1897), 734-747.

Smith, Morton. *Clement of Alexandria and a Secret Gospel of Mark*. Cambridge: Harvard Univ. Press, 1973.

Sobhy Bey, George. "Education in Egypt during the Christian Period and Amongst the Copts." *Bulletin de la Société d'Archéologie Copte*, 9 (1943), 103-122.

Solihin, Sohirin Mohammed. *Copts and Muslims in Egypt: A Study on Harmony and Hostility*. Leicester: The Islamic Foundation, 1991.

Sonbol, Amira. "Society, Politics, And Sectarian Strife." In I. M. Oweiss, *The Political Economy of Contemporary Egypt*. Washington: Georgetown Univ. Center for Contemporary Arab Studies, 1990.

Sonnini de Manoncourt, Charles Nicholas. *Travels in Upper and Lower Egypt*. Trans. Henry Hunter. London: J. Stockdale, 1807.

Sourdel, D. "The Abbasid Caliphate." In *The Central Islamic Lands from Pre-historic Times to the First World War*, Vol. 1 of *The Cambridge History of Islam*. Ed. P. M. Holt, A. K. S. Lambton, and B. Lewis, Cambridge: Cambridge Univ. Press, 1970, pp. 104-139.

Southgate, Horatio. In *The Spirit of Missions*, 6 (1841), 369.

Staffa, S. J. *Conquest and Fusion: The Social Evolution of Cairo A.D. 642-1850*. Leiden: E. J. Brill, 1977.

Starobinski-Safran, Esther. "La communauté juive d'Alexandrie à l'époque de Philon." *Alexandrina: Héllénisme, Judaïsme et Christianisme à Alexandrie: Mélanges Offerts au P. Claude Mondésert*. Paris: Éditions du Cerf, 1987, pp. 45-75

Stern, S. M. *Fatimid Decrees: Original Documents from the Fatimid Chancery*. London: Faber and Faber, 1964.

Strothmann, Rudolf. *Die Koptische Kirche in der Neuzeit*. Tübingen: J. C. B. Mohr, 1932.

Tamura, Airi. "Ethnic Consciousness and its Transformation in the Course of Nation-building: The Muslim and the Copt in Egypt, 1906-1919." *Muslim World*, 75 (1985), 102-114.

Tcherikover, Victor. *Hellenistic Civilization and the Jews*. Trans. S. Applebaum. New York: Atheneum, 1975.

Telfer, W. "Episcopal Succession in Egypt." *Journal of Ecclesiastical History*, 3 (1952), 1-13.

Thornton, Douglas M. "The Education Problem in Egypt in Relation to Religious Teaching." *Church Missionary Intelligencer*, 57 (1906), 651-658.

Three Byzantine Saints. Trans. Elizabeth Anna Sophia Dawes and Norman Baynes. Oxford: B. Blackwell, 1948.

Timbie, Janet. "The State of Research on the Career of Shenoute of Atripe." In *The Roots of Egyptian Christianity*. Ed. Birger A. Pearson and James E. Goehring. Philadelphia: Fortress Press, 1986, pp. 258-270.

Tisserant, Eugène and Gaston Wiet. "La Liste des patriarches d'Alexandrie dans Qalqashandi." *Revue de l'Orient Chrétien*, ser. 3, 3 (1922-23), 123-140.

Trevijano, R. "The Early Christian Church of Alexandria." *Studia Patristica*, 12 (1975), 471-477.

Trigg, Joseph Wilson. *Origen: The Bible and Philosophy in the Third-century Church*. Atlanta: John Knox Press, 1983.

Trossen, Jean Pierre. *Les Relations du patriarche copte Jean XVI avec Rome (1676-1718)*. Luxembourg: Imprimerie Hermann, 1948.

Tsirpanlis, Constantine N. "The Origenistic Controversy in the Historians of the Fourth, Fifth, and Sixth Centuries." *Augustinianum*, 26 (1986), 177-183.

van den Bent, Ans J. ed. *Handbook: Member Churches*. Geneva: World Council of Churches, 1985.

Vansleb, J. M. *Histoire de l'église d'Alexandrie fondée par S. Marc que nous appelons celle des jacobites-coptes d'Égypte, écrite au Caire même en 1672 et 1673*. Paris: Veuve Closier et Pierre Prome, 1677.

Vatikiotis, Panayiotis Jerasimo. *The History of Egypt*. 3rd ed. Baltimore: Johns Hopkins Univ. Press, 1985.

Veilleux, Armand. *Pachomian Koinonia*. 3 vols. Kalamazoo, Mich.: Cistercian Publications, 1980-1982.

Verghese, Paul, ed. *Koptisches Christentum: Die Orthodoxe Kirchen, Ägyptens und Äthiopiens*. Stuttgart: Evangelisches Verlagswerk, 1973.

Viaud, Gérard. *La Liturgie des coptes d'Égypte*. Paris: Maisonneuve, 1978.

- - - - - - - . *Magie et coutumes populaires chez les coptes d'Égypte*. Sisteron, France: Editorial Présence, 1978.

Vivian, Tim. *Saint Peter of Alexandria: Bishop and Martyr*. Philadelphia: Fortress Press, 1988.

Volkoff, O. V., ed. *Voyageurs russes en Égypte*. Cairo: Institut Français d'Archéologie Orientale, 1972.

Volney, M. C.-F. *Travels through Syria and Egypt in the Years 1783, 1784, and 1785*. London: G. G. J. and J. Robinson, 1787.

Wakin, Edward. "The Copts in Egypt." *Middle East Affairs*, 12 (1961), 198-208.

- - - - - - -. *A Lonely Minority: The Modern Story of Egypt's Copts*. New York: William Morrow, 1963.

Warburgh, Gabriel R. "Islam and Politics in Egypt: 1952-1980." *Middle Eastern Studies*, 18 (1982), 131-157.

Wassef, Ceres Wissa. *Pratiques rituelles et alimentaires des coptes*. Cairo: Institut français d'archéologie orientale, 1971.

Watterson, Barbara. *Coptic Egypt*. Edinburgh: Scottish Academic Press, 1988.

Wellard, James Howard. *Desert Pilgrimage: Journeys to the Egyptian and Sinai Deserts: Completing the Third of the Trilogy of Saharan Exploration*. London: Hutchinson, 1970.

Wiet, Gaston. *L'Égypte arabe: de la conquête arabe à la conquête ottomane 642-1517 de l'ère chrétienne*. Vol. 4 of *Histoire de la nation égyptienne*. Ed. Gabriel Hanotaux. Paris: Librairie Plon, n.d.

- - - - - - -. "Qibt." *Encyclopédie de l'Islam: Dictionnaire géographique, ethnographique, et biographique des peuples musulmans*. Leiden: E. J. Brill, 1927.

Wikan, Unna. *Life among the Poor in Cairo*. Trans. Ann Henning. London: Tavistock Publications, 1960.

Williams, Rowan. *Arius: Heresy and Tradition*. London: Darton, Longman, and Todd, 1987.

Wipszycka, Ewa. "La Christianization de l'Égypte aux 4ème-6ème siècles: Aspects sociaux et ethniques." *Aegyptus*, 68 (1988), 117-165.

- - - - - - -. *Les Ressources et les activités économiques des églises en Égypte du 4ème au 8ème siècle*. Brussels: Fondation égyptologique Reine Elisabeth, 1972.

Wisse, Frederick. "Gnosticism and Early Monasticism in Egypt." In *Gnosis. Festschrift für Hans Jonas*. Ed. B. Aland. Göttingen: Vandenhoeck und Ruprecht, 1978, pp. 431-440.

- - - - - - -. "The Nag Hammadi Library and the Heresiologist." *Vigiliae Christianae*, 25 (1971), 205-223.

Wooley, R. M. *Coptic Offices*. London: SPCK, 1930.

Wordsworth, John. *Bishop Sarapion's Prayerbook: An Egyptian Sacramentary Dated Probably about A.D. 350-356*. 2nd ed. London: SPCK, 1923.

Worrell, W. H. *A Short Account of the Copts*. Ann Arbor, Mich.: Univ. of Michigan Press, 1945.

Yanney, Rodolph. "Light in the Darkness: Life of Archdeacon Habib Guirguis (1876-1951)." *Coptic Church Review*, 5 (1984), 47-52.

Young, Dwight W. "The Milieu of Nag Hammadi: Some Historical Considerations." *Vigiliae Christianae*, 24 (1970), 127-137.

- - - - - - -. "A Monastic Invective against Egyptian Hieroglyphics." In *Studies Presented to Hans Jakob Polotsky*. Ed. D. W. Young. East Gloucester, Mass.: Pyrtle and Polson, 1981, pp. 348-360.

Young, George. *Egypt*. London: Ernest Benn, 1927.

Zanetti, Ugo. *Les Lectionnaires coptes annuels: Basse Égypte*. Louvain-la-Neuve: Institut Orientaliste, 1985.

- - - - - - -. *Les Manuscrits d'Abu Maqar: Inventaire*. Geneva: Patrick Cramer, 1986.

Index